JOHANNA GARTON

EDGE OF THE MAP

THE MOUNTAIN LIFE OF CHRISTINE BOSKOFF

MOUNTAINEERS
BOOKS

MOUNTAINEERS BOOKS is dedicated to the exploration, preservation, and enjoyment of outdoor and wilderness areas.

1001 SW Klickitat Way, Suite 201, Seattle, WA 98134
800-553-4453, www.mountaineersbooks.org

Printed in the United States of America
Distributed in the United Kingdom by Cordee, www.cordee.co.uk
23 22 21 20   1 2 3 4 5

Copyeditor: Amy Smith Bell
Cover and book design: Jen Grable
Cartographer: Martha Bostwick
Cover photograph: *Tibetan prayer flags on a mountain pass* (© guenterguni)
Back cover photograph: *Christine Boskoff at Everest Base Camp* (Mountain Madness Collection)

Library of Congress Cataloging-in-Publication data is on file for this title at https://lccn.loc.gov/2019047353 LC (paper); https://lccn.loc.gov/2019047354 (ebook)

Mountaineers Books titles may be purchased for corporate, educational, or other promotional sales, and our authors are available for a wide range of events. For information on special discounts or booking an author, contact our customer service at 800-553-4453 or mbooks@mountaineersbooks.org.

♻ Printed on recycled paper

ISBN (paperback): 978-1-68051-288-5
ISBN (ebook): 978-1-68051-289-2

An independent nonprofit publisher since 1960

FSC
www.fsc.org
MIX
Paper from
responsible sources
FSC® C005010

For Mom and Joyce

CONTENTS

This is a work of creative nonfiction, based on hundreds of hours of interviews and research. The details contained within are true to the best of the author's knowledge. All scenes with dialogue have been re-created based on the accounts of living participants in those conversations. In the few cases where all parties are deceased, the author relied on the accounts of persons still alive to whom those conversations were described shortly thereafter, as well as on selected books, newspaper and magazine articles, photos, and audio/video recordings.

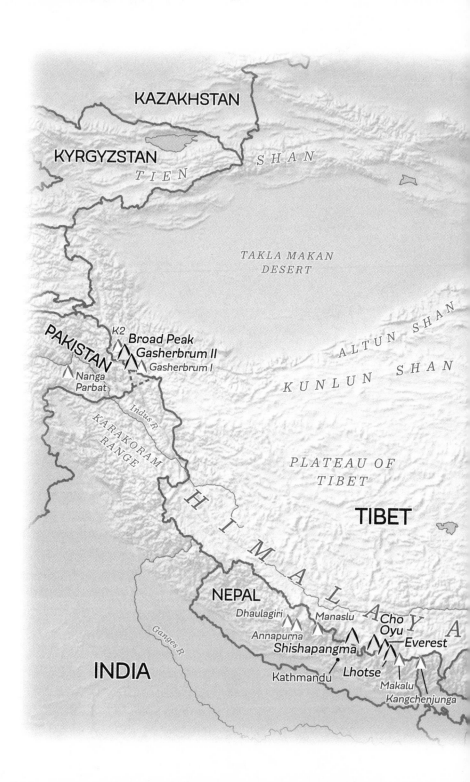

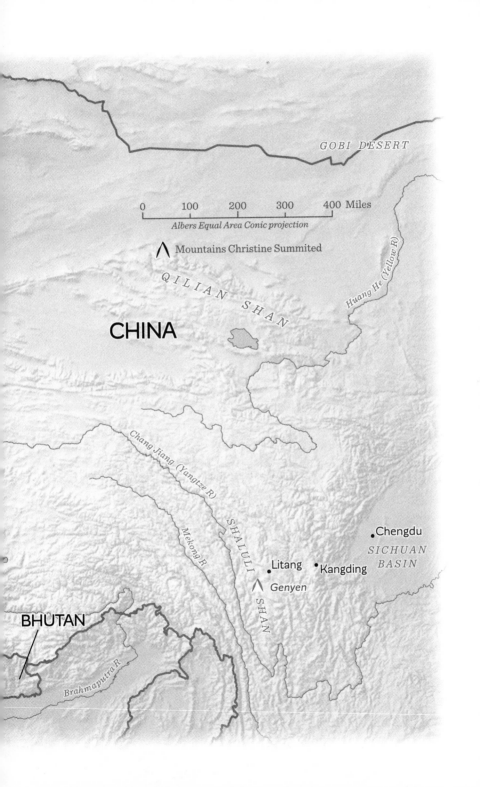

GOBI DESERT

0   100   200   300   400 Miles
Albers Equal Area Conic projection

∧ Mountains Christine Summited

Q I L I A N   S H A N

Huang He (Yellow R)

CHINA

Chang Jiang (Yangtze R)

Mekong R

S H A L U L I

∧

S H A N

•Chengdu

SICHUAN
BASIN

•Litang   •Kangding

Genyen

BHUTAN

Brahmaputra R

8000-METER SPECIALIST

—Bruce Barcott, writing for *Outside* magazine in 2001

WHAT DOES IT TAKE TO become one of the world's premier high-altitude mountaineers? If Christine Boskoff is any example (and she certainly is), the answer is speed, stamina, brains, experience, and the ability to persevere with a smile. "Christine takes pain very well," says Peter Habeler, the legendary Austrian climber who guided with Boskoff on Everest in 1999. "She can suffer without moaning, which few Westerners can or want to do anymore." Her ability to endure in the Death Zone has led the 34-year-old Wisconsin native to the top of the world's highest mountains. In the past six years she's ticked off six of the fourteen peaks above 8,000 meters (Everest, Cho Oyu, Gasherbrum II, Lhotse, Shishapangma, and Broad Peak), in addition to becoming the only female expedition leader among the elite guide services operating on Everest. "She's got great inner confidence and experience," says American climber Charlie Fowler, who scaled Tibet's 26,291-foot Shishapangma with Boskoff last fall. "I haven't seen anybody stronger."

Five years ago Boskoff was stuck in an Atlanta cubicle, engineering flight simulators for Lockheed Martin. Off-hours she built her endurance engine by working the crags near town, whipping off ten-mile runs, and scrambling up frozen waterfalls during the Southeast's brief ice-climbing window. A spring 1993 mountaineering trip to the Bolivian Andes whetted her appetite for more substantial peaks, including the Himalayan massifs. "I'd quit my job every time a big expedition came up—Broad

Peak in '95, then Cho Oyu in '96," she says. Eventually, she abandoned her office post altogether for a less tethered career; she moved to Seattle to help take over the Mountain Madness guide service in 1997, a year after the company's founder, Scott Fischer, died on Everest.

This spring, Boskoff will be back on Everest as a guide for Mountain Madness, which may yield her second summit on that peak. She'll then attempt K2's dangerous SSE Spur with Fowler. A view from the 28,250-foot pinnacle would put her halfway to becoming the first woman to climb all fourteen 8,000-meter peaks. Thing is, she's so modest about her ability, male climbers who approach her at climbing crags have no idea who they're flirting with. One day last year at Skaha Bluffs, in British Columbia's Okanagan Valley, she was besieged by a crew of twentysomething lads trying out their best lines on the attractive alpinist.

"What do you do for a living?" one asked her as she limbered up a 5.10 line. "Oh," said Boskoff, who had recently topped out on Mont Blanc and the Matterhorn, "I run a travel business."

CHAPTER 1

MISSING

LIGHT MIXED WITH DUST POURED through a grimy window in the police station conference room. As more officers crammed inside, standing room became scarce. *God, this is too much,* thought Ted Callahan. *What the hell do they think they're going to see here?*

It had taken more than twenty-four hours for the police to grant Callahan's request to open the bags, and suddenly it was time. The Chinese Public Security Bureau (PSB) here in far western China initially acted as though his request to unlock Chris's and Charlie's duffels had been overstepping bounds. Now, it seemed every desk clerk and janitor in the building had packed into the small space, all waiting to see the bags reveal their secrets.

The buzz from the Chinese police officers collided with the tranquil scene just outside the station. The streets of Litang were home to Tibetan Buddhists, most of them dressed in traditional clothing of richly woven fabrics made from yak hair. Oblivious to the drama inside the station, the locals were focused instead on impending weather systems and the impact to their barley crops.

Two oversize duffels lay in the middle of the room, each secured with a lock. Callahan fiddled with each one, tugging to see if he could jimmy them open. No luck. He'd been operating on wisps of sleep and too much coffee since heading up the search-and-rescue operation a week ago. Or was it a search-and-recovery? The differences muddied his exhausted mind. Setting them aside felt like the only way to move forward.

Callahan had left his academic fellowship in Kyrgyzstan as soon as he'd been alerted to the disappearance of Chris Boskoff and Charlie Fowler by Mountain Madness, Chris's Seattle-based guiding company. Having solid experience dealing with the Chinese and a grasp of the language, he was a good match to head the on-the-ground operation. Chris was a friend and Charlie was a climber he'd known and admired for years. The couple loved climbing more than anyone he knew.

At age thirty-two, Callahan was an accomplished mountaineer himself who'd led trips for Mountain Madness and understood the draw of remote peaks in this part of the world. Both the terrain and the people in the area near the Tibetan border had captivated Charlie for decades, and now Chris shared his fascination. It was an area they'd returned to again and again.

This time, no plan had been left to track their whereabouts. No permits had been requested to help aid the massive hunt. In short, nobody knew where the hell they were. *Christine, dammit woman,* Callahan thought, *please tell me you've left something in here to give us a clue where you've gone.* "Can we get a bolt cutter in here?" he asked. The nearest PSB officer paused for a moment, stymied by Callahan's Mandarin accent. He tripped over a colleague's foot as he pushed out the door, heading for the police toolbox.

In the week since Callahan had arrived in China, he'd been mostly holed up in Chengdu, Chris and Charlie's last confirmed location, following leads. It took a sizable reward to tease out the information needed to land him in this police station in the city of Litang, three days west of Chengdu on the Tibetan Plateau. The air was thin in this part of the country, altitude 12,900 feet.

The caravan leaving Chengdu a few days ago had included a CNN crew. Chris and Charlie's disappearance had started to grab headlines in the United States. A trio of climbers on Oregon's Mount Hood had vanished just weeks earlier, feeding the nightly news reports for several days. The Pacific Northwest drew climbers from around the United States, as there was no finer place in the country to prepare for attempting any of the world's fourteen 8,000-meter peaks. As the drama from the slopes in Oregon turned from a rescue of live climbers to a recovery of their bodies, the story unfolding in China stirred the public's desire for a happy ending. A Christmas miracle. It was December 23, 2006.

The CNN crew was eager to join the search team as it headed west. But going west meant a gradual increase in elevation. Passing through Kangding at 8,399 feet and on to Litang, altitude sickness hit the journalists in waves, and by the second day, Callahan was shaking their hands as the beleaguered reporter and his cameraman descended to the oxygen-rich air of Chengdu.

"Sorry, man," Callahan said as they crawled into their getaway vehicle. "I wish we had some better visuals for you guys, but that's just not how things work in China."

"Yeah, no worries," the reporter mumbled. "Just call us if something transpires and we'll come back up."

BACK IN THE POLICE STATION, Callahan's mobile phone rang as he waited for the tool he needed to open the bags. Checking the caller ID, he saw it was the CNN reporter, no doubt catching word of this development through a leak and upset that he was about to miss some important shots.

A smoky haze filled the room from the cigarettes hanging off the lips of the Chinese spectators. Litang hadn't experienced anything this thrilling in years—certainly nothing involving Westerners. Officers—all men—wearing pale blue uniform shirts leaned against stark white walls. Each sported a standard-issue navy tie.

"Whose bags are these?" the dispatch officer asked as he joined the crowd inside the conference room.

"Some foreigners who came through here a few weeks ago," his colleague replied, offering him a smoke.

"Are they stolen?"

"No, they left the bags with a driver and went to climb somewhere."

"They haven't come back?"

"Not yet. This guy's been trying to open the bags for twenty-four hours, but got caught up in all the bullshit at the provincial level and finally made a fuss with the consulate."

The dispatch officer sized up Callahan, needling his colleague for more details. "What is he? Italian? Swiss?"

Callahan smirked, nodded his head at the unsuspecting officer, and replied in Mandarin. "Neither. I'm American." The embarrassed officer laughed as his friend shoved him.

Callahan was all muscle, with fair skin, blue eyes, and ginger-blond hair cropped close. He had the face of a schoolboy, but he'd been guiding with Mountain Madness for a few years since being hired by Chris. Never one to stay still for very long, he had traveled the world on various contract gigs, learning languages as he went.

Reaching down, Callahan ran his fingers over the duffel bags again. Yellow luggage tags hugged the straps of each one, imprinted with the name and city of their owners.

Charlie Fowler
Norwood, Colorado

Back in the States, friends of Charlie in Colorado had turned their lives into full-time efforts to find him. Charlie was a superstar in the climbing community, and surviving scares in faraway places was nothing new. Among his greatest feats was walking away from a 1,500-foot fall during a winter climb in Tibet in 1997. The accident left him without several toes, lost to frostbite after he'd crawled for several days to the safety of the nearest road. Now fifty-two, Charlie steered clear of publicity, preferring to quietly explore the desert rocks near his home base outside Telluride.

The tag on Chris's bag bore a similar address. She'd recently bought a small house on a plot of land in Norwood. Close to Charlie but still allowing personal space. The simple address in a sleepy Colorado town was in contrast to the business cards she attached to her duffels when departing from Seattle:

Christine Boskoff
Owner, Mountain Madness

4218 SW Alaska Street
Seattle, Washington 98116

At thirty-nine, Chris was the only woman owner of a major climbing outfitter in the Pacific Northwest. Mountain Madness had been her life since 1997. The financials had been frightful in those early years, but the company name was strong. Launched by Scott Fischer in 1984, Mountain Madness drew clients from all over the world, taking them to the top of the highest peaks on Earth. After Fischer perished on Mount Everest in 1996, the company struggled until Chris stepped in. Bringing it back to life had been not only a passion but a means to an end.

Chris had started late in the sport of mountaineering, having given up a successful career at Lockheed in Atlanta and risen like a rocket in her effort to create a life that would sustain her need to climb. The bravado that infused the climbing community in the Pacific Northwest failed to affect her. Instead she was modest, remaining understated about her accomplishments even as she made a name for herself.

A "mediocre athlete at sea level," as she called herself, Chris's real gift was the ability to breathe the thin air at high altitude with ease. Training in Seattle often consisted of getting out of work on a Friday afternoon, then driving a few hours south to the base of Mount Rainier with a girlfriend. The two of them strapped on helmets, busting past groups of climbers who'd spent multiple days on the ascent. Chris and her friend climbed fast and planned to be home for dinner on Saturday. Leapfrogging groups of climbers, the two women with blond ponytails sticking out of their helmets came out of nowhere.

"Where'd you come from?" climbers would ask. When Chris casually answered that they'd come from the parking lot, the looks on the others' faces were priceless. By 5:00 a.m., they'd reach the summit, taking a moment to enjoy the view before making a brutally fast descent. Chris glided over rocks and snow effortlessly. Reaching the car, the two friends would enjoy a postclimb snack—Diet Coke and a bag of SunChips.

Chris was always laughing, constantly in motion, radiant and down-to-earth. She drew a crowd of admirers everywhere, though she barely noticed. Now, when she had vanished in the mountains of western China, the crowd aided the search for her from afar, wanting her back beyond measure. Friends remained awake at night. Mountain Madness rallied their overseas guides and business partners to assist. Her mother, in a quiet Wisconsin city, prayed. This level of attention would have made Chris cringe, yet here it was: unwelcome yet necessary.

THE PSB OFFICER RETURNED TO the conference room, gripping a bolt cutter. He handed it to Callahan, who turned to Charlie's bag first. Several officers jostled forward, hoping to be the first to spot clues spilling from inside. The men leaned over one another, their body odors blending in the drafty space. Callahan reached in to clip the lock, his elbow momentarily bumped as the onlookers pushed each other closer. "I need a little room to breathe, please," he said.

The chatter dimmed. A handful of digital cameras emerged from pockets to document the findings. An officer stepped forward, clipboard in hand to record the contents for the US Consulate. He seemed mildly nervous as he shifted on the cold marble floor.

Snapping Charlie's lock, Callahan slowly unzipped the bag, feeling oddly reluctant. Disrespecting his hero by rifling through his belongings in a police station in rural China hadn't been on any Christmas wish list he'd drawn up. Reaching inside, he pulled out the pieces of Charlie's life: a sleeping pad, a pair of jeans, a small silver pocketknife, a wall adaptor, watch batteries and instructions for a Timex, a single titanium ice screw, disposable razors, rubber sandals, nine rolls of 35-millimeter film, a bus ticket from Kangding to Litang, a business card for the driver in Litang, a US one-cent coin. *Charlie, you eternal cheapskate,* Callahan said to himself, smiling.

Charlie wore the badge of "dirtbag climber" unapologetically from day one. Putting together jobs guiding and writing, he did what he could to minimize his consumerism and maximize his time on rocks. Presentable when he needed to be and far wiser than most people understood, this penny in his duffel would no doubt be spent on a necessity of life back in the United States. *If I can just get him back there,* thought Callahan.

Reward money had been offered to the driver who'd led Chris and Charlie here, but emptying Charlie's black duffel had left Callahan with nothing more than dirty socks and lip balm. And—aside from the ice screw—no climbing gear: no ice axe, ropes, or crampons. *Dammit,* he thought, *they took their climbing gear.*

Littered among the three weeks of searching had been hopeful rumors that perhaps the pair had been abducted or thrown in a Chinese prison. Not a likely scenario, given that all the bits and pieces were pointing to the obvious conclusion: they'd gone to climb.

"What are you looking for?" asked an officer next to Callahan. Clipboard man shooed away colleagues who'd started to touch Charlie's belongings spread out on the floor.

"Something more than . . . this," Callahan said. "Something to tell us where they went. Definitively."

"Are they friends of yours?" asked the officer, nodding to the door, where one of the flyers created by the search team hung, attached with masking tape.

Callahan glanced at it. "Yeah, they are." Chinese characters spelled out the basics on the flyer:

Charlie Fowler and Christine Boskoff
Last heard from in Litang on November 7
Missed flight back to USA on December 4
If you have seen either or both of these people or have any informa-
tion regarding their whereabouts, please contact us immediately.

In the photo on the flyer, Chris was offset against yellow tents in the background. She wore a scarlet-and-black down parka and a white Mountain Madness baseball cap. Smiling broadly, her cheeks were flushed deep red from high-altitude sunburn.

"She's beautiful," the officer said.

"Yes," Callahan responded.

Charlie's picture showed him in a gray polo shirt against the backdrop of a rock field: rumpled salt-and-pepper hair, leathered skin, famously not smiling, looking every bit the confident, ass-kicking climber he was.

Charlie and Chris's relationship had lasted six years. Whether they'd end up together forever was anyone's guess, but they loved each other, and the river of respect they had for each other ran strong.

Clipboard man cleared space for Chris's green duffel to be unpacked. Callahan looked back at the picture of Chris as her duffel was moved into place. He'd heard her voice just four months ago, in August 2006.

"Come on, Ted," she'd whispered, "I can just get on your shoulders." The two of them were leading Mountain Madness clients up Russia's Mount Elbrus, the highest peak in Europe, at 18,510 feet. A night before the climb to Elbrus Base Camp, they'd stayed out too late. In the chilly Russian midnight, the guesthouse holding their beds for the night was locked.

"You're joking, Chris. Can't we find some other way to get in?" Callahan knew before she answered where this was headed. The glint in her eye calmed him.

"I'll just pop in the window and open the door for you." Looking at him with conviction, she placed her hand on his shoulder, gently pushing him lower so she could step up.

Marveling at her free spirit, he kneeled and sank a little into the soft ground. "Oh god, all right. Up you go. Don't hurt yourself."

"I'm totally fine," she said. "Let's do the damn thing."

Callahan could still feel the weight of her 120 pounds on his shoulders as he severed the padlock and unzipped her duffel. He knew what he was looking for. Reaching in, he pulled out a thin, canvas diary. It fell open to reveal pieces of the puzzle that searchers on two continents had struggled with for weeks: the climb of Elbrus in southern Russia. The ascent on Cho Oyu, on the China-Nepal border, in October with three clients. Meeting Charlie in Hong Kong. Climbing two lesser peaks in Sichuan Province, including well-known and challenging Yala Peak. A detailed account of how well they'd bargained and how cheaply she and Charlie had managed to live.

And finally, the plan. In Chris's loopy, almost childlike handwriting, a rough itinerary put them at the base of Mount Genyen. Genyen Massif, a holy mountain rising up 20,354 feet from Lenggu Monastery on the Tibetan Plateau. Their prize.

Callahan dropped the diary back into the duffel and punched in numbers on his mobile phone, connecting him to his colleague Kara Jenkinson in Chengdu. "Hey, it's me. I've got the bags open and the driver was for real. The reward money worked. It's Genyen. My god, that's where they are. Tell Seattle and Telluride we're heading out first thing tomorrow."

CHAPTER 2

MIDWEST GIRL

WITH A POPULATION OF SEVENTY-FIVE thousand and an altitude of only 790 feet, Appleton, Wisconsin, situated on the Fox River, is about as far away from Sichuan, in southwestern China, as one can travel. The nearest significant mountains are the Rockies, a thousand miles and several tanks of gas to the west. The paper industry, including Kimberly-Clark (the personal care company that produces big-name brands Kleenex and Huggies), provides thousands of jobs in the community.

Aside from the river, perhaps the most noteworthy natural feature in the community is High Cliff State Park. Ten miles from Appleton, High Cliff sits on the shores of Lake Winnebago, a vast body of water in the middle of northeastern Wisconsin. Dotted with limestone cliffs perfect for bouldering, the park became Chris's destination of choice on trips home to visit her family. Strapping on a heavy backpack to add to the demand on her body, she'd run the ten miles there and back, training for summits of 8,000-meter peaks on the other side of the world.

Proximity to Canada gives Wisconsin natives a distinctive accent. Nasal, sharply articulated phrases are a novelty to those outside the Midwest. Drinking fountains are "bubblers." Stoplights are "stop-and-go-lights." Deep-fried cheese curds are as common as french fries and are paired with Friday night fish fries and bottles of locally brewed beer. Chris's Wisconsin accent never left her, a tribute to the fact that she'd lived in Appleton all seventeen of her formative years. Long after she'd moved away, her love for Wisconsin Danish kringle and the Green

Bay Packers remained, as did her strikingly friendly disposition that caused her to drum up conversations on all manner of trails and rocks. Engaging others in pleasant chatter marked Chris as a Midwest girl, while Wisconsin's frigid winter months left their mark for future climbs by preparing her to endure subzero temperatures.

Winters give Appleton and Wisconsin a bad rap, say locals. Yes, the temperature can cause massive, temporary migrations to Mexico. The salt dumped on roads to melt ice eventually makes them appear to be made of white concrete. But April through November are a delight. The town is full of blooming flower beds, and kids zoom all over on bikes, eventually stopping at one of many ice cream parlors. Why would anyone ever leave?

Downtown Appleton in the late 1970s and early 1980s—Chris's childhood years—boasted Conkey's Bookstore, a cocktail lounge called Cleo's, and the brand-new Paper Valley hotel, named in honor of the community's leading industry. It was a place of relative quiet. A city filled with Lawrence University professors and engineers living next to line workers and truck drivers. Sunday mornings, Chris and her family attended Good Shepherd Lutheran Church.

Chris was the youngest of four children, and the only girl. Her mom, Joyce, had given birth to Chris at age thirty-nine and watched her daughter battle for position in the weekend flag football games on their lawn. Joyce recalled: "Her brothers would get her out there playing with all the boys and Tommy would yell at her, 'Just get in there and push those boys aside, Chrissy!' She wasn't big, but she'd run for a touchdown as she scrambled right around them. They made her tough."

NOW NINETY-TWO, JOYCE EXUDED THE energy of a best friend more than a grandmother. With a laugh that carried from one room to the other, conversation and stories came easily in her presence. Her build was somehow sturdy yet delicate, perhaps because of her height—no more than five feet. She joked: "I used to be five-two but then I shrank." Taking herself too seriously would be tragic, draining the pleasure out of simple things left to enjoy, such as her great-grandchildren and the book club at her retirement home in Appleton.

Reminiscing about her daughter, Joyce referenced a childhood friend of Chris's. "Nadine is the one to talk to! She knew Chrissy well. Oh my, did those girls get into some antics when they were teenagers!" Waving her hand in front of her face, she broke into a huge grin, the stories of her teenage daughter trickling between the edges of her memory.

NADINE GREW UP TO BECOME a landscape designer, but back in the day she was simply Chris's best friend. Both girls came from families of boys, and they became thick as thieves in seventh grade when they met at Madison Junior High School. "We were total tomboys," Nadine recalled. "We signed up for the basketball team and both of us sucked, so we sat on the bench together. We weren't tall, and neither of us were good shooters, but we had fun."

Eventually the girls were so attached that they rode double on Nadine's banana bike. Sunny weekends were filled with lying on blankets in the driveway, slathered with baby oil. When Chris's brother Paul was out on dates, the two girls shut themselves in his room and listened to his records, playing Chris's favorite album, *Rush 2112*.

"Basically, we were just a couple of girls messing around and getting into trouble," Nadine said. "We figured it would keep us from getting into trouble later. Whenever Chris got in hot water, I'd knock on her bedroom window and give her a Tab."

By the time they hit high school at Appleton East, the girls had expanded their list of activities. Chris joined the tennis and softball teams, took up playing flute in the marching band, and sported a classic eighties short haircut that was so uneven on the sides that she earned the nickname "Little Spike." Hanging out with Nadine's family gave Chris the chance to experience opportunities she wasn't getting at home. Her family took the occasional trip up to remote northern Wisconsin, but many of Chris's big adventures were with Nadine and her parents, who were still in their thirties.

In the winter of 1983, the girls were at Nordic Mountain in central Wisconsin. "I can't believe you're in tenth grade and you've never been downhill skiing before," Nadine said to Chris. She looked at her friend, who was gazing up at the mountain. Although it was a foothill compared to what Chris would be on in a decade, the mountain was the first to irresistibly entice her.

"I don't need the bunny hill," Chris said. "I wanna go with you. I can handle it."

Nadine wasn't so sure. "I've been on skis since I was four years old. That's probably not the best place to start, way up there." But she lost the argument and the pair took the lift up, scooching off at the top and inching closer to the mountain's smooth, downhill slope.

"Just give me a little push! I'll be fine," Chris said as she positioned her skis parallel as instructed.

Watching Chris begin her first descent, Nadine's tummy knotted. Wind blew against her neon down jacket as she took off behind her friend. Gaining speed, she picked the fastest line to catch up to Chris, who appeared to be disobeying Nadine's five-minute lesson on how to slow down or stop. "I couldn't catch her," Nadine recalled. "She went straight down, and I found her at the bottom, just sitting on the snow, smiling."

Joyce and her husband, Robin, saw to it that their children went through confirmation and were properly educated. The loving parents told their kids repeatedly that they could pursue whatever they wanted. All four were sent off to college with strong Midwestern values and the drive to squeeze as much as they could out of life. Joyce pressed particularly hard for Chris to go to college "since Mama didn't get to go." The decision to stay home and raise four children had fit with the times, yet Joyce was adventurous by nature. In the 1950s, she trained to be a beautician and worked for a spell at a local department store, but ultimately she felt her calling was at home with her three sons and Chris.

For a time, it looked like the University of Wisconsin–Oshkosh would become Chris's home for the next four years. Robin had a fierce work ethic, which his daughter emulated, resulting in high school grades that would allow her the freedom to be selective with her education and career choices. A career in nursing sounded promising and would be a choice her parents could understand. But Chris changed her mind at the last minute. Instead of pursuing a nursing degree at Oshkosh, she decided on engineering at the University of Wisconsin–Milwaukee, an hour farther from Appleton than Oshkosh. A daughter going to school in engineering seemed an ocean apart from anything Joyce had known. *Never mind,* she thought. *Chrissy will do more in her life than I've done in mine.* As with many a mother and daughter, their differences seemed stark, though similarities would arise with time.

In 1985, when Chris graduated high school, Joyce was close to sixty years old. She'd lived through the Great Depression, a World War, and Vietnam. She'd watched a moon landing, two Green Bay Packer Super Bowl championships, and the rise of the women's movement. Life had treated Joyce well, and with four grown children off on adventures, she prepared to enjoy their every step.

Draped in red, white, and blue, the graduating seniors at Appleton East prepared to walk into the gymnasium. For Joyce, it was the end of a life at home with kids. Her days would turn to volunteering and even grandchildren soon.

Dear Mom,
All is well at school. Studies tough, but I'm surviving. The class-rooms are cold. Really cold. Can you please send a pair of my mittens?
—Chrissy

Joyce sent the mittens. She knew her daughter well. Chris hated being cold. When the Wisconsin winters subsided and the school term ended in summer, Chris returned to Appleton. Working at a bakery brought in needed college funds, while spending time with her friend Nadine remained a constant. And not far from Appleton was the home of the Experimental Aircraft Association (EAA), a nonprofit dedicated to aviation enthusiasts that held a fly-in convention every July; Chris caught the flying bug.

"She jumped into new adventures with everything she had," Nadine remembered. "She was tenacious that way. If you were with her and you wanted her to stay longer, she'd say that she simply had something to do, without bragging about what it was, even if it was something major like climbing a mountain. That summer in college she took one visit to the EAA convention, thought it was cool, and invested her entire being in it. Not standing from a distance watching others fly. She needed to do it herself. She needed to fly."

Learning to fly consumed the rest of Chris's summer days, and she earned her pilot's license by college graduation. For Mother's Day, she took Joyce up in a rented plane so she could show her how it all looked from the air: circling Lake Winnebago, the Fox River, and the family home. Chris Feld was already learning to love the view from the top.

After graduating from college in 1991 with an electrical engineering degree, Chris made Atlanta home, where she'd gotten a job at Lockheed Aeronautical Systems. Entering this world as one of the few women in the room wasn't new to her; she'd experienced it at home in Appleton and in her undergraduate classes in Milwaukee. At Lockheed, her talent for leadership was noticed, and she was assigned to guide a team designing software for a lighted control display for the C-130J Super Hercules, a military cargo plane.

Challenged but still restless, Chris sought outside activities to battle the tedium of her nine-to-five routine. Her desire for something more than a fancy job was about to lead her down a new path.

CHAPTER 3

A NATURAL

EYES GLUED TO THE PAGE of a North Face catalog, Chris sensed something click. The climber in the photo was on a summit in Alaska. Below him a layer of wispy clouds hung as the sun set in golds and crimson. Making it to the top of Nordic Mountain in Wisconsin had been a thrill, but this . . . *this* seemed a thousand times more exciting.

Just enough to intrigue her, the image led Chris to a presentation at the Atlanta Climbing Club in early 1993. The speaker had recently returned from Argentina, where he'd climbed Aconcagua, the highest peak in the Western Hemisphere. His slides showed a gradual ascent over the course of roughly twenty-one days. In the final shots, he kneeled on top, smiling. At 22,837 feet and lit by a sky of liquid blue, the alpinist looked elated.

Chris was fascinated. The speaker talked about the hardships, altitude sickness, the climbers who'd failed and those who'd arrived unprepared. "I've only been at this a few years, but the physical challenge is addictive." Dressed in jeans and a crew-neck T-shirt, he was appealing in a rugged sort of way. And older. He looked to be in his forties. The fact that he was talking about something she was increasingly fascinated by was a bonus.

"So after all this," he said, "if you feel like climbing is something you might want to take a crack at, you should go big." Ending the talk, the speaker added, "I'm heading to Bolivia in a few months. That's what I'd consider challenging! If any of you are takers, come on up and chat. I'll stick around for a while."

Chris rose, waiting for the crowd around the climber to thin. When he seemed free, she eased forward, full of wonder as she approached. "I think I might be hooked," she announced, shaking the speaker's hand. Their eyes connected as he laughed at her opening line. His hair was streaked with gray, matching his moustache. The energy she felt from him during the presentation proved stronger up close. He seemed a mix of wise and dynamic, and she sensed immediately that they'd get along.

"I'm Christine Feld. I loved your presentation."

"Keith Boskoff," he said. "You've got a little experience in you for something like Bolivia?"

She hadn't. "Not tons, but I pick things up pretty quickly. Just took one course at the Sporting Club at Windy Hill. Did a little climbing with a friend of mine in Michigan, too."

"Michigan? You're from the Midwest?"

"Wisconsin."

"A cheesehead! A Wisconsin girl goes to Bolivia. I'm liking this image," Keith said. "Got any gear after that course at Windy Hill?" He shifted his weight, crossing his arms as he sized up the short blond woman in front of him. Her build was solid. Not lithe or wiry like the women at the climbing gym he was used to seeing. She looked strong, capable of endurance—qualities he knew were important trekking miles at altitude.

"A backpack," Chris said. "That's it. But I just got a raise, so my credit card is ready to be put to use. You might look at me and think I'm not up for it, but I've got three older brothers so I can handle myself. I'm into all kinds of sports. Tennis, barefoot waterskiing, running, racquetball."

Keith looked at the fiery woman before him. She seemed like the real deal. "Tell you what. Let's get together, rope up, and I'll give you a few more pointers."

Chris and Keith began training together, a partnership that turned into romance with ease. He was seventeen years her senior and owned an architectural firm, a career that allowed flexibility and enough money to support his climbing habit. Chris committed to her new interest by purchasing gear and absorbing the knowledge she'd need for the sport she would grow to love. She was an uncomplicated girl from the

Midwest. Yet at age twenty-six, she was a natural for the sport. Years as an engineer had sharpened her analytical skills. Patience had grown from struggling to keep up with her brothers and then leading teams of men at Lockheed. And she was resilient—a gift from her German-bred, pragmatic parents.

THE SPORT OF CLIMBING, SOME say, is misunderstood. What the average person might see as a sport for the selfish or those simply needing an adrenaline rush, climbers observe as a way of life. Athletes capable of sorting through technical challenges rise in the sport. Those at the top of their game are typically articulate and astute about the risks involved in scaling rock, ice, and high peaks. Their wish to survive and enjoy the thrills captured by being in nature generally outweighs their desire to walk close to death. They don't have a death wish, but a wish to live in a way that few others understand. Elite athletes and those involved in extreme sports have a focus and drive that underlies their approach to each move.

"It's a type of alive—not like a party, but like being at one with the world. It's being in tune," notes Eric Brymer, a professor of exercise and sport science at Manchester Metropolitan University in England. "These athletes may have more to tell us about what it means to be human than the rest of us."

Mountaineer Conrad Anker, who has spoken frequently of the ethos of climbing, states, "If you're not scared at least once a week, maybe once a month or once a year, you're not living life. Some may think it's a very frivolous pursuit, obviously we're not curing cancer, we're not even curing the common cold, but there's this drive that humans have to explore and to see what's over the horizon." While climbing does indeed foster a connection with the world in a unique way, it's hard to argue that the sport is not also one wrapped in danger. Entering the orbit of climbing means hearing refrains like these:

My family told me when I got into this that they're worried they'll lose me.
I was warned that I was going to lose people I loved.

If you can't handle death, you shouldn't be in the business of climbing.

Given that new methods and equipment are constantly being developed, breaking climbing down into all its varieties is a nearly impossible task. Rock and ice climbing are perhaps the most accessible and well-known forms. The advent of climbing gyms has allowed beginners to swiftly master new skills no matter what the topography or climate of their surroundings. Once adept at working with the necessary gear, climbers can incorporate what they've learned into mountaineering, which often includes both rock and ice climbing.

Chris dove in, training under Keith's watchful eye. His vocal, high-energy temperament contrasted with her private, steady nature. As she did with all new interests, she wanted to excel and put silent pressure on herself. In Chris, Keith saw a tenacious partner who could push him as much as he pushed himself. Since losing his parents in a plane crash in his twenties, he'd felt alone in his life. But he felt close to Chris, who soon became the primary recipient of his love and attention. The pair fell in love over the next two months. "It's the greatest love I've ever had," Keith wrote in his journal. "I love every move she makes and everything she says."

In turn, Chris fed off Keith's knowledge, gobbling up every bit of information he provided on how to become a better climber. They spent weekends rock climbing in Georgia, North Carolina, and Tennessee. During the week they'd go to the climbing gym or strap on seventy-pound packs and run up Stone Mountain to gain the endurance needed to summit Tarija Peak in Bolivia. Visiting from Wisconsin, Joyce marveled at her daughter as she ran up and down the mountain four times in the time it took Joyce to hike it once.

Unaccustomed to having a climbing companion able to keep pace with him, Keith found his passion for the sport and Chris growing exponentially. Chris continued to push herself and often hiked to the limits of her ability to build endurance. Glancing behind his shoulder on one of their weekend training sessions, Keith noted the look of frustration on Chris's face. He forged ahead as she tried to keep up, tripping over rocks as her legs felt heavy. He told a fourth, then fifth story about a climb he'd enjoyed. Each story had a goofy sidebar punctuated by hand gestures and impressions.

"Come on, Chris. Not much longer," he said. "Turnaround point is just up over this ridgeline."

"I'm fine," she said, in an unconvincing tone.

He stopped and turned, shifting from storyteller to cheerleader. Chris slumped onto a boulder, unlacing her boots.

"Look, this isn't going to happen overnight," he told her. "You've been sitting in a cubicle at Lockheed for two years. Don't expect so much from yourself."

"Dammit, Keith. I said I'm fine so just . . . space, please." Her exasperation exposed, she reached down and pulled off both boots. In a flash, she threw them beyond the path, watching them roll down into dry brush. Head in her hands, she sat unwilling to make eye contact or admit weakness.

Keith hadn't seen this side of her before. He leaned on his trekking pole as he reached down to retrieve the boots. "You'll need these. Like I said, the turnaround point is just up over that ridge." He handed her the boots with a gentle smile, which she briefly returned. They continued the hike, finishing in silence laced with triumph.

WITH THREE WEEKS TO GO before the Bolivia trip, Chris found herself in Colorado undergoing a crash course in ice climbing from well-known mountaineer Thor Keiser, who would be the lead guide on their climb. Just a year earlier, Keiser and French climber Chantal Mauduit had been rescued by climbing greats Scott Fischer and Ed Viesturs on K2, perhaps the most treacherous of the world's 8,000-meter peaks. Chris had begun to master the lingo and dig into the personalities in the climbing community. Her time in Colorado was an opportunity to expand these skills.

Keiser took Keith and Chris to climb a classic pillar of ice in the Vail area called *Rigid Designator*, which rose 115 vertical feet. With a cauliflowered base rising into an upper column of beautiful ice, if Chris topped out on her first visit here, she knew it would be quite an accomplishment in her young climbing career. On day two of their attempt to scale *Rigid Designator*, Keith had Chris roped, and he stood below her on solid ground, belaying her from thirty feet. The day prior, he'd fought all the way up, while she'd managed to scale only about half of it before stopping in exhaustion and rappelling down. She'd vowed to get to the top before they left Colorado. Confident in her skill, Keith placed a bet with Thor, the loser paying for dinner in Bolivia.

Passing her previous stopping point, Chris paused, adding long ice screws into the frozen wall as she rose. She swung her ice axe, making contact with pale blue and splintering frozen shards that bounced off her helmet. Higher she climbed, taking a moment to rest, turn back, and look at the view. The altitude, often a factor for new climbers, failed to bother her. Her breathing remained smooth, her heart rate low, and her head clear. On a wall of ice at nearly nine thousand feet, Chris felt challenged but strong.

As her breath created puffs of white, Chris came close. With a final, calculated hack into the ice, she pulled herself to the top of the pillar. A hundred feet below, Keith let out a hoot. He and Thor stood amazed at the feat, which had taken only a few hours for a relative novice. Keith gripped the rope in his guide hand, leaning back as she slowly descended.

"You owe us dinner in La Paz, dude," Keith told Thor, laughing. Almost mumbling to himself, he said, "I've got to marry this girl."

MOUNTAIN GUIDE HECTOR PONCE DE LEON heard Chris laugh. Not just once, but many times, interrupting the intensity of the climb. The clients on his 1993 guided Bolivia trip seemed drawn to Chris's energy. At altitudes over twenty thousand feet, she seemed untroubled by the difficulties with food and physical limitations that usually worried novice climbers. Keith had expressed concern about her pushing too much, too fast, wondering if she realized how hard the challenge would be. But Chris's first foray outside the United States showcased her ease in places far from home and high in the clouds. She appeared to be made for life in a tent on a high ridge.

"I just didn't feel like I was guiding her. Not at all," Ponce de Leon said. Thor had asked the Mexican guide to help him lead their small group on climbs of several peaks in Bolivia, and he recalled being surprised by their tenacity. "Chris and Keith wanted more than regular clients. They asked for an extension of the normal itinerary. She wanted extra climbs everywhere we went. Her physical and mental strength were outstanding. I was impressed." Ponce de Leon remembered her laughing a ton, "having a great time ... she was just all over the place. She was putting up tents and doing things that we weren't expecting clients to do. After that, I knew I needed to keep track of her."

Guides often gripe about high-maintenance clients, but Chris brought lightness to the team. Still a beginner in the world of climbing, she inhaled everything about it. Wrapping her arms around the sport, she was learning that climbing wasn't always comfortable. It was full of snow, cold temperatures, and potentially sleepless nights in thin air. But she relished the hardships that scared away many mountaineers. In South America, Chris hit her stride while Keith and the guides watched with admiration.

Their climbing journals shed light on this glorious experience:

[Chris] It's my first time in a third-world country. I'm with Keith and I'm loving it. What could be better? This is like everything I dreamed mountaineering to be and then some. I think this trip is going to be a turning point in my life. Actually, Keith was it first. I love him dearly. He thinks I'll be the next [pioneer climber] Kitty Calhoun. I have to prove myself and be tough and aggressive and show no pain. I think I'll find out what I'm really made of.

• • •

[Keith] Chris is like a wide-eyed kid. She loves this place and appreciates the culture and the atmosphere more than any woman I've ever met. She is amazing, unusual and loving. If we do K2 in 1995, she'd be the first American woman. Anyway, one step at a time.

LESS THAN A YEAR AFTER taking to climbing and mountaineering, Chris closed out 1993 by summiting 19,341-foot Mount Kilimanjaro in Tanzania with Keith. He had proposed to Chris on a hike, and she said yes enthusiastically. They raised glasses of whiskey after their summit, toasting the future, and married the next year in Atlanta. The wedding was attended by Robin and Joyce Feld. Their daughter's wedding cake was made of bagels and bananas, a far cry from the traditional butter-cream version the Felds had envisioned for their baby.

"I kept going to Atlanta by myself to see them," Joyce recalled. "They were full of adventure and I liked adventure myself." Adventure for the newlyweds included a honeymoon in Asia. It was October 1994 and 22,500-foot Ama Dablam in postmonsoon Nepal called to the pair, who sought to become the first American couple to summit that peak. Completing their goal on October 25, Keith and Chris were jubilant, deciding to remarry at the base of the mountain in the village of Pangbouche. Music blared from speakers set up by villagers. Once word had spread that an American couple planned to marry, the village came alive. A Buddhist monk provided blessings. Chris and Keith became instant celebrities, draped in traditional Nepalese clothing. They danced to local music that spilled into Michael Jackson. Chris's hair was caked with celebratory yak butter as Ama Dablam rose in the distance.

Ama Dablam—technical to ascend and stunning to behold—was the highlight of their mountaineering career so far, both as individuals and now as a couple. Mountaineers who summited the highest peaks in the Himalayas often visited historian Elizabeth Hawley in Kathmandu after their expeditions. With sharp attention to detail, Hawley questioned them closely to confirm their ascents. She spent decades verifying the achievements of climbers and recording them in an extensive database, which is still used today (Hawley continued her work until her death in 2018 at age ninety-four). With their summit of Ama Dablam, Chris and Keith received their first mention at her hand:

Ama Dablam in the post-monsoon. A total of 50 men and women summited Ama Dablam this season, including Americans Keith Boskoff and Mrs. Chris Boskoff.
—Himalayan Historian Elizabeth Hawley, American Alpine Club Journal

THOSE WHO CLIMB FREQUENTLY BECOME aware of a spectrum concealed in the upper echelon of the sport. Therein lies a vast array of attitudes about the element of danger. In perilous conditions, often the most compelling for elite climbers, the margin of safety is thin. It can be an illusion. The point where the reality of safety ends and the illusion begins differs for each individual. Reducing the risks in elite climbing is an effort involving speed, efficiency, and safe practices. When all three of these systems fail at the same time, extreme danger surfaces. Putting yourself in the same situation over and over again and walking away can feel like a gift of survival, when really the odds are no different than they are at a Las Vegas blackjack table. Or as one Seattle mountain guide explained: "It's like an all-you-can-eat buffet for some of these climbers. Those first four plates taste delicious, but it's that last piece of bacon that might send them over the top."

Chris had been climbing a few years with some success, and she found the exhilaration of the sport addictive. In Appleton, she frequented a new climbing gym whenever she was home visiting her parents. The locals, unaccustomed to a climber of her caliber, gave her a wide berth. "When she came in, it was pretty much all business. She was totally on a mission," remembered Paul Kuenn, who owned Vertical Stronghold, the Midwest's first climbing gym north of Chicago. "People would generally let her do her thing, but they'd definitely stare. Every now and then I'd overhear someone saying, 'Man alive, that woman has been on the wall for over two hours and she hasn't put her feet down.' She crossed from one end to the other."

Kuenn had arranged the holds so Chris could travel 170 feet sideways by going around the bouldering area, changing directions, and coming back without stopping to break. "This is Wisconsin, so there weren't exactly tons of people who knew who she was as her ascents became bolder," he said. "But eventually she was in all the climbing magazines. It's funny, she really didn't care about any of that. She wasn't into celebrity. She'd come to the gym and bring her mom to watch. The two of them together—decent, humble Midwesterners."

CHRIS AND KEITH CONTINUED TO scrape together vacation time, finding long weekends to flee Atlanta for greater challenges throughout 1994 and 1995. On one such getaway, New Hampshire was the destination. Relative to the mountains of the Greater Himalayas or the Andes,

Mount Washington in the White Mountains of New England pales at 6,289 feet. Yet its proximity to the intersection of several storm tracks makes it one of the deadliest mountains in the United States. Catching storms from every direction, the mountain faces brutal gusts that can come out of nowhere. Small outbuildings at the peak are chained to prevent destruction. In 1934, a wind speed of 231 miles an hour was clocked at the mountain's observatory, a Northern Hemisphere record that still stands.

Wind buffeted Chris and Keith as they began their attempt on Mount Washington's northern face. "Ready, Chris?" Keith called. He stood a distance from her, on a wall of steep ice.

Unanchored but roped to Keith, Chris looked down, double-checking the toe straps on her crampons. "Yeah, one sec. I wanna make sure I've got these tightened." A blast of air trapped her words, carrying them away before reaching Keith. Leaning over, she caught a glimpse of the rope, furiously uncoiling. Reacting immediately, Chris jumped hard on her ice axes with her body to arrest Keith's slide. He had been caught by the gust, knocked off balance, and was plunging down the ice in a near free fall. Digging into the ice with her crampons and tools, Chris stopped his fall, hoping the axes would hold.

A sharp pain rocketed through her hand, radiating up her arm. Sensing that the axes were holding firm, she peered down and saw her husband's face—a look of horror as he lay flat against ice. His fall had been stopped. Silently, Keith made his way back to her, relying on his crampons and pulling only gently on the rope as he heard his wife's cries and saw it wrapped around her hand.

"Keith, are you okay?"

"I'm okay. Don't move. I'm coming to you. Don't move your hand."

Her left hand gripped the ice axe, her right hand was limp against the handle of her second axe, bones crushed underneath skin. "I think I broke my hand, Keith. Dammit."

"You broke your hand but you saved your husband," he said. "You saved my life, you ridiculous woman!"

The chill of the snow was no match for adrenaline. Chris and Keith held each other, breathing heavily. Her hand was battered, but her confidence high. She'd weathered her first big test. Keith leaned over and kissed her. She smiled, then winced.

"That's enough for today," he insisted. "Let's go fix that hand."

Walking to the car, she said, "I'm ready for more."

"More? How about we talk about more after dinner once you're in a cast?" He knew she was ready for the big ones. "Those eight-thousand-meter peaks are no joke. You're gonna need both hands for those."

"I can be ready," Chris said. "By summer. Broad Peak. Scott Fischer will be there and it's our time, too."

"Scott's been climbing for ten years. He's done K2 and Lhotse. He could probably do Broad Peak in his sleep," Keith said.

"I'm not going without you," Chris pressed. "Are you in or out?"

"After today, I owe you one. I'm in. Broad Peak, it is."

CHAPTER 4

AN INDUSTRY BOOMS

OF ALL THE CITIES IN the country to establish a foothold in the climbing industry, Seattle in the 1980s and 1990s loomed large. Located on the Puget Sound in the Pacific Northwest, Seattle offered proximity to the Cascade Range and the Olympic Mountains, providing a wealth of opportunity for climbing at every ability. Longtime residents included iconic climber Fred Beckey and the Whittaker brothers, Jim and Lou, who'd learned the art of outdoor adventuring in the local mountains. They had put their skills to test on peaks all over the world, including Everest, which Jim had summited as the first American in 1963.

Successful, growing businesses such as Microsoft and Starbucks drew employees who wanted to spend their weekends and days off skiing and climbing in the nearby peaks and ski areas. Local outdoor retail companies Eddie Bauer and REI fed the appetite for cutting-edge gear, while recreation experts of all stripes established guide services that provided full-service expeditions for those interested in adventures. In 1987, Vertical World opened, billing itself as the nation's first climbing gym. By the time Chris's hunger for climbing began, Seattle had expanded its pitch to those across the country seeking the same rush.

Gambling that he could make a go of it in the adventure travel business, Scott Fischer and his partners had opened the doors of Mountain Madness in 1984. He and his wife, Jeannie, had moved to Seattle thanks to her job as a pilot for Alaska Airlines, which afforded Scott the chance to climb mountains and launch the business. Seduced by climbing from a youth filled with National Outdoor Leadership School (NOLS) courses, Scott began by guiding friends. Mainly, he crafted the company to take clients to the peaks he loved. Scott made no secret of the fact that the business was born out of his desire to link his sport and his income.

Scott's strength and skill at scaling mountains were formidable. He loved telling stories in which he was the punch line, blurring the divide between novice climber and master. Treating everyone, from Sherpas and high-altitude porters to clients, as equals became a hallmark of his expeditions, along with honoring the environment, which Scott believed was as important as treasuring its beauty.

Among Scott's earliest supporters was Geri Lesko, who had come to the sport of mountaineering in her late forties. Geri had gained an appreciation for the outdoors from summers at a family camp in Yosemite. Mountaineering became a natural passion, and she pursued fourteen-thousand-foot peaks in California and Colorado. In 1990, she found herself in Washington attempting to summit Mount Rainier, where she met noted Seattle climber Ed Viesturs. She was introduced to Scott in 1995.

"The first time I met him," Geri recalled, "he extended his hand to escort me from the cab. I'd arrived to view a pre-expedition slide show in Seattle for a trip I was taking with him to Pakistan. I looked up and said, 'Scott, you *are* just as gorgeous as everyone says you are, but are you any good?' He laughed and said, 'You'll see.'" Fifteen years older than Scott, Geri became a confidante and trusted adviser, lending her ear as he worked to establish himself as a leader in international guided expeditions.

Sponsorships were necessary to turn a profit on big climbs, and Scott's bold personality and attractiveness made perfect marketing material. In addition to being the face of the company, he needed to prove his worth to draw clients. Mount Everest became priority number one. Without an Everest summit on his résumé, clients would turn to other companies before his. The competition grew increasingly fierce as guide companies perfected their business models. Though the demand in the industry proved real, it came with growing pains. Scott practiced alpine-style climbing. This method focused on highly trained climbers who packed light. Efficiency and speed were carefully balanced with safety. Alpine-style climbers rarely turned to supplemental oxygen, medication, or high-altitude workers to aid their climbs.

Though alpine style was a respected method, the reality for guided adventures was expedition-style climbing, which required monumental planning. A push to the summit was no longer two individuals and all they could carry. Expedition-style climbing enlisted high-altitude workers who spent time fixing ropes on trails in advance of clients. Supplies were shuttled up mountainsides with tents pitched to shelter clients at higher camps. Supplemental oxygen (known as "Os") and drugs to counteract the side effects of increased altitude were widely embraced. Such climbs came with a price, upward of $60,000 at that time for an expedition that lasted many weeks and without a guaranteed summit.

The race to meet the demand for adventure companies exposed a divide between those who'd been raised on alpine-style climbing and those who were seeking expedition-style adventures. Guiding companies were launched by those with climbing experience, talent, and raw energy. These were necessary assets, but the business knowledge was sometimes missing. Clients were looking for the full package: companies that could provide the training, handle the logistics, and get them up the mountain. Furnishing perks while providing a focus on proper training and safety set in motion an incongruity that persists today.

The year 1990 marked a milestone for Scott and subsequently for Mountain Madness. Lhotse, a next-door neighbor to Everest and the world's fourth highest mountain, remained unclimbed by Americans. With little fanfare, Scott and his climbing partner, Wally Berg, climbed to 27,940 feet until there was no longer mountain to climb.

Next up was K2, second to Everest in height, but a brutal and more technically challenging mountain. Nestled in the Karakoram Range, K2 is one of the range's few peaks over 8,000 meters, each marked by glaciers and steep, dark slopes that exemplify the Turkish translation for Karakoram—*black stone*. Partnering with Ed Viesturs, Scott's trip up the mountain in 1992 started and ended with drama. An early fall from a loose ice block dislocated his shoulder, stranding him at base camp for two weeks until it healed enough to try again. A subsequent attempt yielded a close call with an avalanche and the rescue of Chantal Mauduit from a high camp. After the rescue, Scott and Ed reached the summit of K2, but during a harrowing descent they were called to a second rescue, this time of New Zealand climber Gary Ball, who was suffering from high-altitude pulmonary edema (HAPE). K2 had lived up to the hype, a reminder that it could be very dangerous to heed the alluring call of its summit.

Everest remained. The world's tallest mountain had yet to find a place on Scott's résumé. He'd attempted it before, in 1987 and 1989, without a summit. Several years later, in 1994, on an expedition billed as the Sagarmatha Environmental Expedition, Scott's ascent to the top was as easy as the other attempts had been difficult. On the climb, he reaffirmed his commitment to the environment, as expedition members and high-altitude workers carried trash off the mountain, long plagued with the remnants of previous climbs.

The market for those seeking to summit 8,000-meter peaks was growing. As it erupted, one demographic played catch-up: women.

MOUNTAINEERING HAD LONG BEEN A sport portrayed in the media through the eyes of men as an escape from domestic life to the wilds of the outdoors. In many societies, being "feminine" meant staying at home, while masculinity was defined as seeking faraway adventures. By the late 1980s, the world of high-dollar, flashy expeditions had erupted. Commercially organized mountaineering tours could take clients as high as their pockets were deep. The influence of money was apparent, both in the gear developed to aid in climbs and in the amount needed to undertake far-flung trips. At the time, the commercial landscape was heavily male-dominated, resulting in women creating their own, all-female trips.

Among the earliest to take this approach was mountaineer Arlene Blum, who in 1969 received this response to her request to join an all-male expedition in Afghanistan:

Dear Miss Blum:

*Not too easy a letter to write as your prior work in Peru demon-
strates your ability to go high, and a source I trust has furnished a
glowing account of your pleasant nature in the mountains.*

*But one woman and nine men would seem to me to be unpleasant
high on the open ice, not only in excretory situations, but in the
easy masculine companionship which is so vital a part of the joy
of an expedition.*

Sorry as hell.

Aside from the perceived intrusion of females at base camp, the ability of women to undertake the same physical rigors as men was called
into question, as Blum discovered. "When I asked why women wouldn't
be admitted to a commercial climb of Mount McKinley that year," she
recalled, "I was informed that women are a liability in the high mountains: They are not strong enough to carry their share of the loads and
lack the emotional stability to withstand the psychological stresses of
a high-altitude climb."

There's little doubt that the physical challenges women face in alpine
climbing are different from those men face. With generally smaller bodies, women shoulder a larger percentage of their body weight than men
when required to carry the basics needed for survival at high altitudes.
Yet many women argue that the mental game women play is more effective and better suited to the stress of climbing. Mountaineer Vanessa
O'Brien, the first American and British (dual citizen) woman to successfully summit K2 in 2017, explained it this way: "I believe women
have a bit of luck, which comes in two forms. The first is their open and
transparent communication style that helps them get where they need
to go. The second is their mental focus that helps them stay the course
when the going gets tough: and the going always gets tough. That's quite
simply, our secret."

WITH LITTLE FANFARE, SCOTT FISCHER invited Stacy Allison to climb
Everest with him in 1987. A friend from his NOLS days, Allison had
the grit and talent to be part of the expedition, no matter her gender.

Though the two didn't summit, in 1988 she attempted again with a different group, this time becoming the first American woman to reach the top of the world's highest peak. The news buoyed Scott, for if anyone could see the strength women brought to the mountains—in practice or in spirit—it was Scott. His own mother, Shirley, had graced Everest Base Camp on one of his trips there, spending time with him in the place he loved.

In 1993, elite rock climber Lynn Hill became the first person to free climb the Nose, a route on El Capitan in the Yosemite Valley. Though she'd already won competitions all over the world, she faced the same challenges as other women in terms of gender discrimination. When some attributed Hill's success to the fact that she had small fingers and a petite frame, she responded:

> *Both are true facts, but there were other sections of the route that were perhaps more difficult for me because of my small size. I think those statements indicate hints of jealousy that come from sexism and the idea that men always have to be better—if a woman does something before a man, some men try to find a reason to undermine the achievement instead of just recognizing the beauty and vision of the ascent. No matter what size you are, you still have to be a very good climber to free climb the Nose, so why couldn't they accept the fact that a woman is capable of making such a breakthrough ascent? I don't see a point in dwelling on people's small-minded ego problems. It's not my problem; it's their problem.*

The conversation of whether women approached climbing differently than men evolved through the 1990s. While it was still not uncommon to recognize the basic physiological differences, people became more cautious about making assumptions based on gender. Chris adopted this approach in her own climbing. Differences existed among climbers, more often between individuals and less between genders.

As she grew in the sport, her source of inspiration remained Polish climber Wanda Rutkiewicz. With nine summits of 8,000-meter peaks to her name, Rutkiewicz perished in 1992. She lost her life on

Kangchenjunga, on the Nepal-India border, just as Chris was falling in love with climbing. "Wanda was a huge influence on me," Chris said. "She played a huge part in establishing a place for women in the high-altitude mountaineering world. Unfortunately there hasn't really been anyone after her."

Christine Boskoff was next.

CHAPTER 5

BROAD PEAK

TUCKED INTO THE BORDER BETWEEN Pakistan and China, 26,401-foot Broad Peak ranks high on the list of 8,000-meter peaks for those in the game of summiting all fourteen. Though steep in sections, the mountain lacks any sheer vertical walls, and there's little technical climbing required. Broad Peak's wide summit stretches a mile long, offering stunning views of nearby K2 and both Gasherbrum I and II.

Accessing Broad Peak requires a trek of a week or more from Askole, the last village in Pakistan connecting climbers to the rest of the world. The hike to base camp funnels expeditions directly along the top of the Baltoro Glacier, a thirty-five-mile-long, three-mile-wide expanse of breathtaking beauty. Dividing the Indian subcontinent from Tibet, this part of the Karakoram Range packs in a few 8,000-meter peaks along with many just below that height, like younger siblings but nearly as formidable. An intoxicating stretch of rock and ice reaches a pinnacle at the convergence of the Baltoro with the Godwin-Austen Glacier. Known as Concordia, the intersection gives climbers their first views of K2 and Broad Peak. The sight has been known to stun and shock mountaineers in such a way that some climbers immediately wither, surrendering any hope of making it to the top.

IN JULY 1995, KEITH AND Chris took leave from their Atlanta jobs to climb Broad Peak. It would be the first attempt at this altitude for both of them. After years of partnering with Keith, Chris was going to get the chance to test her fortitude with others, including Scott Fischer. Scott had gathered a team of friends suited to the challenges of the mountain. He'd also hired Lopsang Jangbu Sherpa, a high-altitude guide, who had become a trusted team member after summiting Everest with Scott. This climbing season bridged the gap between Scott's 1994 clean-up expedition to Everest and the Everest expedition he was planning with clients for the next year.

When they arrived, Broad Peak Base Camp bustled with activity. Its proximity to K2 meant that climbers attempting that lofty peak need only take an easy hike of an hour to visit with those on Broad Peak. The Mountain Madness camp welcomed climbers both established and unknown. Among the more famous was Peter Hillary, the son of legendary alpinist Sir Edmund Hillary. He'd be attempting K2 with British mountaineer Alison Hargreaves, who just months earlier had reached the summit of Mount Everest without the assistance of Sherpas, fixed ropes, or bottled oxygen.

Unlike Chris, Alison had climbed for decades before arriving at K2 in 1995. But like Chris, she'd risen without much initial notice in the sport of mountain climbing. In a field packed with men, the women in Europe who'd gained notoriety had often been heralded more because of their gender than their accomplishments. This move ran counter to Alison's core, just as it did with Chris, who thought of herself as a climber and not as a "female climber." Following her recent success on Everest, Alison knew that her passion for climbing raised eyebrows. The reason: she was the mother of two young children. The press and critics within mountaineering communities created a narrative that accused her of "acting like a man" and attempting to "have it all." As a leading professor of sport sociology at Brunel University in London put it: Alison's "heroism was conditional upon her safe return to her children. No such demand is placed upon men: their deaths are the purest symbols of heroism."

Nevertheless, she carried forth with a life dedicated to both climbing and her children. Writing in her journal at K2 Base Camp, Alison said, "It eats away at me—wanting the children and wanting K2. I feel like I'm being pulled in two." Being a father to young children and a mountaineer himself, Scott respected Alison in a way others didn't. At Broad Peak Base Camp, he and Alison chatted about kids and Everest. High-end coffee and booze flowed while satellite phones stayed busy as the K2 alpinists checked in with the outside world.

Chris and Keith watched at a distance, setting up their tent and planning to move higher onto the mountain. They'd come to Broad Peak at the same time as Scott's team but planned to climb independently. Nonetheless, they couldn't help noticing the staging going on all around. The Mountain Madness camp buzzed with life, and the expedition members and high-altitude support team looked comfortable with their surroundings and their leader. Scott's energy radiated to those around him. Though they'd heard of his accomplishments, the Boskoffs felt secure in their own. They busied themselves preparing gear while absorbing the fact that they'd finally made it to the foot of an 8,000-meter peak. Camp itself was a mess of tents, each one serving a purpose for cooking, sleeping, or getting medical attention. Chris couldn't get enough of taking in the scene and the divergent personalities of the climbers and support staff.

Scott seemed the antithesis of Chris but also a potential match. His charisma allowed him to easily navigate a multitude of personalities, while Chris guarded her privacy. She and Keith kept to themselves, focusing on their goal of summiting. In a sport that required patience and calculation, Chris worked to find the balance. Her determination was an asset but also a danger as she longed for a summit. Her hunger for the top meant she was prepared to persevere, but she was still apt to overlook small details that more seasoned climbers noticed. Meanwhile, Scott felt a symbiotic relationship with the mountains and was content to wait as long as it took for the perfect weather window to move higher.

During a day of rest, Scott invited Chris and Keith over to his camp nearby. "You're pretty new at this, I hear?" he asked the couple as they pulled up camp chairs.

"Compared to you? Big time," said Keith, with a laugh. His broad smile put Scott at ease. Both men were from the East Coast, animated as they spoke.

"I can tell you, the big peaks—there's nothing like it," Scott said. "I did Everest last year and am hoping to go back again next year."

"You think you'll stick with it?" Chris asked as she reached for the mug of coffee Scott offered her.

He'd been on expeditions with women before, but Chris's aura was more purposeful. It was less about the trappings and more about the experience. "I don't know," he said. "It's what I do and I do it well. I've got a company to run and it helps to get publicity for these big peaks, but there are plenty of other things I'd like to get done. I've got a couple of kids at home. They'd like to see more of their dad, and I'd love to be around for them more than I have been."

"You know, Chris is going places," Keith said. He looked at his wife, amazed at his good fortune. "We've got solid business experience between us. Wonder if we could help out somehow?"

"Oh yeah?" Scott waved to his guides who were organizing gear just beyond the tents, then focused on Chris. "You've not done any of the big peaks, but you're a decent athlete and you feel okay up here at fifteen thousand feet?"

Chris shrugged. "Truth be told," she said, "I suck at sea level. But I've got the right genes. I feel good, the altitude doesn't bother me, and I'm fast."

"You've got this," Scott said, grinning. "Stick with us for the climb and then let's talk about ways I can get you involved in Mountain Madness. I think I'd be decent at running a business if there weren't other things I'd rather be doing."

Raising her eyebrows, Chris glanced at Keith as he leaned back in his chair, smiling. "Sounds good," she said. "We're gonna make a push for the summit tomorrow and see what happens."

"Tomorrow?" Scott cautioned, "You see those weather reports calling for wind and snow up top? Avalanche danger is real up there. Just chill down here for a bit. You've got oxygen for the final summit bid, yes?" He'd stopped paying attention to the guides, now compelled to understand the logic in Chris and Keith's pushing for the top in the face of a possible storm.

"Yes to the weather reports and no to the Os," Keith said.

"Suit yourself," Scott said, "but take it easy up there. You don't want your first to be your last."

The Boskoffs thanked Scott for the coffee and returned to their tent to prepare for the next day. Their decision concerned Scott, but their resolve—especially hers—reminded Scott of himself.

WATCHING THEM LEAVE BASE CAMP the next day, Scott turned to another climber on his team.

"I don't know, man," he said. "The mountain doesn't feel ready. The slopes are loaded—primed for avalanches. I'm not convinced they should be out there."

"She's strong, Scott," observed the other climber. "Look at Alison. She just summited Everest less than three freaking months ago. No Sherpas. No oxygen."

But Scott wasn't worried about Chris. "It's him," he said grimly about Keith. "He loves that woman. I can tell. He'll do anything for her, including going beyond where he's capable of going." Scott walked to the expedition's high-powered telescope. Wrestling with it, he fixed the tripod securely between rocks and trained it on the steep cliff leading out of camp.

LEAVING BASE CAMP, CLIMBERS HAD options as to where they'd lay their heads each night. A series of camps, each consisting of no more than a few tents, led up the mountain. At roughly 6,000 meters sat Camp 1. A second camp was set up at 6,500 meters. Camp 3 was located at 7,100 meters. A fourth camp just above that, referred to as High Camp, was the last stop before the summit. In preparation for reaching the top of any high peak, climbers spend weeks on rotations going up and down the mountain between the various camps. Each rotation brings them to a higher camp until the final push to the top, known as the summit bid. This lengthy process helps the body gradually acclimatize. By spending days pushing their bodies to higher altitudes, then returning to a lower altitude to rest for several days, mountaineers adjust properly and more safely than a straight shot up the mountain which would result in almost certain death.

Keith and Chris had done their rotations and were prepared for their summit bid. They targeted Camp 2 for the first night. What looked like decent weather when they'd started the climb from base camp became gloomy. Night painted the mountain and with it, winds. As they huddled in their sleeping bags, the sounds of the storm grew. By morning, the fate of the couple for the next four days was solidified. Locked in, Chris and Keith were battered in their tent by 100-mile-an-hour winds. Combined with snow, the blizzard proved survivable yet kept the pair captive inside day after day.

Finally able to descend on the fifth day, Chris and Keith recounted the experience to Alison and Scott, who couldn't believe they'd survived.

"She only hit me once!" Keith joked.

"I couldn't help it!" Chris said. "Holy crap, I wasn't sure we were going to make it. The tent flattened on our faces. We had to hold it up with our ski poles. I was sure the tent would rip or the poles would bust."

A few days later they made a second attempt, much to the shock of the others who watched the couple leave and trudge through waist-deep snow. This time, as they got closer to the summit, Keith's eyes became blurry and he got a painful headache. They turned back and returned to base camp. Scott's group had not yet tried for the top, but when they did, Chris intended to be ready.

Despite the deep blackness of the night sky, Keith's sunglasses covered his eyes as he lay in the tent a couple of days later. He'd been diagnosed with a high-altitude retinal hemorrhage. The lack of oxygen had caused dilation of blood vessels in his retinas, rendering him temporarily unable to see clearly.

Keith had accompanied Chris back up to Camp 2, but his days trying to summit Broad Peak on this expedition were over. At the opposite end of their tent, Chris strapped rope onto the outside of her pack. The steaming cup of sweet tea she was drinking sat next to her. She made sure to take in each sip, eager for the liquid before she started the ascent. Though she knew Scott's team was capable of leading her to the top, leaving Keith felt foreign. They'd always climbed together. Chris knew he was disappointed, but she had trouble reining in her enthusiasm for a third chance to the top. Keith reached out a gloved hand, pulling her to him and held tight, the gap in their experiences about to widen.

CHRIS CAUGHT UP WITH THE departing climbers, stepping in behind the small group from Scott's expedition. A stream of headlamps lit the way as the group pushed for the summit well before dawn. At a pitch of fifty degrees, the sharp angle of the mountain surprised her, even on this third attempt. It was the equivalent of climbing a double black diamond ski run. The team was making good time, their bodies rested, while Chris's legs felt heavy from the two previous attempts. With Scott in the lead, they made it to Camp 3 within a few hours, assessed, and moved on. Chris was thirty minutes behind, each step now requiring several breaths.

Crampons digging into snow and ice, the last stretch of the ascent tested each of them. Snowpack from recent days required breaking more trail than they'd expected. As they cleared the final hundred feet, a hypoxic fog covered Chris's brain in a way new to her. Channeling Keith, she willed herself forward.

By 10:00 a.m., the climbers stood atop the wide apex of Broad Peak. Chris had summited her first 8,000-meter peak. She looked across at the swath of mountains, which included K2, where Alison Hargreaves and Peter Hillary were climbing at that exact moment. The view also included Gasherbrum I and II, favorites of Keith. Glancing down at the Baltoro Glacier and then to base camp, she hoped Keith was recovered enough to look up at her with the telescope.

"Congrats, Chris!" A member of the expedition offered his hand and she shook it.

"Hell yes, you did it!" Scott added. "How does it feel?"

"It feels awesome, and you were right—there's nothing like it."

Scott grinned at her, then checked with the members of his group. "Ready to go down? The weather's held, but it looks like it might change." The landscape of the Karakoram could be placid one moment, volatile the next. Competing air masses could strike each other at any time with no regard for who was on these mountains, nor the victories they'd achieved.

Chris had suceeded on her first 8,000-meter summit, but all she could think about was how cold she was and getting back to Keith.

"Let's do it," she said.

Descending Broad Peak, Chris's legs ached for rest. Normally fast when moving down, this time she lagged an hour behind the others. High camp had consisted of only a couple of tents, and all of those had been collected by the time she reached that point. The team had decided to retreat all the way to Camp 3. The decision was no doubt a nod to the weather. From the north, the storm Scott had seen gathering was coming to life. Winds gusting up to a hundred miles an hour from China pounded the slopes. Snow kicked up, blinding Chris's view and covering the tracks she'd been using as a guide.

Though she was relatively new to high-altitude mountaineering, Chris was an expert in engineering and specifically in analyzing data. With a keen eye for following scientific observations, she plotted the contours of the mountain, although she was barely able to see. Remembering the angles of the path the team had taken up the mountain, she knew that if things got desperate, she had a sleeping bag and could hunker down for the night.

With each movement, Chris longed to be lower. The lessons of the past few weeks played in a loop, her mind reciting each one. Patience. Deference to the weather. Listening to those with more experience but finding space to follow one's inner voice.

As daylight began to fade, her anxiety increased. The path to Camp 3 had been obliterated by wind and snowdrifts. Then a break in the clouds yielded a few seconds of sunlight. Chris scanned her surroundings, terrified to realize she was heading right off an ice cliff. Black spots marked an area far ahead, which she recognized as Camp 3. Chris stumbled forward, darkness and crippling cold engulfing her. Two hours passed until the black spots became the intoxicating sight of tents. Crawling into her tent at Camp 3, she heard the winds screaming. She had made it to safety, as had Scott's group. Broad Peak's position had sheltered it from the worst of the storm.

Nearby, the team on K2 wasn't as lucky, however. Peter Hillary had sensed the danger and retreated, leaving a band of climbers to proceed upward to the summit earlier in the day. At higher altitudes, the unsteady air and winds had initially seemed tame. Lower, the intensity of the storm trapped climbers in their tents. The catastrophic winds raced up the slopes of K2, hitting those still on the mountain's highest points late in the day.

THE NEXT MORNING, THE SKIES were clear. The weary Mountain Madness climbers arrived at Broad Peak Base Camp, and Chris was reunited with a relieved Keith. There, surrounded by warmth, the climbers tracked the progress of their friends descending K2. By radio, the group listened as Canadian climber Jeff Lakes made his way down from Camp 3, buoyed by the encouragement of his waiting teammates. "You're almost there, Jeff. You're almost there," they called over their radios. After stumbling into his tent at Camp 2 at 1:30 a.m., Lakes died a few hours later, a victim of a combination of altitude sickness and hypothermia.

Scott's telescope was positioned for a scan of the mountainside, hoping to see signs of life. Alison and several other climbers were still unaccounted for. "I'm looking at something that looks like a slide path," he said. His sunglasses were off, giving him better vision as he looked through the scope. Lopsang inched forward, then Chris and Keith, who'd walked the short distance from their tent to join the vigil.

"It's . . . I'm looking at about a fifteen-hundred-foot slide path, and I see something at the very end of it," said Scott. "Oh god, I think it's a body." He stepped away from the telescope, giving others a turn to confirm. One by one, the group verified what they saw. A body was lying in a snowfield, most likely having been picked off the summit of K2 in high winds and tossed down the slope. Another day would pass until the body's distinctive clothing would be identified by teammates as that of Alison Hargreaves.

Chris squinted into the telescope at two figures digging in the snow at a point lower on the mountain. Her gaze stayed fixed, hoping it was only an illusion. She stepped away, horrified. The climbers were digging a grave for another teammate, further driving home the danger of this sport.

As their Broad Peak expedition closed out, Chris knew several things to be true. Her skills as a climber were exceeding Keith's, as she noted in journal entries referencing her conflicted desire to begin climbing routes she knew he was incapable of. She realized that, unlike Alison, she was limited in her ability to climb and be a parent, later telling a reporter she couldn't envision having children at that moment in time—"I don't even own a plant!" she'd said. As for her own family, Chris's parents were ever-present in her mind.

I dream about my mom and dad quite a bit now. The older I get and they get, the more I miss them. I realize I have the best parents in the world!

THE FOLLOWING MORNING AS THE Broad Peak group made plans to trek out, they were met by climbers returning from K2, including Peter Hillary. Scott led them to the telescope, where they lingered, looking for any indication that other remaining teammates might have survived. Finding none, they turned to the task of alerting the world. Peter Hillary placed a sat phone call to his father, Sir Edmund. Scott reported the news of Alison's death via *Outside Online*, the newly launched web version of *Outside* magazine.

The days and months following saw a rash of criticism about Alison's "selfishness" in choosing mountains over motherhood. Chris ignored those opinions, focusing on Alison's fortitude and her own future on alpine slopes.

CHAPTER 6

TURNING POINTS

GERI LESKO HELD THE PHONE to her ear as she listened to Scott ramble. It was a few months after he'd returned from Broad Peak. They'd been talking for over an hour, covering the expedition and how he'd handled the climbing team and their colorful personalities. Geri had come to know Scott as more than a climber. His children occupied much of his time when he was in Seattle. He loved being a father; that role added a layer of tenderness to the exterior everyone else knew. At present, though, his voice gushed with excitement about some recent ice climbing and the upcoming expedition he was leading to Everest.

"The ice climbing in Ouray was awesome, but nothing compared to what Everest will be," he said. "Geri, you really should think about coming."

"Maybe next time, Scott. You got me to a big peak in Asia once, but this spring I'll be hiking in Yosemite." Since meeting Scott, she'd admired his spirit. The business wisdom he lacked seemed overshadowed by pure passion for the outdoors, which was captivating. In return, Geri had become a trusted adviser. Scott respected her opinion and generally wanted her input on many things, personal and professional.

"Suit yourself," he said. "I'll check in with the office, so call them if you want the scoop and I'll send periodic dispatches through *Outside Online*." The media outlet was sending him with a talented writer and climber named Jane Courage. "She's top notch," said Scott. "She'll do great. She's the right one for the job."

"Sounds like it," Geri said. "If I don't talk to you before you leave, be safe. It's so thrilling, but be careful up there. What day do you plan to summit?"

Scott was always safe. "We're aiming for May 10, but you know how these things go with the weather . . . Hey, enjoy Yosemite."

Geri thanked him and replaced the handset on the receiver, making a mental note of May 10.

TENGBOCHE MONASTERY IS AT 12,687 feet in the Khumbu region of northeastern Nepal and is the largest Tibetan Buddhist monastery in the area. Given its location on the path to Everest Base Camp, the surrounding village caters to mountaineers heading off to achieve their dreams. Beginning in April, when the spring climbing season kicks off, the village hosts tent cities and lures climbers into such delights as buying cake from some of the highest bakeries in the world. The views from the village provide stunning moments of realization about the journey ahead as Everest rests behind several other notable peaks, each one a gut check to climbers hoping to summit. Before heading out along the river valley to Everest Base Camp, climbers and high-altitude team members traditionally stop at the monastery, where many hope for an audience with a Tibetan monk to receive blessings on their expedition.

There exists a natural tension between those wishing to scale mountains in this part of the world and those who believe the peaks are sacred and should remain undisturbed. Whether deference is given to those seeking to protect the mountains is often a very personal decision. Some climbers look for signs or meaning in the words of spiritual leaders, while others remain focused on goals unhindered by such influences. Few laws exist to provide guidance for alpinists or spiritual figures— only the laws of the heart.

Jamling Norgay, the son of Tenzing Norgay, the first Sherpa to scale Everest, with Sir Edmund Hillary, once spoke about this balance:

You know we look at the mountains as sacred, and to this day some of the Himalayas remain off limits to us. They are such holy mountains that to climb them would be wrong. For many of us, especially on Everest, mountain-climbing has become our livelihood. But we go to the mountain with respect. We know that Chomolungma [the Tibetan name for Mount Everest, meaning Goddess Mother of the World] lives there, and so prayer and ceremony must precede any attempt to climb the mountain. We place prayer flags wherever we go. The mother goddess of the world lives on Everest, and our prayers are sent to her by the wind horse. The flags blowing in the wind are the sound of our prayers, our communication with the goddess. In prayer, we learn the respect with which we must approach the mountain. The deities can be defiled by people who abuse the mountain, who pollute it with garbage or try to climb it without showing proper respect. Ignorant people sometimes climb mountains. They climb only as an expression of their ego. It is very important that climbers respect the mountain and the people who live here.

Scott's 1996 Everest expedition team had made the hike to Tengboche, and they settled in for the night.

"The evening was clear, cold and calm," Jane Courage recalled. "The peaks were exhilarating. A natural, euphoric high." She prepared to file a report with *Outside Online*, one of many that would be sent back to the United States over the following months.

As the team organized their gear and swapped stories, Scott spent time alone with the monks at the monastery. Upon his return to their tents, his usual upbeat mood seemed muted. The monks had warned him about the dangers on the mountain and the unfavorable timing of the ascent. Astrologically, the conditions were not good for climbing Everest, they said. Balancing the spirituality of the mountain and the needs of his clients, Scott pressed forward, listening to snow avalanche down distant slopes.

GERI FOLLOWED THE NEWS OF Scott's expedition, preferring the personal connection with the Mountain Madness office to the option of navigating the world of online news sites. She called on Friday, May 10, when she was on the way to Yosemite with a climbing partner. Lengthy ring tones gave way to the sounds of laughter. The gas station pay phone in her hand suddenly felt weightless. Celebration in the Mountain Madness office was under way.

"It's Geri. I'm just calling to see what the news is from Scott? I take it by the sounds I'm hearing that it's good?"

Juggling a plastic cup full of champagne, the office staff member said, "Yes, Geri! A pile of them made it to the top. We're still waiting to hear about Scott, but it's thrilling news so far!"

Geri asked for clarification, straining to understand. "I'm not sure I heard you. Did you say that Scott hadn't made it yet?"

"As far as we know, but . . . it's Scott. Call back tomorrow and I'm certain I'll have more good news for you!" Geri hung up the phone, not quite satisfied.

Back in Seattle, all but a couple of the staff members continued to toast the success of the expedition. The two without champagne glasses were the only climbers in the office. "All I recall," one of them remembered, "was turning to my colleague and saying, 'I don't know why everyone's celebrating right now. They're not down yet.' We just knew it was premature."

The four-hour drive from San Francisco to Tuolumne Meadows in Yosemite took Geri and her friend through the Sierra National Forest. Hiking the next day in 64-degree weather, she envisioned Scott on top of Everest, his mirrored glasses reflecting neighboring mountains. She knew how he longed for this commercial success to make Mountain Madness more solid financially. Returning to their cabin that evening, Geri reached out and pulled a note off the front door. In scrawled handwriting were instructions for her to call Mountain Madness immediately.

She called to learn that Scott was missing. A freak storm had hit the mountain on the descent, and he was feared trapped in the area of the mountain above 8,000 meters known as the "death zone," where oxygen in the air decreases, becoming a precarious environment not meant for human survival in long stretches. She made a second call a few hours later. Scott was still missing, now presumed dead.

Disbelief gripped Geri's heart. She and her friend collected their gear and made the drive back to San Francisco to await confirmation. "I was in shock, unable to believe he was gone," Geri said. "He was supposed to come back. He always came back."

MONDAY MORNING, MAY 13, 1996. Geri walked slowly around her kitchen. Sleep had eluded her all night. She tried to ring Mountain Madness, but the phone lines had been constantly busy, the media relentless as outlets across the globe sought details on what happened. None of it mattered. Scott was gone.

She noticed a pile of mail lying neatly stacked on a rectangular table in the front foyer. Her husband had brought it in, though it could have been days ago. Mail seemed bothersome to Geri, but this stack drew her attention. A few letters. Several bills. A magazine. Nothing noteworthy, except what lay on top of the pile. A postcard.

Picking it up, she found herself looking at an image of soft snow covering the tops of a mountain she recognized instantly. Unnaturally blue skies framed the edges of the postcard. At the bottom, just one word: Everest. The metered stamp indicated it had been mailed several weeks earlier, no doubt carried out of base camp and sent from Kathmandu long before the ascent. She'd later learn the postcard had actually been mailed by Jane Courage, who'd said goodbye to Scott and left the mountain before he began his final climb.

Turning it over, she saw Scott's bold handwriting, filling the postcard with just a handful of words. Reading them, her heart swelled with elation, then took a dive not unlike the plunge of a roller coaster on its last loop.

Geri,
You should have been here. It's a good one!
—Scott

FAMILY AND FRIENDS OF EIGHT climbers received unimaginable news as a result of the storm on Everest in May of 1996. Four others had died on the mountain that year, making it Everest's deadliest season to date.

Stories from survivors packed the pages of books, most notably *Into Thin Air*, an account by journalist Jon Krakauer, who had been embedded with the New Zealand expedition that was also on the mountain at the time. His retelling of the disaster became a bestseller. The book resonated within the climbing community, most notably in Seattle, where Mountain Madness lay in turmoil, its leader, for the first time, not coming back.

For those seeking controversy, the disaster on Everest and those that followed on other mountain expeditions provided ample material. Each one laid out a new palette of issues to be debated: decisions made based on inaccurate assumptions; minds clouded by hypoxia at altitudes not meant to sustain human life; weather reports gone bad; egos that transcended judgment. The narratives differed, but the end result was often the same.

Chris and Keith received news of Scott's death at their home in Atlanta. Preparing for her second ascent on an 8,000-meter peak, Chris paused, and she and Keith made plans to fly to Seattle for Scott's public memorial. As fresh as her climbing career was, she'd already been exposed to its dangers and had lost several friends to the mountains.

Scott's friends gathered in Seattle from throughout the region and across the globe. A memorial service had melted into a gathering at a local brewpub. Hours later, Geri and three new acquaintances, including Keith and Chris moved on to Ray's Boathouse. Also at the table was Henry Todd, a popular Everest outfitter from Scotland. Ray's hummed with the sound of steady conversation. The restaurant was a fixture in Seattle, with sweeping views of Puget Sound and the Olympic Mountains beyond. It was several weeks after the disaster on Everest.

The four chatted about Tibet, where Chris, Keith, and Henry intended to travel in a few months before attempting a summit of Cho Oyu. They teased Geri about taking a pass on another 8,000-meter peak. "It's the easiest eight-thousand-meter peak of the whole lot," Henry told her. "You can practically walk up it."

"God, you sound just like Scott," Geri said. "I was told I needed to do McKinley before I considered anything at that altitude." The waitress arrived, momentarily stopping conversation.

"I'll have an Indian Lady Martini," said Henry.

"What's *that*?" asked Chris. Geri, Henry, and Keith smiled. Decades and hundreds of cocktails ahead of Chris, they'd been around the world and back while Chris, just twenty-nine, was eager to learn.

Back to the issue at hand, Keith pumped Henry for details on Cho Oyu. "So what you're saying is that Chris and I shouldn't have an issue with the summit?" His voice pulsing with excitement, Keith used his hands and facial expressions liberally to make points.

"God, no," said Henry. "I think the two of you could walk it in the dark after hearing what you survived on Broad Peak last year."

Leaning forward on his elbows, Keith tried to drive the conversation, Geri sensed, but Chris's interest in the topic of their upcoming climb was equally relentless. Listening to every word, Chris said little, but when she did, her words were thoughtful. As the evening progressed, she peppered Henry with questions about the Tibetan culture, the people, and his attitude toward mountaineering. Geri could tell that at forty-seven, Keith had more climbing experience, but Chris's youth and physicality were a major asset. What she lacked in years, she made up for with enthusiasm and a hunger to grow.

The conversation continued, drinks were served, and a bottle of Bombay Sapphire gin appeared, complete with a likeness of Queen Victoria on the front. Chris looked at the bottle, beaming as she took a sip of her Pabst Blue Ribbon. Keith smiled faintly but seemed intent on returning the conversation to Tibet. Dinner ended, and as the group moved for the door, Henry announced he was entirely without a place to stay for the night.

"Geri, he can stay with you!" Chris said spontaneously. "You said you've got a huge hotel room!" She was full of zest.

Geri was beginning to like Chris more and more, despite the unwanted invitation she'd just offered Henry. "He can stay with me," she said, "but where's he gonna sleep?"

"I'll get my sleeping bag!" Chris said, jumping up to head to the car. "We're going to do some badass rock tomorrow, but I can get it from you before we leave in the morning." Shrugging, Keith trailed behind her.

"They seem motivated," said Geri.

Glancing at Chris and Keith as they left, Henry took a sip of his second martini. He'd seen hundreds of mountaineers rise and fall. "Yeah, they seem to have what it takes, but I bet she's going to outclimb him soon. And it seems like he might have a problem with that."

WITH THEIR BROAD PEAK EXPERIENCE still fresh, Chris and Keith were back in Asia in September 1996 for a go at Cho Oyu. Located twenty miles northwest of Mount Everest on the Tibet-Nepal border, Cho Oyu rises 8,201 meters. Its name is typically translated to "Goddess of Turquoise" in Tibetan, as it glows in this color when seen from Tibet in the late-day sun. Alternatively, some have translated Cho Oyu as "Bald God" to mirror a Tibetan legend in which a bald god known as Cho Oyu had his back turned to Chomolungma (Mount Everest) because she refused his marriage proposal.

Considered a relatively simple ascent, Cho Oyu often receives attention as one of the first peaks alpinists attempt over 8,000 meters. With very few technical sections, predictable avalanches, and decent weather much of the time, the mountain sees a fair amount of traffic. Because of its location straddling the Tibet-Nepal border, Cho Oyu Advanced Base Camp has occasionally more drama than the usual bouts of high-altitude mountain sickness. The glacial pass of Nangpa La is just beyond base camp, overlapping part of a trade route between Tibet and Nepal's Khumbu Valley.

Though 1996 was uneventful, ten years later Chris would return when the world's attention was drawn to the plight of Tibetan refugees attempting to cross the border into Nepal.

HENRY TODD'S PREDICTION HAD BEEN correct: the Boskoffs moved swiftly up the mountain. It was Keith's first 8,000-meter summit and Chris's second. Back home in Atlanta, struck with mountain fever, Keith and Chris planned their next ascent in early 1997. As they trained for an attempt on Lhotse, the world's fourth highest peak, it became apparent that climbing could become a full-time endeavor for them. Working to gain sponsors for their next trip, they talked about a move to the Pacific Northwest. Mountain Madness had been put up for sale. Scott had left the books in poor shape, and the conversations they'd had with him before his death about the business were still on their minds.

Hiking up Stone Mountain with a seventy-pound pack, Chris had reached a point of fitness she had never before achieved in her thirty years. Her age and stamina allowed her to lead their training hikes, with Keith, carrying his own heavy pack, in the back chatting about their next moves. Reversing roles had come, as Henry Todd guessed, with a price. Keith's pride was slightly tarnished by his wife's rise. Chris had begun to notice that people asked if Keith was her father, and she continued to silently question the extent of his mountaineering ability over the long haul. Meanwhile, she was still working hard to improve her speed, something he was starting to see as a threat. As he wrote in his journal: "It is quite obvious that Chris has to prove to me she is quicker uphill, downhill, and on straight, flat areas."

As a businessman, Keith saw the potential to capitalize on Chris's success. If she summited Lhotse, she'd be the first American woman to do so. If Mountain Madness didn't pan out, the two mused about other options. A bagel shop. A clothing business. A rafting company. Keith took long strides as they hiked, working hard to keep up with his wife's brutal pace.

Chris loved her life with him, but doubts about their partnership were ever-present. As she wrote in her journal: "I don't know how much more I can take with my climbing. He's holding me back. Always panicking on the climb. I feel I might force him to go too far just because he wants to keep up with me. I have some major decisions to make. I guess I'm confused as to what to do."

Two months later, on May 25, 1997, Chris and Keith rested in a small, two-person tent on a ledge carved into the side of Lhotse. They'd spent weeks establishing camps at several levels up the mountain. The climb through each stage had been brutal, with strong winds following them constantly. They'd traversed the legendary Khumbu Icefall, going across waves of ice blocks with the help of aluminum ladders. They'd acclimatized properly and avoided frostbite. Now, what they'd hoped would be summit day looked unconvincing. Chris's stomach churned; their food supply was down to a can of Pringles and a tub of cheese spread.

Melting snow for tea, she felt Keith's body warm against hers. Positioned in the center of the tent, her legs hung over the edge of the cliff. Safety ropes assured that she'd stay put, but her mind felt numb, depleted of oxygen as they lay in the death zone. She closed her eyes and tried to sleep.

Lhotse rose to 8,516 meters and every step was earned. The peak had been climbed by only one other woman, Chantal Mauduit, just a year earlier. The day was spent stuck at twenty-six thousand feet, sleeping restlessly until 2:00 a.m., when Chris's altimeter watch sounded its alarm. The winds had died. A summit push was ahead.

Waking Keith, Chris reached for her boot liners, aghast to realize they'd slipped to the part of the tent hanging over the cliff and were frozen. She had no choice but to put them on, knowing her feet would warm them. Slipping on an oxygen mask, Chris messed with the gauges on her tank. She hadn't used Os on her first two ascents, but Lhotse had other plans.

Three hours later, the couple left their tent for the summit. Starting up a forty-five-degree snow face, Chris felt strong. She pulled ahead of Keith, few words exchanged between them. They both knew that slowing to wait for her husband wasn't a viable option at this altitude. She looked ahead to a gully that weaved its way up the last bit of mountain. She moved upward, every breath borrowed in the thin air. Two hours ahead of Keith, she used her hands, feet, and crampons to scale the last two hundred feet of rock face to the summit.

Alone she sat. The second woman ever and the first American woman to experience the peak of Lhotse under her boots. The view of Everest that she'd hoped for was obscured by incoming clouds. Fifteen minutes passed before it was time to descend.

An hour and a half into her descent, Chris met Keith, still heading up. "Keith, the weather's turning. I don't know how smart it is to keep going."

"You made it," Keith mumbled, pulling off his oxygen mask. "God, that's incredible."

"I did, but the views were crap. The storm is back." She knew it was critical to not spend much time talking. She also knew the decision was his.

"I hear you," he said. "Let's go down. I want to be with my kick-ass wife."

A rush of relief carried her through the next few hours. The wind and the snow came as expected. By the time they'd reached Camp 3, it was a whiteout. Chris had slipped into the sliver of clear weather and the history books with her ascent.

Lhotse, First American Female Ascent. It was reported that on May 26, Christine Feld Boskoff became the first American woman—and second woman ever—to climb Lhotse. She had climbed to Camp IV by [sic] *her husband, Keith Boskoff. After waiting out a day of storms, Keith was not up to the ascent, so Christine continued on alone to the summit, which she reached at 12:30 p.m.*
—*Himalayan Historian Elizabeth Hawley,* American Alpine Club Journal

GERI'S PHONE RANG IN HER San Francisco home in November 1997. The caller ID showed "Keith/Chris Boskoff." The three had stayed in touch since their meeting in Seattle over a year ago for Scott's memorial, but it had been a few weeks since they'd talked. Geri picked up, preparing to hear Keith talk about life since quitting their jobs. Or perhaps another ascent was planned for spring.

"Geri," said Keith, "you won't believe what we just did."

"Oh boy, should I sit down for this one?"

"Perhaps you should. Chris and I just bought Mountain Madness."

CHAPTER 7

EMBRACING MADNESS

CHALK DUST PERMEATED THE AIR at Vertical World in Seattle. Rising on all sides were brightly colored walls speckled with holds on which climbers placed their hands and feet. Jane Courage pulled on her climbing shoes, preparing to spend an hour in escape mode. The eighteen months since her time on Everest with Scott and the Mountain Madness expedition had been a blur. She'd stepped away from all of it, but not from the rush of the climbing gym. Standing, she reached around to the small of her back, dipping her hand into the chalk bag.

"Hey, you must be Jane, right?"

Glancing over, Jane saw a woman smiling broadly at her. This freckled tomboy had an aura that felt light, and Jane was drawn to her, despite not having a clue as to how the woman knew who she was.

"I am, yeah." Somehow, she felt . . . familiar.

"I'm Chris. Chris Boskoff. I heard you hang out here."

In that moment, it all made sense. "Oh, Chris! You're Chris! I've heard about you." Scott had told Jane all about the Boskoffs. "You and your husband just bought the Madness, didn't you?" Chris offered her hand to Jane and the two shared a chalky handshake. Jane felt at ease instantly, looking eye to eye with the woman she'd heard so much about.

"We did," said Chris. "For better or worse! Keith and I bought it a few months ago."

"Good for you. Scott talked about the two of you. He liked you a lot. God he'd be happy that it was *you* who ended up with the business."

"He mentioned you a bunch, too."

"How's it going so far? It's gotta be way different here than it is in Atlanta." Jane shifted her stance, intrigued with what the answer might be.

"I dunno," said Chris. "Okay, I guess. A lot to learn, and running a business really isn't what I thought I'd be doing with my life right now, but it's cool. I'm just in this to climb."

Chris's words resonated with Jane, who'd always embraced the challenges that life threw at her. In 1973, she'd graduated high school early and traveled alone across Europe and North Africa, and then took the Trans Siberian Railroad across the Soviet Union before returning home with eighty cents in her pocket. She went on to the University of Washington, where she got a degree in Mandarin Chinese, then worked as an interpreter and eventually devoted herself to a combination of writing, rock climbing, photography, and raising two young daughters.

The Everest tragedy still weighed on her, but in the moment, Jane was enjoying her uncanny connection with Chris as she listened to her backstory. Both women had brothers. Both loved to be outdoors. Both had grit. Both had lives that unfolded in this sport flooded with men. Scott's description of Chris had focused on Chris and Keith as a pair, but the woman before Jane seemed wholly singular. Untethered to the need to talk big, Chris seemed to be an understated straight shooter. Impressed with her humility and authenticity, Jane forgot about the escape she'd come for.

"Wanna do some routes?" Chris asked.

"Let's do it. I can't promise I'm as strong as you, but I'll try to keep up!"

Lining up routes next to each other to allow them to stay on the same rope, Chris and Jane took turns belaying. They pushed each other to exhaustion, chatting the entire time, making fun of themselves and each other. A partnership had been created that would last a lifetime.

OPERATING A GUIDING BUSINESS ISN'T usually a wildly profitable venture. The overhead can be extreme and the profits low. At any given time, just one lawsuit can take down a company without adequate protection. It's a brutal profession best suited for those adept at handling financial uncertainty, temperamental clients, the occasional injury, and even death. It's also a dream come true. The dream of immersing oneself in a life of all things outdoors with the potential to make money pulls many into the profession.

The Boskoffs moved to Seattle and officially took the reins of Mountain Madness in December 1997. Shopping for their first home together, they found a cozy house on a slope overlooking Puget Sound. While most buyers searched for such things as large kitchens and open floor plans, Keith felt drawn to a room in the basement. Unfinished and not particularly fancy, he took one look at it and felt it was a sign. The space could become their gear room: shelves stacked high with ice axes, harnesses, boxes of carabiners, and coils of rope. It was, Keith told a friend, destiny. The room would be the perfect size and location to store the collection of all that had brought and held the couple together.

It had been a year and a half since Scott had died on Everest. The company books were grim. With only two confirmed clients when they moved to Seattle, Chris and Keith faced a financial challenge in a world they knew little about. On top of their obvious need to turn the company around, the pair felt the pressure of being outsiders. Keith's gregarious nature often made him the center of attention, yet it wasn't enough to make up for the fact that he was a driven, no-nonsense East Coaster who'd spent little time in the Cascades.

For her part, Chris's accomplishments were noteworthy, but she could be reserved, didn't care about sponsorships, and shunned the drama that sometimes swirled around other climbers. Like Scott, she cared about respect from other mountaineers and wasn't into the gossip about her reputation. Nor was she willing to spend gobs of time on marketing or publicity work. She merely wanted to build a solid business and climb while doing so.

Scrambling to learn how to bring the company back into the black, Chris and Keith received an unexpected wave of attention with the recent release of Jon Krakauer's book *Into Thin Air*, the account of the 1996 disaster on Everest that had taken the life of Scott and seven other climbers. Chris in particular wrestled with the idea of capitalizing on the media surge in order to increase the brand awareness of Mountain Madness. Instead, they worked hard to educate people on the importance of being well-prepared for large-scale expeditions. Mountaineering was fast becoming known as the only sport that could allow people to essentially buy their way to the ultimate prize. For a price tag, anyone could join an Everest expedition. The concept equated to buying one's way into the Super Bowl—a troubling trend.

Aside from providing general education on climbing, Chris and Keith tried to move forward, largely ignoring the notoriety that naturally followed as the book became more popular. Keith provided color while Chris and her accomplishments slowly helped turn the business around. Chris became the focus. The perfect profile for the press, her unpretentious style, beauty, and steady coolness drew people to the sport and to Mountain Madness.

A former client recalled: "A week before we were supposed to go on an expedition, I called Mountain Madness and she happened to answer." He assumed he was speaking with a member of the staff. "I had no idea it was Chris. I made some comment like, 'I hear there's some woman running your company now,' and she laughed a bit. She didn't identify herself. A week later we gathered for the trip and I introduced myself. She smiled and told me we'd met once before, on the phone. I was humiliated, but she just shrugged it off. That was just Chris."

ONE OF THE BOSKOFFS' FIRST priorities for the business was strengthening ties with mountaineering contacts in Nepal. They'd visited the country several times and were convinced it was ready to be developed for more Mountain Madness expeditions. Scott had successfully developed climbing operations in Africa, and Nepal seemed to be the next logical location for Mountain Madness to focus. A chance encounter with the right individual helped make this a reality.

Buried between mountains and clouds in the Khumbu Valley of northeastern Nepal is the village of Chaurikharka. Westerners stumble over its name when they see it, so some remember its loose translation: "Yak Pasture." By foot, one can trek from Chaurikharka to the airport in the neighboring village of Lukla in roughly thirty minutes. It is known as one of the world's most dangerous airports; planes land and take off at the edge of a sheer cliff that drops two thousand feet. Lukla's airport is most notable as the starting spot for folks heading to Mount Everest. Built with funds from a foundation set up by Sir Edmund Hillary, the airport is where many climbers disembark from planes, carrying with them fancy gear and backpacks full of dreams.

In the early 1970s, it was not uncommon to see a young boy from Chaurikharka standing behind the fence that lined the still-unpaved airstrip. He'd watch the planes land, eyes wide. As dust from each landing wafted to his perch behind the fence, the boy would imagine talking to the Western climbers. Without a grasp of English, the task seemed staggering. His father, Da Nuru Sherpa, was a member of the Sherpa ethnic group; he'd lived several years in Bhutan, where construction work was plentiful. By the late 1960s, Da Nuru and his young wife became parents. They named their son Kili Sherpa.

Kili's family eventually moved back to Nepal, where expeditions to the mountains surrounding their hometown were becoming more common. When Kili was just a few months old, his mother passed away, leaving his father to care for their infant son. Resolved to make a life for his child, Kili's dad worked with climbing expeditions of every nationality. Kili thereafter lived with his grandparents, so his father could capitalize on the income generated from guiding Western clients. The wealth from foreign pockets seeped into the village in the form of education as well. Kili went to the local Hillary School, which had been built by Sir Edmund Hillary after his successful ascent of Mount Everest in 1953. Kili watched as Hillary hauled lumber with locals from the Khumbu Valley to build the school, and became a student, eventually making it through the fourth grade. In those years, Kili's primary interest was standing on the airport grounds at Lukla. When climbers got off planes, he watched as they collected their bags, stuffed with expensive sleeping bags and mountaineering boots that cost the equivalent of six months' salary for a local Sherpa family.

NOW SITTING IN HIS EXPANSIVE Kathmandu home, eyes wide, Kili recalled his youth. His voice strengthened, the errors in English no match for the power of recollection. "I'd go after them and talk to them. I followed them. I didn't know how to speak English, but sometimes

I used sign language. If they needed a place to sleep, I grabbed them and brought them to my grandmother's house." Tanned and muscular, Kili's arms rose as he laughed, remembering his boyish confidence. The memories are decades old, but they describe the spark that led him to Kathmandu, his wife, and his profession.

Once a Sherpa boy with no discernable English skills, Kili found that his innocent approach to unknown Westerners yielded this life. "They didn't trust me, but then I told them I had relatives in the village," Kili said. "I got jobs for many people." By then, Kili's dad was working expeditions to the highest peaks in the world: Everest, Makalu, and Kangchenjunga. He'd climbed with Reinhold Messner, an Italian mountaineer who, with Austrian Peter Habeler, had been the first to stand on top of Mount Everest without supplemental oxygen.

Though Kili had lived close to Mount Everest nearly his entire life, the moment he first saw the peak up close when he was twelve altered him forever. "I saw there is a sun shining on the mountain and just seeing it I feel so warm. After that, I have been constantly going to Everest Base Camp many, many times." Year after year, Kili helped his father haul loads out of base camp at the end of foreign expeditions. His father had become adept at maintaining the Khumbu Icefall, an ever-moving expanse of rock and ice. Massive crevasses along the icefall required ladders to be set so climbers could safely maneuver the route to the Everest summit. Then and now, the treacherous job fell to Sherpas, whose risk tolerance was high given the economic rewards in doing the job well. Those who took on this deadly task were known as the "icefall doctors."

Kili's experiences with his father led to opportunity. By 1985, Kili was being hired directly by foreigners to act as a porter for expeditions to local mountains. At nineteen, he started a rotation of joining expeditions, followed by trips to Kathmandu to find more climbing work. The pay provided by foreigners was generous, though Kili's financial acumen was weak. Spending as fast as he earned, each penny went to waste on booze until he realized something needed to change. He'd begun dating a young Sherpani woman named Maya who would become his wife.

Together, the couple decided that Kili should try to launch a career as a Khumbu trekking guide.

Kili became skilled at approaching foreigners on the streets of Kathmandu and proposing to lead them on treks. It was a rudimentary business model not uncommon as large-scale expeditions moved into Nepal. Meanwhile, his boyhood training ground at the Lukla airport took hold. His English was now decent. He began writing letters to foreigners abroad whom he'd met in Kathmandu who planned to return. The concept for growing a trekking company seemed within reach but lacked a major component. Since Kili had no telephone or email account, potential clients had no means to contact him.

What he needed was a box at the post office. A place where foreigners could respond to his offers to guide. "I needed to get this box very badly. The post office guy told me I needed one thousand rupees for the box"—the equivalent of ten dollars. Kili didn't have it. Knowing his livelihood depended on it, Kili turned to his assets. In addition to the wages he'd gathered during his last expedition, the Koreans he'd led gave him a good sleeping bag and a brand-new backpack. Gambling that he'd be provided such items again on a future expedition, Kili marched into Thamel, the area of Kathmandu laden with climbing shops. He sold both the sleeping bag and the backpack, pocketing 1,100 rupees—and bought the PO box.

Over time the mailbox filled with aerograms from all parts of the world, from thrill seekers looking to add Nepal to their list of destinations, and from others, who'd return year after year, wanting Kili to guide them. The PO box connected him, inspired him, taught him, and put food on his table. "Without this box, my life would be different," Kili said. Decades later, the box is still checked daily.

SPICED CURRY POTATOES SIZZLED IN Kili and Maya's kitchen. Maya, now forty-eight, poked her head into the room to check on Kili's mug of masala chai, smiling as she filled it. A mix of cloves and cardamom coated the top of the creamy blend. Steam rose, begging to be inhaled as his lips touched the warm ceramic.

By 1996, the couple had married. He began taking trips to the United States to work at a summer adventure camp in upstate New York with an American he'd met. On one of these trips, Kili heard that a man he'd known from his childhood was coming to speak at a conference in New York City. It was worth his time, he thought, to go see the man. Taking the train into the city, Kili carried with him a few sheets of letterhead from a recent expedition. His name was inscribed on the left side of the paper, along with the names of the expedition members. What he sought was a recommendation letter, and this man was his chance.

At the end of the man's speech, Kili approached him without pause. A simple *namaste* and a mention of his hometown of Chaurikharka was all it took for Kili to be assured he'd leave with his recommendation. The man effusively greeted Kili, then happily reached for the letterhead, scrawling a few simple sentences before handing it back. Now, decades later, Kili opened a three-ring binder on his dining room table and flipped to a page holding the original letter protected by a thin sleeve of plastic.

As far as I know, Kili Sherpa is a very pleasant and no doubt competent individual. He comes from the village of Chaurikharka where we have built schools and medical clinics. He certainly speaks excellent English and looks strong and energetic.
—Sir Edmund Hillary

IN THE SPRING OF 1997, Kili Sherpa stood at the edge of Gokyo Lake. Turquoise waters reflected back at him as he paused to take a break from leading a group of Brazilians to Island Peak, a 20,300-foot mountain just south of Lhotse and Mount Everest. Mountaineering consumed him now, along with its many facets and characters. The tragedy on Everest the previous year that killed Scott Fischer and seven others had made international headlines. Kili's youth had involved drinking away the pay he earned on expeditions, but now that he was in his thirties, he knew there was more ahead. What or who it was had escaped him . . . until this moment.

Alone at the lake, a series of thoughts passed through his mind. Eager to expand his mountaineering business, Kili had worked hard to improve his English, something he knew would help him pick up more clients. Still, he felt pulled to something greater. He began talking out loud, startled at the sound of his own voice. "I asked for help. I promised I would work hard and make a good life. I asked to meet American climbers who had business for me." The thought seemed so bizarre that he quickly forgot about it. Carrying on with his guiding work, Kili climbed Island Peak with his clients. Three days after his moment at Gokyo Lake, a pair appeared on the trail. An American man and a woman, a sight Kili hadn't seen often. Her bouncy ponytail was in stark contrast to the standard baseball caps worn by men in these parts. Keith and Chris Boskoff were on the move to Lhotse.

"We talked just briefly," Kili recalled. "I met them and she was strong. Friendly. Laughing all the time. They told me they were thinking of buying Mountain Madness. I gave them my contact information. They said they might like to hire me if it happened."

A few weeks later, Chris summited Lhotse, leaving Keith behind as she became the first American woman to reach the peak. Upon their return to the United States, they kept in touch with Kili, true to their word. Mountain Madness soon became theirs, and Nepal and Kili were in their sights. Kili Sherpa's call for help had been answered.

Back in Kathmandu, twenty years after that first meeting on the trail, Kili turned pages in his three-ring binder. He stopped at a sheet-protected page holding a yellowed letter addressed to Kili Sherpa at PO Box 3438 in Kathmandu. "This was a big letter. Chris and Keith had told me many things that other people had told me before. 'We will hire you. We will be back in touch with you.' So I was unsure. But she wrote to me."

The big news is that Keith and I have bought Mountain Madness, Scott Fischer's company. Business is very good here at Mountain Madness . . . We are very interested in forming a partnership in Nepal similar to our very successful partnership that Scott started

*in Africa . . . Forming a business partnership with you seems like
a very good idea . . . We are very anxious to see you again and we
feel we can make Nepal Mountain Madness's next big destination.
Please respond quickly so we know if you are interested with our
plan.*

Best regards,
Chris Boskoff
President, Mountain Madness

CHRIS AND KILI WOULD GO on to climb together, work together, and grow
Mountain Madness in Nepal. Before Scott's death, he had mused about
the Everest climbing route, saying, "We've built a yellow brick road
to the summit." Over time, these words would play out, as hordes of
hopeful trekkers and climbers flocked to the pristine flanks of Everest
and other alpine playgrounds. The economic gains for the Sherpa community were notable during these years, accompanied by a myriad of
complex issues. Tasked with the most dangerous jobs on the mountain, many Sherpas were exploited, working long hours for low wages.
Throughout his career, Kili sought to provide fair wages for the young
Sherpas he led into the business. Striving to help them obtain financial
freedom and opportunities in education, Chris and Kili agreed on their
goals for the business.

Carrying his son on her shoulders, Chris and Kili walked the streets
of Kathmandu prior to expeditions, collecting supplies. A room in his
basement became her de facto storage closet, where she'd organize and
restock on visits to Nepal. Transcending differences in gender, culture,
and language, Kili and Chris became business partners but also close
friends.

"If she hadn't been in my life," Kili said, "I would not be where I am
now." He leaned onto a pillow, having moved from the dining room into
the bedroom. At fifty-one years old now, Kili was less apt to hide emotions. Reaching for a sleeve, he wiped his eyes. "This story of Gokyo Lake
I have not told in twenty years," he said, as his voice softened.

CHAPTER 8

LOSS AND RESILIENCE

BY EARLY 1999, MOUNTAIN MADNESS had risen bit by bit into prosperity. With three 8,000-meter peaks on her résumé, Chris looked for ways to enjoy the mountains while Keith used both of their accomplishments to promote the business. Ahead was an attempt at Gasherbrum II, with an expedition to Everest not far behind. Working on marketing plans, Keith was constantly in motion designing trips and drumming up clients.

Since leaving Atlanta for Seattle in 1997, Chris and Keith had met people through their profession, and soon Chris had a group of friends for routine climbs of Mount Rainier and other local peaks. While Chris found it easy to make friends, Keith failed to find his footing in their new life. His leadership style could be brash, and several of the guides Scott Fischer had hired found the change unwelcome from Scott's laid-back style. Chris was more easygoing. The stresses of the business rolled off her in ways that impressed Keith. Though devoted to each other, the pair sometimes seemed a mismatch. Their arguments could be loud, but they were brief and followed by periods of calm. It seemed nothing more than the stress of moving and buying a struggling company that was now in the spotlight.

On January 25, Keith had arranged to have a meal with a colleague to talk about the year's upcoming events for Mountain Madness. They expected that 1999 would be a boom year. Trips were going to be promoted online, the newest thing at the time. The office phone rang shortly before noon. Keith answered.

"What do you mean? I'm starving!" The office staff had grown used to hearing Keith's memorable East Coast accent. He remained upbeat even as his lunch date was canceled. "That's okay," he said. "I'll just pack it in a little early and leave Chris here to close up shop."

Reassuring his lunch date, Keith hung up the phone.

LATE THAT RAINY AFTERNOON, CHRIS returned home, soggy but anxious to go over her day and hear about Keith's. She opened the door to their home in West Seattle, calling his name. Greeted by silence, she moved from room to room, peeking inside each. The windows looked out over Puget Sound and the Olympic Mountains. Neither Chris nor Keith had rushed to spend time on decorating when they'd moved in. Instead, their home was utilitarian. Enough space for slides from their trips. Closets large enough to hold their expedition packs. For Keith, the kitchen appliances were ideal for quick gear fixes. When Chris wasn't looking, he would sneak pieces of rope upstairs to the kitchen, sealing frayed ends on the stove burners. He knew the act would push beyond her sensibilities, and he whispered to friends not to give him away. His wife wasn't a neat freak, but littering the stove in their home with shards of rope would bother her—something he avoided when he could.

Rain pelted the windows in the master bedroom. Though Seattle natives were used to this weather, January had been particularly gloomy. Not finding Keith upstairs, Chris walked back to the first level, then to the door leading to the basement, and continued downstairs. It was a large space opening out to the back lawn. Exposed rafters ran across the ceiling and into the windowless room that had been converted into their gear room. Stepping into this room for the first time when house hunting, Keith had felt its magic. The pair had spent hundreds of hours in this space together, organizing helmets and stacking coils of rope. Each trip began and ended here. Neither of them were prone to micromanaging other parts of their lives, but the gear room was unique. Its contents were neatly arranged and captured the essence of their dreams, their individuality, and the milestones in their marriage.

Entering the basement, Chris looked up. Here, in their beloved gear room, she became a widow. Outside, the rain continued, pouring in sheets.

BATTERED BY SHOCK, CHRIS STOOD before a small gathering of friends in a local lodge that now doubled as a place to hold a memorial service. At thirty-one, she was without her husband—a concept she'd considered only vaguely in the context of losing Keith to the mountains.

After the service, a running partner approached Chris, her last conversation with Keith still fresh. He'd seemed so upbeat just hours before the suicide. So absolutely sure of himself. "I'm so sorry, Chris," said her friend. "I'm just so sorry. If you need anything, I'm just a phone call away. Just call me."

Chris appeared dazed. The words she'd shared about Keith with the crowd had included silly quips about his personality. They'd felt awkward, and those gathered knew these superficial vignettes were cover for grief. "I think I'll take you up on that," she told her friend. "I'm kinda numb right now, but a lot of running will be good, won't it?"

Waves of disbelief passed through the layers of people in Chris's life. Keith's darkness had woven itself into his days largely unseen, manifesting in ways unfamiliar to those around him. The loss was jarring, prompting speculation in the weeks following. He'd been so jovial, friends recalled, without any sign of depression or loneliness. Perhaps the mood masked the other pieces in his life that could've caused strain. The Seattle weather. Acquiring the business. And then there was Chris's wild success in mountaineering. It had been an unforeseen, meteoric rise that opened doors neither Keith nor Chris had ever considered. Her climbing career was on the upswing. His perhaps was on the down. Theories crowded conversations until all that remained was silence.

Years had passed since Chris sat in church with her mother, Joyce, in Appleton. Chris worshipped the mountains now. They had become her passion, her inspiration, her temple. She coped quietly, in a way that surprised many.

"After Keith died," Kili Sherpa said, "she didn't talk about it much." To some, Chris came across as stoic and resolute as she learned to move on and lead Mountain Madness on her own. Others worried about how guarded she seemed, not understanding it as a product of her upbringing. One friend remembered that "after she lost Keith, she conveyed that she believed there was something beyond this life. A place where we'll be able to see our loved ones again. . . . It was a source of comfort."

Chris seemed to use the business and her climbing as ways to heal. A colleague noted that it was almost as if Chris had "doubled down," resolving to run the company and find new training partners. She went on regular training hikes on Mount Rainier, Tiger Mountain, Mount Si, and Mount Adams, often with packs holding fifty pounds of free weights wrapped in towels. Her sessions at the climbing gym with her friend Jane Courage lasted hours, each of them pushing their bodies into exhaustion as they worked to improve their techniques. "It became even more important for her to have truly meaningful relationships in her life," Jane said. "Whether she thought about it or not, each person in her life filled a purpose. Scott's friend Geri was a steady hand—solid, balanced, loving. Chris adored Geri, just as Scott had. And for the two of us, it was all about climbing."

Chris's climbing continued but, at least temporarily, her journaling stopped.

NOT LONG AFTER KEITH'S DEATH in early 1999, the international climbing community experienced two more mountaineering losses, British alpinist Ginette Harrison and American Alex Lowe. Rather than prioritize her own goals, Chris began to seek fulfillment in the accomplishments of others and in the worlds she traveled to for adventure.

"I feel like my peak happiness doesn't have anything to do with climbing sometimes," she told her friend CJ one afternoon as they laced up to run Mount Si. "My favorite moments are when I wake up on a glorious morning on a dirt floor after sleeping in a tiny hut in the middle of nowhere. I see the landscape, feel the sunshine, and just feel so . . . alive being out in the vastness of the world." It was a few months after Keith had died, and Mount Si had become a haven for her. The steeply inclined mountain trail in North Bend east of Seattle was one they frequented.

"It seems like you're letting go of the chase a little bit?" CJ offered.

"Maybe. I mean, you know I'm not in this for the glory," Chris said. "I hate that crap. All the bullshit climber ego stuff. I still feel most alive when I'm in the elements and I know I'm on the knife's edge of life and death." More and more, Chris realized she liked seeing other people achieve their goals, giving them new things to aim for.

"Like . . . just get to the next rock?" CJ asked.

With her shoes tied, Chris pushed herself off the back of her old Land Rover. A small cooler inside wedged itself between piles of fleece, holding snacks and several cans of beer, her usual cheap brand. "Exactly," she said. "Just nudge them a bit further so they know they can do it. It's all mental, you know?"

"I do," CJ agreed. "Look at you. You've become a pro on rock and you're admittedly not naturally built for it, but you've got the right attitude and the right mental toughness."

Chris laughed, leaning over to sock him in the arm before taking the lead up the trail. Turning back to him, she said, "That's your polite way of saying I'm a tank, isn't it?"

CJ knew her pace would quicken within minutes. "It's my way of saying you're built like a truck and not a sports car. But you crush me at altitude. Positively crush me."

It was true and Chris knew it. "I breathe easy up there, and on rock I am good in my head. So that counts. It feels like a chess game to me when I'm up there trying to figure out the sequencing."

"Well, you're an engineer, Chris."

"In a former life, yes," she said. "Now I can't even use my camera properly." She recounted a hilarious story about running into Sir Edmund Hillary in Kathmandu, huffing as she took a sharp turn up an embankment.

"The real deal? What did you get yourself into this time?" CJ asked, as he looked down and noticed his lace was coming untied. He paused to tie it, knowing the 4,167-foot mountain was daring him to catch up with Chris. She had become friendly with Sir Edmund over the years, which CJ could not quite wrap his head around. "He's how old now?"

"He's like eighty years old or something," Chris said. "But sharp. Great conversationalist. And he invited me for dinner."

"Sir Edmund invited you for dinner? I cannot believe your life. Continue." Chris's ponytail stuck out from under her Mountain Madness cap. CJ kept his eye on it as he ran, waiting for the punch line.

"I go to his place for dinner. It's lovely. Wonderful food, laughter, stories. Near the end of dinner, I ask if I can get a photo with him."

"You're kidding! Why have I never seen this photo?"

Chris laughed. "Hang on, I'm getting there. So this friend who was there takes a photo with my camera. I thank Hillary. Tell him I'll see him next time." As they bounded over a boulder in the middle of the trail, Chris landed the punch line. "On the plane home, I take out my camera to rewind the film . . . There wasn't any film in the damn camera!"

Incredulous, CJ stopped, hands on hips and doubled over chuckling.

"I'm a dope," Chris said, smiling. Nearly out of breath now, they continued running, the top of Mount Si waiting.

SIX MONTHS AFTER KEITH'S DEATH, Chris frequently stayed late at the Mountain Madness offices. Based in West Seattle, the staff worked out of a series of nondescript tiny rooms in a historic brick walk-up. Pulling together the slick catalog of trips the company provided took time, and it was a job that Chris relished. Expeditions were listed by altitude in descending order, and each one had a yellow, horizontal block beside it to map out the weeks and months of the year that clients would need to take leave from family and jobs to climb. Trips she'd cultivated recently were marked with a badge labeled "NEW!"

"I'll never forget meeting her," recalls one of Chris's friends. "She was upstairs in a back office. It was late at night and she was working on the catalog only by the light of the computer. I'd heard a lot about her, of course, but I didn't have a clue what to expect. As soon as we met, she gave me the warmest hug. I knew right away we'd be friends. She was such a bright light. A few years after we met, I lost my husband. I'll never forget Chris coming over to sit with me. Not talking, but just being present. She understood suffering and loss at a young age."

Part of moving *through* loss and not *around* it meant carrying on in the mountains alone. In the summer of 1999, Chris traveled back to the Karakoram. This time, her hope was to scale the 8,035-meter peak, Gasherbrum II. The mountain had been a favorite of Keith's. Without him, the trip would be another in a series of "firsts" that she'd have to achieve. The team was composed of Chris and ten men, along with a documentary film crew that had come to chronicle her journey up the mountain. The resulting film would be titled *Ascent on G2*.

Alpinist Steve Swenson overlapped with Chris at Gasherbrum II Base Camp. The expedition had its bumps, with bad weather, complaints by team members that logistics were botched, and leadership missing. Steve recalled talking with Chris and commending her on her resiliency. Things may not have been seamless, but the fact that she followed through and focused on the goal of overseeing the team in the midst of her grief was a feat.

Accompanying Chris on the expedition was Hector Ponce de Leon, the guide who'd led her on her first big climb in Bolivia with Keith six years earlier. He remembered Chris's tenacity in the middle of heartache: "She was the face of determination in Pakistan. I think a lot of people didn't think she was ready to be back in the mountains, but she stood her ground. She was a lioness."

MOUNTAINS BATHED IN WHITE frame a moving image of Chris in knee-deep snow. Climbing with her body weight leaning into an aluminum trekking pole, she looks at the camera and smiles. The contrast with the peaks behind her is breathtaking. She wears a cardinal-red down jacket, bright purple pants, and tall, canary-yellow mountaineering boots with crampons.

It's the opening shot of the film, with Chris's voiceover: "I look at women and men as the same—equals. I don't look at this as 'because I'm a woman I can't do this.' The main thing is that you do what makes you happy. The thing that really intrigues me about climbing is not only the adventure and the excitement, but it's also going into a different land and seeing the people. Experiencing their culture. Going where hardly anyone else has ever gone."

The entire team disembarks from their vans to stock up on supplies for the expedition. Chris was becoming more recognizable in Pakistan than in Seattle, and the eyes of the local men are on her—a lone woman who appears to be running the operation. The expedition members wander from stand to stand, and she chuckles, making note of the contrast in the goods drawing interest from team members: "Well, the woman had to buy mangoes and the men had to look at guns."

THE TEAM IS ON FOOT, trekking through the valley on the way to base camp. Crossing rickety bridges, the Balti porters hired to carry supplies look at ease shouldering massive loads. Chris stops to address an ox blocking the trail. Looking at the camera, she comments in a moment of levity, "I'm trying to talk him into carrying me to base camp, but it seems like he wants to go the other direction."

As the expedition moves up the mountain, it becomes clear how challenging their task will be. Opting against using porter assistance beyond base camp, the team climbs without supplemental oxygen. Refueling stations are established at incremental marks up the mountain. Camp 1 at 5,898 meters. Camp 2 on a shoulder of the mountain at 6,400 meters. Camp 3 at 6,797 meters. Camp 4 at 7,407 meters, at the start of the last traverse. Then a few thousand more feet to the summit, a trek of eight hours to the top of Gasherbrum II at 8,034 meters.

The days are spent judging the weather, then moving up and down from camp to camp to let their bodies adjust to the increase in altitude. An avalanche hits base camp, leaving Chris to shuttle down to assess the damage, which thankfully is minimal. Between the daily training climbs, Chris and her teammates perfect the art of boredom, a required part of any expedition, as one of them explains, "This is what mountaineering is all about. It's about ninety-five percent exhaustion, boredom, and tedium and five percent abject terror and thrill."

With plenty of time to think, Chris is caught in a moment rarely seen on camera or in person. Looking down and away, her hair blows across her face as she talks about her loss. Eyes cast away from the camera, she says: "My husband Keith passed away on January twenty-fifth." She pauses, taking a breath. Bits of snow graze her cheek, her nose painted white with sun protection. "This is my first expedition without him. This was a peak that he'd always wanted to climb. It's given me his spirit that hopefully I'll carry through. It's hard sometimes when you sit there and think, 'Can I climb without him?' I think time will tell."

After two summit bids are thwarted because of weather, Chris reaches the top on her third attempt. On a gorgeous day, she and the remaining two team members make their way to the top. Falling slightly behind, she pauses before the summit. "I don't like to quit," she says. "It took so long to prepare. The training and logistics. You might as well finish it. Sometimes when I'm climbing with someone behind me, I pretend it's Keith and he's saying, 'Come on, let's go—you can do it.'"

Pulling tight, the fixed rope leading to the summit slips through her mittens as she kneels on top with her two teammates. Music swells as the film reaches its climax. Chris, now the first North American woman to reach the top of four of Earth's highest peaks, gives a slight grin and calls down to base camp to report their success.

"This is a peak for Keith," she declares. "I was going to leave Keith's wedding ring here, but I decided against it. I'm not ready to leave it at the top. Maybe some other peak. But I did this peak for Keith."

CHAPTER 9

EVEREST

SIPPING SOFT DRINKS, PASSENGERS ABOARD a 747 peeked out the window, a vision of vastness. Clouds mixed with empty skies. At a cruising altitude of thirty-five thousand feet, the very thought of being on the other side of the jet's thick steel walls seemed absurd. Yet just outside, and a mere seven thousand feet below, this height was Chris's playground. Her body wasn't naturally bred for altitude, which made the scenes on the mountains she climbed all the more unbelievable.

"I remember being with her on Cho Oyu," one of her climbing colleagues said, "and the clients were a mess that high, but she looked perfectly normal. Like she was out for a stroll, and when she hung out at camp, she was entirely focused on breaking out the high-end cheese and crackers." What was happening to Chris's clients while she ate cheese and crackers was common; Chris's response was a little more unusual.

Although the percentage of oxygen in the air at higher altitudes remains the same 21 percent it is at sea level, the weight of air (the barometric pressure) decreases the higher a person ascends. Less pressure means that the air itself is less concentrated so not as much oxygen is taken in with each breath.

Less oxygen makes it harder for the body to perform work and think clearly. When ascending too high, too fast, some individuals experience high altitude illnesses. The most common is acute mountain sickness (AMS) in which appetite may disappear; those affected may also experience nausea, poor sleeping patterns, fatigue, or difficulty thinking clearly. A nasty headache is the most common symptom. If these symptoms are ignored or those affected continue to climb higher, two less common but more serious illnesses may occur: high-altitude pulmonary edema (HAPE) and high-altitude cerebral edema (HACE). HAPE, the more common of the two, is associated with edema fluid accumulating in the lungs, leaving climbers with increasing difficulty supplying the body with vital oxygen. In the case of HACE, the edema fluid accumulates in the brain, resulting in impaired thinking and behavior, loss of stability in walking, and eventual loss of consciousness.

The question as to what it is that allows humans like Chris to acclimatize more easily than others has fascinated scientists for generations. Is the ability to adapt influenced more by genetic components or by environmental factors? The answer at present seems to be that it could be a little of both, with ongoing genetic research leading to new attempts to explain why some people do better than others at altitude.

In Chris's case, fitness also played into the equation. Endless climbs of Mount Rainier had no doubt prepared her body well. Keith had schooled her in the proper methods of strengthening her lungs and heart with long runs carrying a heavy pack. With each successive trip higher, Chris's ability to adapt improved.

As a doctor and client of Mountain Madness, Dr. Julio Bird was in awe of Chris. He recalled her as a student of climbing who approached each day as a scientist approaches a lab experiment. "Her conditioning was incredible," he said. "She just raced up those mountains. She didn't know what it was, but she knew she had a gift to breathe at high altitude." Chris stayed on top of her health and that of her clients by measuring the oxygen saturation in their blood with pulse oximeters clipped to their fingers. "We were all ninety to ninety-one percent saturated," Julio said, "but she was always ninety-seven to ninety-eight percent."

Eighteen months after Keith died, Chris was at the apex of her career. She had climbed four 8,000-meter peaks. Her business was flourishing. Public interest in mountaineering was at an all-time high. The time seemed perfect to turn her sights to the world's highest mountain. Billed the "Everest Millennium Expedition," the marketing material from Mountain Madness requesting sponsor dollars spoke for itself:

"At 8,848 meters high, Mount Everest is the highest mountain in the world. Christine has chosen the pre-monsoon season to make history. Please join us to make possible Christine Feld Boskoff's bid to become the only woman in North America to summit five 8,000-meter peaks."

TO COUNTERACT THE EFFECTS OF extreme altitude, ascents above a certain level typically require supplemental oxygen. This precious gas fills aluminum cylinders and is often carried by Sherpas and other high-altitude workers whose job it is to monitor clients on large expeditions. Os are sometimes administered at an altitude predetermined by expedition leaders and at other times on an as-needed basis.

While the vast majority of expedition members on 8,000-meter peaks happily use supplemental oxygen, the story differs among elite climbers. Many climbers see the absence of bottled oxygen as a more "pure" way of attaining a summit. Others argue that climbing without oxygen is preferable to reduce the number of empty bottles discarded by climbers in an attempt to lighten their loads. Whatever the viewpoint, the topic has been debated since 1978, when Mount Everest was first summited without oxygen by European mountaineers Reinhold Messner and Peter Habeler—a feat that had been previously thought unattainable.

Twenty-two years later, Peter Habeler wanted to try again, with Chris as his partner. "She invited me and I was so happy to 'meet' Everest again after such a long time," he recalled. "I had heard about Chris and knew she was an incredible, strong climber, but I came to also find her warm and respectful." The Austrian climber had maintained his conditioning over many decades. Now fifty-eight, he felt confident he could summit again without supplemental oxygen. When he heard Chris was ready to attempt Everest, he grabbed the opportunity. His climbs with Messner in the 1970s and 1980s had been in the alpine style, carrying light loads and spending minimal time on the mountain. Peter had always felt that a quicker ascent was the safer way to go.

The Mountain Madness Everest team in 2000 consisted of a small number of like-minded climbers. Chris wouldn't be leading clients but rather attempting her own first ascent on Everest. This would allow her to climb more rapidly instead of tending to others. They were one of fourteen teams attempting the summit that year, and the permit issued by Nepal's Ministry of Tourism & Civil Aviation listed the name of the Mountain Madness team leader as "Mr. Christine Feld Boskoff."

Also joining Peter and Chris would be Nazir Sabir. A friend of Scott Fischer, Nazir was meant to be on Scott's fateful 1996 expedition, before pulling out due to schedule conflicts. A renowned mountaineer from Pakistan, Nazir had attempted Everest once before, in 1997. If he reached the top this time, he'd be the first Pakistani to do so. Kili Sherpa would also be on Everest. As planned, he'd helped Mountain Madness dig deeper into the Nepal market, stepping up to fill part of the void left when Chris lost Keith. Having been to the base of Everest many times, Kili himself was still looking for a summit. He'd been high, but never to the top of the world. He hoped the year 2000 with Chris, Nazir, and Peter would be it.

OUTSIDE THEIR TENT, THE WINDS had picked up again. Kili and Chris lay in their sleeping bags wondering if it was time to descend. The two had made it to Camp 4 on the South Col of Everest in early May 2000. Nazir and several team members were in other tents, all of them feeling the force of the sixty-eight-mile-an-hour winds. This last section before the summit was notorious for wind. Already this season had been marked with similar winds that had forced many climbers to seek safety in lower camps.

Up to this point on the climb, Chris and Peter had been formidable partners. Her strength and ability to adapt at high altitude challenged him. Keeping pace with each other on training rotations traversing the Khumbu Icefall, the two got through it in forty-five minutes, while most other climbers needed three hours. Though Chris was still on the rise, Peter's celebrity had caused a stir at base camp. A friend recalled just how his presence had played out:

She [Chris] told me that at one point on the expedition a couple climbers came up to the two of them all unrecognizably bundled up and asked excitedly about whether they'd heard legendary

Peter Habeler was on the mountain. Chris loved it and so did he.
He played it up with her standing right next to him, saying, "Oh
my gosh, you're kidding? Peter Habeler? Really?" And then he kept
it going and said, "Hey, you know you should ask her because she
hangs out with the big boys." He pointed to Chris, who laughed,
shook her head, and said she'd be on the lookout.

According to this friend, Chris's assumption "was that these climbers would never have guessed Peter was standing in front of them because, after all, who could imagine he would climb with a woman? They probably assumed he was a guide and she was a client." Years later, Chris's humor was perhaps one of the most compelling attributes that Peter remembered. "Something I really value in mountaineers is a sense of humor," he said. "She had a wonderful sense of humor and I just loved that and thought it was so important. You simply had to like her, if not to love her."

The duo stuck together for weeks on Everest, coaxing each other through winds and snow that hadn't been seen at that level in years. After his first two attempts at the summit failed because of weather, Peter began to feel the effects of altitude. His lungs rattled, a sure sign of HAPE. Any ambition of ascending Everest a second time without oxygen was dashed. He went down to a lower camp, eventually giving up his summit bid and reporting that "an old man should not try to climb Everest without oxygen."

Meanwhile, Chris and Kili rested in their tent at Camp 4. They'd entered the death zone and were unable to sleep. The wind threatened to blow them off the slopes. A lone cylinder nestled between them, its regulator adjusted to allow a constant flow of precious oxygen. Tubing stretched to a mask cupping Kili's mouth and nose. He turned his head to look at Chris. Her breathing was slow and mouth uncovered. She'd refused oxygen, hoping to be the first American woman to summit Everest without it.

Kili paused, not accustomed to giving advice to the woman he respected so greatly. His memory of first meeting Keith and Chris at Gokyo Lake felt bittersweet without Keith here now. Kili had been a steady force since Keith died, and Chris in turn had carved a path for Kili to a new life. If there were anyone he'd give his life for, it was Chris. He removed his mask, allowing words to be exchanged.

"Chris, you should use oxygen. We're at South Col. You need it now."

"I don't want it," she said. "Even if I did, I don't have a tank."

Kili nodded, pulling his mask off and holding it out to her. Her blue eyes looked tired. Her voice weak. The space between them felt strained by the disagreement. "Yes, I know," he said. "You can use mine. If you're beaten up by altitude, it's a big problem here. Even myself, strong Sherpa, I get very tired."

She balked at the idea. "I really wanted to do this without Os, Kili. I did. Peter did, too."

"You have come to climb Everest, Chris. You are strong. Stronger than me. But if you get sick . . . " Kili couldn't begin to think about her falling ill on his watch. They stared at each other, neither budging until Chris spoke.

"Just to get through the night?"

"Yes, just that."

She reached for the mask in silence as Kili adjusted the dial on the regulator. Placing it over her mouth and nose, she inhaled, closing her eyes. Oxygen poured into her body, precious and life-sustaining. As she drew in three more breaths, her body softened into the sleeping bag. She removed the mask and handed it to Kili, who took three breaths of his own. Taking turns with the mask, the two gradually fell into hypoxic sleep.

ON THE MORNING OF MAY 24, Chris reached the summit of Everest, her fifth 8,000-meter peak. The moment was fleeting. It was her fourth attempt at the summit in just a few weeks, and she was without Kili, who'd decided 2000 was not his year. After several attempts thwarted by wind, he'd departed, returning to base camp and leaving Chris to pursue the summit with one remaining high-altitude guide and more bottled oxygen.

The only picture of Chris on that morning shows her kneeling on the summit, her ice axe wedged into a thick wave of snow at her thighs.

Grasping the base of her oxygen mask with a gloved hand, she's wrapped in a black and bright red hooded down suit. The mask shrouds most of her face, the rest covered with goggles. It's impossible to see a smile, a moment of elation or pride. Before descending, she placed a call to Joyce from a satellite phone, telling her, "Mom, I'm on top of the world." The call was brief, shortened by Chris's knowledge that the trip down would be just as perilous as the ascent.

Asked later by journalists what she thought about at the top, Chris said, "First I felt relieved because we'd been there so long. It was the first time I had thought of going home. I also thought a lot about Scott Fischer and I was hoping he was proud of his company. You think about the people that have helped you, who are there rooting for you. Then you think of going down to get some tea. You know, you are only halfway there when you get to the top. You still have to focus to get down safely and live to tell about it."

The descent from Everest exemplified Chris's strength and spirit. What often takes a couple of days took her just nine hours. Passing through Camp 4, she refused to rest and continued down to base camp.

Nazir Sabir became the first Pakistani on top of Everest a week before Chris. Though she was not with him at the time, Mountain Madness received credit for his success, with the Pakistani press reporting that his expedition had been led by "American lady Christine Feld Boskoff."

The year 2000 also marked the year the first Nepali woman reached the top of the mountain. Just twenty-six years old, Lhakpa Sherpa led a group of Nepalese women and reached the summit a week before Chris. Returning year after year, she would go on to hold the record for the most number of ascents on Mount Everest by a woman and crush the perception that Everest was only for men. "I want to show that a woman can do men's jobs," Lhakpa said. "There is no difference in climbing a mountain. I climb for all women."

In June, Chris returned home to Seattle. Friends wrapped her in warmth and praise, though her thoughts were elsewhere. The adrenaline rush of the past seven years had caught up with her, as she wrote in her journal.

After getting back from Nepal I had mixed feelings about my future with the business, climbing and love . . . I knew I had serious decisions to make with the state of Mountain Madness. I was also frustrated with where my own personal climbing ambitions were taking me . . . disappointed I ended up using oxygen for my final summit attempt. I was tired of having everyone tell me what my limits were, assuming because I was a female there were certain limits I could not obtain . . . for example, summiting Everest without oxygen. I wanted advice, but didn't know where to turn.

Frustrated and full of self-doubt, Chris penned a final sentence that few mountaineers have ever fathomed writing: *Everest was not a challenge for me.*

CHAPTER 10

CHARLIE

NORWOOD, COLORADO, IS ONLY A thirty-minute drive from Telluride, but a contrast to the ski town in every way. The politics lean conservative, with water rights being an ever-important topic of conversation in the local diners. Around town, the vehicles are mostly trucks that haul firewood and ranch dogs, a far cry from the SUVs in Telluride adorned with ski racks and fancy GPS systems. In the year 2000, the population of Norwood was 438, and the Norwood High School Mustangs played eight-man football. With its one-storied shops and utilitarian downtown, Grand Avenue is the main drag of Norwood, splitting off to side streets lined with small, sturdy homes built to withstand wind and snow.

Easing his way onto Charlie Fowler's street just beyond Norwood's center, Keith Brown wondered what he should expect from their dinner date. Charlie had jumped at Brown's offer to pick him up and bring him back to his place for a home-cooked meal. Cooking wasn't Charlie's thing, though he'd worked hard in recent years to perfect one of his favorite dishes, "Hotter Than Hell Chicken." Brown knew the conversations were worth the drive there and back. In the short time he'd known Charlie, he'd come to appreciate his authenticity. A meal with Charlie would be without bullshit, void of self-importance, and perhaps not even touch on the stories and adventures that made him one of the most iconic rock climbers of all time. It would just be . . . dinner with

Charlie. Getting him solo and outside the masses of the climbing scene in Telluride was the key to unlocking his charm.

Brown parked in front of Charlie's yellow and white cabin, a 1920s, two-room structure with a dilapidated roof. The sun had set, bringing the spring temperature down to 30 degrees, as he knocked on the door. After a moment, Charlie opened it, his laconic drawl welcoming Brown with, "Hey, cool, come on in." The 550-square-foot home held not much more than a wood stove, prayer flags, climbing books, boxes of gear, and Kodachrome slides. Buried in the attic was a beautiful set of china from Charlie's grandmother's collection. A mahogany desk took space in the living room, also from his grandmother's house in West Virginia. While *things* were not important to Charlie, family was.

Stepping inside, Brown realized the temperature mirrored the cold outside. "What's up with the heat?" he asked.

"Oh yeah, well, truth be told I never got around to bringing in wood for the stove this year."

"This *year*? So, no heat this winter?"

"Nope. Don't need it," Charlie said. "A pain with all that wood anyway."

Brown felt momentarily stymied, unclear how to respond to something missing that seemed critical in the frigid Colorado winters. Although he longed to return to the warmth of his car, Brown understood the reason for Charlie's absolute comfort in the chill of his own home. Charlie's lean, 5′8″ frame was packed tightly into a down expedition suit complete with hood, very likely the same one he'd recently worn climbing in the Himalayas.

Weathered by decades of wind and sun, Charlie's face was lined in a way that made it known he was an outdoorsman. His hair, a mess of gray and dark brown, had a perpetually tousled look. Peering from under the hood, Charlie's eyes were clear and inviting. Now in his early fifties, he looked full of life, quite ready for Brown to hand him an ice axe or thermos of hot tea and point to the nearest crag.

"Let's go," Charlie said. "I'm starving." Grinning, he stepped out into the bitter twilight, leaving Brown with his first Charlie story of the night.

THE SLIGHT SOUTHERN ACCENT THAT Charlie spoke with came from years growing up in Virginia. His father, an Episcopalian minister who died when Charlie was twenty-one, spent two decades teaching his son to hike and camp in the nearby Smoky Mountains. From his librarian mother, Charlie learned to seek fulfillment outside social norms. Calling his mom a "left-winger with heavy Marxist leanings" in her, Charlie had a lifelong advocate. Nurturing his love of the outdoors and his disdain for the establishment, Charlie's mother watched him race through a degree in environmental science in three years at the University of Virginia. On the day of his last final in 1975, he packed his car with climbing gear and moved to Boulder, Colorado. Hooked on the sport of climbing already, he'd led several classic climbs up in New York and West Virginia.

For the next several decades, Charlie focused on cutting a trail for himself that combined work he enjoyed with his love of climbing. Among his job titles were furniture maker, writer, bag designer, computer programmer, and trip leader. Each position was designed to add value to his lifestyle (his sewing work eventually led him to make backpacks, patch clothing, and add pockets to simple lawn chairs that he'd sleep on during camping trips) while allowing the greatest amount of time for climbing. Eventually he'd pursue his American Mountain Guides Association certification, contracting his services with the credentials highly sought by wealthy clients.

By the mid-1980s, Charlie had become known for his first ascents in the Tetons, the Wind River Range, Canyonlands, Red Rocks, and Yosemite. In his thirties, he began traveling outside the United States, to Patagonia, Bhutan, Nepal, and Tibet. Following his trips, Charlie put together slide shows to share in Telluride, sometimes at private homes, sometimes at pizza joints. The visuals were astounding: Charlie exploring remote Communist China in the early 1990s; Charlie bumping along dusty roads in the Peruvian countryside; Charlie's tent staked to dry brush in rural Nepal. Each journey seemed unencumbered, as if nothing else in the world mattered but the moment at hand. Even in times of seeming distress, his outlook resonated positivity.

In one memorable 1984 experience, Charlie teamed up with Boulder climber Alex Lowe for a winter ascent of the Diamond, a vertical to overhanging thousand-foot wall that started at thirteen thousand feet on the east face of Long's Peak in Colorado. To begin, the pair dodged an avalanche, an event that would have caused many other climbers to hightail it to safety. For Alex and Charlie, it was simply a sign that the coast was clear. With snow falling, thick layers accumulated against the flat rock as the two ascended, unroped. Then, without warning, a wind slab broke from under Alex's feet, hitting Charlie square on and sending him falling over the cliffs and down the smooth rock face.

Charlie later described the fall: "As I began to free-fall I thought, *This is really going to hurt.* Much to my surprise, I landed softly in a sitting position, in a huge pile of new-fallen snow. It didn't hurt that much at all. No one seemed too surprised by our story; by then I already had a reputation for an uncanny ability to cheat death."

UNLIKE OTHER CLIMBERS WHO SOUGHT partners with equal or greater ability, Charlie never shied from the chance to be on rock with beginners. Nor did he seek the glory of mastering popular routes or the money that called to him from big sponsors. His sweet spot was discovering challenging, unexplored places that could push his limits and increase his skill set, regardless of who he climbed with. In a sport that could be ego-driven, Charlie sought only to pass on his enthusiasm.

"He was one of my original heroes," remembered friend Mark Kroese:

His skills were off the charts and he knew it. He didn't need to prove himself to anyone. I remember being nineteen years old at Yosemite with a friend and climbing the Nose of El Capitan for the first time. Charlie was there with a less-experienced partner and they passed us on the way up. Right after that, his partner took a 160-foot fall. They retreated, passing us on their way down and his partner's eyes were as wide as saucers but Charlie seemed unfazed. We were completely freaked out, but trying to stay cool.

*Years later I interviewed Charlie for a book I was writing and
he asked if we'd met. I reminded him about the incident and he got
a big kick out of it. Though I had remembered clearly how I'd tried
to stay cool, his recollection was just as clear. He had a vivid recollection of two young climbers who were totally paralyzed by the
fall they'd just seen.*

BY THE MID 1990S, CHARLIE had been climbing twenty-five years. He'd
mastered every climbing discipline he tried, with many first ascents
(first successful summits) to his credit. Rock, bouldering, ice, free
climbing, and alpine-style mountaineering: his climbing résumé burst
with accomplishments too numerous to fit on a single page but not well
known because he rarely made mention of them unless questioned by
others.

Charlie spent years working on his form and technique, but perhaps
the biggest shift in his climbing career came in October 1997 when
he was in his early forties. Climbing in western Tibet, he guided two
younger but experienced climbers up Gurla Mandhata, a mammoth,
25,242-foot peak. Already acclimatized from previous, smaller ascents,
the trio estimated they could summit in two days in alpine style, moving fast and carrying only enough to survive the up and back. Day one
progressed as planned. Day two began and ended just as quickly, with
the weather turning poor. By day three, with fingers and toes beginning
to freeze, it was apparent that the snow and cold would keep them from
undertaking the technical maneuvers they'd need to summit. These
were the moments in which Charlie shined. A climber and guide who
was old-school and classical, he would only take the next step when
he was ready and rarely took unnecessary risks. It was time to retreat.

Tied together on a 150-foot rope, the three climbers descended until
. . . a slip. Sliding down a steep slope, they hit a serac (a peak of ice on a
glacier) that launched them three hundred feet into the air. After sailing a total of 1,500 feet, they landed on a pile of snow that cushioned
their fall. The younger men were relatively unhurt, while Charlie had
badly twisted his leg in the fall but was alive. Awestruck that they hadn't

suffered greater injury, the men managed to retrieve their gear, then bivvied (created a small, improvised shelter) for the night in the crater they'd created. Charlie's account of the experience, published in a 1999 edition of the *American Alpine Journal*, described the following days and weeks without the drama that actually ensued, including the frostbite all three suffered; the multiday hike that involved crawling at times to get to base camp; the feet that swelled and oozed pus; the hallucinations; the rescue by infectious disease doctors; the one-week, hanging-on-by-a-thread road trip to Kathmandu; and the amputation of several of Charlie's toes.

Instead, his words described only the pragmatic approach he took once the team had spent a night in cold shock after the fall: "The next day they took off for help while I suffered alone. They arrived at Base Camp late that night. Kwang [the Sherpa they'd hired to assist prior to their ascent] turned right around the next morning, and with two local yak herders he had recruited, helped me down that day. Base Camp was quickly dismantled and we hit the road for Kathmandu and home."

Charlie made his way back to Oregon, to the home of his sister, Ginny, where he sought medical advice in an attempt to save the rest of his badly frostbitten toes. In the end, he lost parts of five toes and his entire right big toe. What might have been devastating for any other climber, Charlie shrugged off by simply strategizing his recovery. "We visited him in Colorado during the summer after his surgery," said Ginny. "We went on a car trip through southwestern Colorado, Utah, and Arizona, and he was the guide. Charlie sat in the front seat with his foot on the dashboard."

What had been a prolific career suddenly became nearly mythical as Charlie recovered. Instead of staying home for his feet to heal, as the rock climbing season took off in 1998, he went to Moab with friends, belaying them from the base of big walls as he sat in a lawn chair. And then he taught himself how to climb again without as many toes. Charlie went on to develop hundreds of difficult routes near his home in Norwood, never complaining about his lack of toes. Instead, according to Ginny, he "just pretended he had them."

CHARLIE'S LEGENDARY FRUGALITY AND SLIGHT social awkwardness for-ever belied his intelligence and wit. Passionate about books, he collected stacks in his home, as they were one of the only things he spent money on. He relished an understanding of other cultures, art, architecture, and performance art. Among the friends who transcended his climb-ing world was Joel Coniglio. Moving from Boston to Norwood, Joel had heard about Charlie. Within a short time, the two had met and begun to explore activities outside climbing.

"We'd road trip to Santa Fe and show up all grungy, having eaten Pop Tarts and nasty fried stuff all the way down," Joel said. "Charlie would say, 'Man, we gotta clean up a bit and shave so we can go into some of these galleries.' He really was able to navigate a lot of different worlds and wasn't just this one-dimensional climber that people tended to see. His frugality offended people, but it wasn't meant to. I would say he was . . . enigmatic. He was the most humble person I've ever known but also quite confident. He didn't want to constantly be talking about climbing. He didn't relish that kind of attention."

If not climbing or reading, Charlie could often be found immersed in photography. He and Joel had come to learn the art of Polaroid trans-fers, a printmaking technique in which instant photos are transferred to another base, such as paper or wood. "Charlie was super curious about exploring and not always for the purpose of climbing," Joel said. "We'd poke around in new areas, make these gorgeous, ethereal images that looked like paintings. Became kind of obsessed with it, really. Because we could do it anywhere, we found ourselves making prints on belay ledges or in bivouacs. Literally printing on the peaks we were climbing."

As Charlie and Joel became better friends, Joel grew to understand him in a way few did. Perhaps the biggest mystery he unlocked was how this somewhat introverted, quirky climber managed to attract women. Charlie's orbit frequently included beautiful, fit women, and though his relationships rarely lasted long, most ended cordially and he wasn't prone to macho guy talk in the wake of a breakup. "It was a source of amusement, really," Joel remembered. "We'd all say, how the hell does Charlie keep attracting these beautiful, athletic women? I just think women were drawn to his lack of bravado, his humility. He wasn't super emotive, and kind of awkward, but also totally unpretentious."

In 1993, *Climbing* magazine spoke to this when a writer asked Charlie when he planned to get married. "Women are more dangerous than climbing," he joked, before adding: "I'm saving myself for the right woman."

CHAPTER 11

PASSION

JANE COURAGE AND CHRIS SWAPPED leads on a rock route on Snow Creek Wall outside Leavenworth, Washington. The route played to their divergent strengths—cracks that demanded technique and strength for Chris, and delicate, airy face sections for Jane. They'd climbed many times here, and it was a challenging classic that gave them both a rush.

At the base of the eight-hundred-foot wall, the bright floral capris they wore stood out against the slate gray. Months before, Jane had bought matching floral capri pants on a whim in Hawaii. Colorful and loud, they were something that Chris would never look at twice, much less purchase. Both women preferred to climb in ratty old favorites and not the latest splashy gear unveiled on the racks at REI each season. Chris's old Land Rover was typically spilling with empty Diet Coke cans, old bags of popcorn, and well-worn climbing equipment. Like her vehicle, her clothes were decidedly utilitarian.

As they sorted gear for the climb, Jane presented the gift. Chris had been a mix of quiet mortification and graciousness until Jane pulled out her matching pair and Chris realized the prank. As Jane often did with Chris, when climbs required formidable grit, she'd make sure to keep it light. This time, the matching pants provided the spoof du jour for their fine day on the wall.

"That's it, sista," Jane called as she moved back from her landing spot at the top of the first pitch. As she belayed Chris up, she called, "How's the rock, babe?!"

After the first pitch, the climb increased in difficulty. Jane led the final pitch, which was a crack that also offered rough protrusions known as chickenheads. At the top of the climb, Jane moved back about twelve feet from the cliff's edge, tying to a tree to secure herself as she belayed Chris up the final pitch. They could no longer hear each other, but Jane knew Chris was heading up as the rope went from tight to slack. Dirt and chalk dust caked Jane's thighs, the colors of the flowers on her capris now muted.

A short time into Chris's ascent, Jane heard a slight snort come from over her shoulder. She knew she had company. Walking toward her, an oversize mountain goat watched her intently, stopping just shy of the tree. "Hi there. I know what you're after, but you're gonna have to wait. My friend isn't up yet and I'm, you know, tied to a tree." Jane's hands gripped the rope, one eye keeping watch on the ledge for Chris. "Coming soon?" she shouted. "I've got a visitor here and he must know I've gotta pee like mad!"

Popping up, Chris took one look at the scene and dissolved into laughter. Jane frantically untied, slipping off her harness and bolting to an open area with the goat giving chase.

"I can't breathe," Chris said, gasping as she laughed. She leaned over, her small, weather-beaten hands cracked from the climb, and rested on her thighs as she tried to pull herself together. "See what happens when we wear hot pants like this? Stalked by a mountain goat for your pee! Hurry and drop your drawers!"

The goat calmly but doggedly walked toward Jane as Chris said, "Hey, goat dude, be polite and give the girl some privacy." By the time the goat made it over for a salty sip, Jane was up and gone. The women sat and watched as the goat finished, gave them an unimpressed look, and walked away.

"Sheesh, this is the first time I've had a goat encounter on Snow Creek Wall," said Jane, catching her breath.

Reaching into her backpack, Chris pulled out two hard-as-rock Power Bars, handing one to Jane. The women had grown close in the years since Keith had passed away, sharing climbs and dinners of sushi, Chris's latest food obsession. She'd taken on the role of godmother to

Jane's two young daughters and had been one of only four people to attend the wedding to celebrate her second marriage. Though Jane relished her role in Chris's life, she sensed that Chris would eventually want a partner who could keep up with her and fill the gap left on high-altitude expeditions since Keith had been gone.

Jane had recently traveled to Mountainfilm, a festival showcasing adventure films that took place every Memorial Day weekend in Telluride. While there, she found herself at a party one night, chatting with a guy who seemed quiet but astute and amiable. They talked about films and China, a country they both loved and hoped to explore more. He carried himself without airs, totally unimpressed by the fact that he was surrounded by powerful film patrons.

"Do you climb?" Jane asked.

"Yeah, I climb," he replied in a flat monotone.

Jane nodded, having no clue how elite he was at the sport, nor the fact that she might be the only one in town who had no idea who the man was. The conversation continued, a mix of Seattle climbing stories and his hopes of traveling to unexplored places in Bhutan and western Sichuan. Being from the Pacific Northwest and not Colorado, Jane knew little about the climbing personalities in Telluride. She only knew she'd been told to find one climber in particular, someone one of her Seattle friends said was an original and worth meeting.

Half an hour passed before Jane paused, wondering whether this man was one and the same. "Wait, what did you say your name was?"

"Charlie. Charlie Fowler."

JANE RESPECTED CHARLIE'S DRIVE AND depth. He wasn't a poser and his passion for the mountains impressed her. So did his ego, which oozed humility despite his vast accomplishments. He was an old-school climber, depending on skills he'd developed over many years of hardcore rock and alpine climbing. She loved that he wasn't into self-promotion, hype, or media. He was simply a nonstop climber. Their conversations continued by email and phone well after she flew back to Seattle. As he started to talk with her about a future trip he was planning to Asia and needing a travel companion, Jane thought of Chris. Her friend could also use a strong mountaineering partner again. Charlie seemed ideal. A dozen years older than Chris, he had the skills, experience, and disposition to be compatible with her.

"I thought Chris and Charlie would be good climbing partners," Jane recalled. "That's it. I wasn't *ever* looking to hook her up romantically—not even close. I just told him, I know a girl."

Jane suggested Chris as a travel and climbing partner, sharing some details about her with Charlie before providing her an email address. Because of the distance between them, Charlie and Chris initially corresponded. Charlie excelled at writing, having already spent many years publishing articles and climbing books. Though Chris held back at first, Charlie's messages to her were full of humor and sincerity. She began to warm to the idea of partnering with him, and over the course of a few weeks in August 2000, a long-distance romance began to blossom. An outdoor sports expo in Salt Lake City in the middle of the month would be their first meeting. Planning for the trip, they talked about their color preferences for potential outdoor photo shoots and the assortment of things they liked to pack, some of them far-fetched.

From: chris@mountainmadness.com
To: Charlie Fowler
This list looks great, but I don't see a surfboard on it. Also, I'm a red color person if we have a choice. Then black. Then blue. Just thinking about photos . . . I look bad in green and yellow.

• • •

From: Charlie Fowler
To: chrisb@moutainmadness.com
Patagonia does, in fact, have a loaner program for their surfboards. I was in San Francisco a few years back with a surfer friend. I went out and shot video even though I'd never been on a surfboard myself. You know what they say, "If it wasn't for the rocks, we'd all be surfers."

Do you know Dr. Jim Duff? I just got an email from him. He's involved with some good work over there in Kathmandu. I'll fill you in later. He says my toes are famous in Australia ... it's a long story. See ya, Charlie

• • •

From: chrisb@mountainmadness.com
To: Charlie Fowler
My brother is a surfer in LA. Well ... he tries. I never went with him, but he doesn't go that much anymore. If he would surf as much as he talks about it, he'd be another Frankie Avalon.
I think I met Jim at Everest. Does he have a wife who's a doc, too? If so, then I know him ... great guy. Toes in Australia? Sounds like a good story! It has "epic" written all over it!
Later, Chris

• • •

From: Charlie Fowler
To: chrisb@mountainmadness.com
You're so insightful . . . . the toe thing WAS epic. Actually, Jim just took a photo of my toes last year, or what's left of them, I should say. I guess the photo was published in Australia. Well, it's a long story, but here's the short version—I fell 500 meters down a peak in west Tibet and crawled out over a few days, got frostbite on my toes, and lost five. Oh well. Toes are overrated if you ask me.
I hope you don't get the wrong idea about me. I'm really a safe climber. I don't make a habit of falling off, honest. And don't worry, I can still climb just fine, too. I do walk slower than I used to. Some people think that's an improvement.
It was interesting to hear you say your role at MM is changing and you're looking at more personal climbing. That's pretty much where I'm at, too. For several years I worked a lot as a guide, which I enjoy, helping people fulfill their dreams. But now I think it's time to focus on my own dreams. My only commitment is to support myself, too, which is not so hard. So I have a lot of independence, can do what I want (within limits, of course). We can talk more about all this ...
More later, Charlie

• • •

From: Charlie Fowler

To: chrisb@mountainmadness.com

Here's some background info, personal goals and ideas from me, so you have a better idea where I'm coming from.

Ideally, what I'd like to do now in life is travel around, have some cool adventures like doing unclimbed peaks in Tibet! Take some photos and maybe video as well. Then come back home and do slide shows, write articles or even books, sell my pictures, etc. I don't have a lot of expenses at home, as I like living simply. Anyway, I get the impression that you may be thinking along the same lines.

It'll be real nice to talk in person. There's too much to talk about.

I think one of the things I like about searching out these unclimbed peaks over there—no tourists or development, lots of pristine mountain terrain. I'd like to get in there before these places get trashed, try to set a good example or tradition of low-impact travel from the start . . .

Anyway, I think your ideas fit with mine, it seems. I imagine we can work on a lot of stuff together. We'll see. Looking forward to seeing you soon and brainstorming about all this.

Bye, Charlie

CHARLIE AND CHRIS MET IN person in Salt Lake City, and the spark was enough that they were soon planning to connect trips they had to Nepal two weeks later.

From: Charlie Fowler

To: chrisb@mountainmadness.com

Hey Dear,

Maybe I should just meet you at the Gaurishanker, so you can do your business. What time do you arrive, anyway, in case I change my mind 'cause I can't wait to see you . . . in any case, let's hook up real soon.

Love, Charlie

• • •

From: chrisb@mountainmadness.com
To: Charlie Fowler
Last night I spoke with Jane. You know what she told me? She said
that you're interested in me. Can you believe that? I didn't tell her
we were already involved. I'm awful, but it was cute listening to her.

• • •

From: Charlie Fowler
To: chrisb@mountainmadness.com
Jane is right. I am interested in you. I'm counting the days till we
meet in Kathmandu.

• • •

From: chrisb@mountainmadness.com
To: Charlie Fowler
I will call you as soon as I know when I'm able to be at the hotel. I
will have to talk with Kili Sherpa a little bit, too. God, I can't wait
to see you!!

THE TRIP TO NEPAL WOULD take them into familiar territory for both of
them. Charlie was planning his first summit of an 8,000-meter peak.
He'd try for Cho Oyu while Chris would be there as well, guiding a trip
for Mountain Madness. The expeditions were separate, but the pair
planned to see each other when they could, then connect afterward to
climb another 8,000-meter peak, Shishapangma. It would be Chris's
sixth 8,000-meter peak.

Arriving in Kathmandu at the end of August 2000, Chris wrote in her
journal of her fascination with this surprising relationship. Where had
it come from? They'd only been together a few weeks and were now fully
in the throes of the excitement of a budding relationship.

August 30, 2000
I'm in Kathmandu. I got hooked up with Charlie Fowler for
Shishapangma. I'm not sure where he came from. Maybe God sent
him. I read his emails more closely and he's actually quite funny.
I felt really geeky emailing this guy back and forth, but I enjoyed

*getting four to five emails a day from him. It was refreshing. I felt
like fifteen years old again!*

*I met him in Salt Lake City at the Outdoor Retailer Show. I
didn't know what he thought—was I too geeky and regimented for
him? So now I'm scared about this expedition and this relationship. I started climbing only nine years ago and I don't have much
guiding experience. I feel like a deer in the middle of I-5 with a huge
semi heading straight towards me. I keep saying to myself to stay
focused, do your best and let things happen. If Charlie thinks I'm
a goof, so be it. Someday I'll shine but now I'm post-holing through
life.*

• • •

September 3, 2000

*We're in Lhasa heading for Cho Oyu Base Camp. I wonder if
Charlie is thinking about me. I wish he was with me. Does that
make me insecure if I miss him or want him?*

*The guys in the expedition went out. I wasn't invited. I honestly
don't care, but it would have been nice to be invited.*

• • •

September 6, 2000

*We made it to base camp! When we got to base camp, Charlie had
already left for advanced base camp. But he left me a note and a
T-shirt for my birthday. What a sweetheart. I still don't believe
Charlie is real. There has got to be some catch. If there is, I'm ready
for it. If there isn't, then I can see spending some long-term time
with him. He excites me like Keith did, but he is different in good
ways. Besides, he will never be Keith. Keith was one of a kind.*

• • •

September 11, 2000

*I think Charlie is the kind of guy I've been looking for, but I'm
not sure if there is a perfect someone. He can make me laugh and
I'm looking forward to spending quality time with him. I hope he
respects me and likes me for who I am and not because of my looks.*

• • •

September 16, 2000
Today was a rest day. We hung out at our camp, listened to tunes
and ate Italian sausage and cheese (big hit!). Charlie stayed over
last night! I think I'm in love, but I can't tell him that. It's too soon.
I'll give this relationship my all. If it doesn't work, I'll become a nun.
I need to stay focused on our expedition. Oh, also I'm going to put
my all into the business. Charlie is right—What would I do if I
didn't have it? Sometimes I just get . . . lazy. God, I'm going to give
everything my all.

AS CHRIS LED HER TEAM on rotations between lower and higher camps,
she remained in contact with Mountain Madness in Seattle. Then,
nearing the end of their expedition and approaching summit day, she
received word that her father had suffered a stroke.

September 20, 2000
Well this entry isn't so pleasant. Yesterday from Camp 2 I found out
my dad was in the ICU. He had a stroke. I went down from Camp
2 in three hours. My mom said any day now they were expecting
him to die. I cried and Charlie came down to comfort me. Should I
go home? Should I stay and climb? I don't know. I spoke to Charlie
and he said whatever I decide is right. I feel like a heel for staying,
but I have a commitment to my team for Cho Oyu. Also . . . I don't
want to let go of Shishapangma. I guess I'm selfish. Climbing is my
savior and my healer.

ROBIN FELD PASSED AWAY ON September 21, 2000, while his thirty-
three-year-old daughter led the expedition members farther up Cho
Oyu for a summit bid. Ultimately her team was turned back by high
winds, and none were able to set foot on top. Charlie, several days ahead
of Chris, made it to the top of his first 8,000-meter peak, meeting Chris
at Camp 1 on her descent. As the two made their way back to base camp
and prepared for a summit attempt on Shishapangma, Chris questioned
her decision to stay. What drove her to remain on the expedition, missing her dad's funeral? Where would her path lead?

September 30, 2000
I probably missed my dad's funeral. I can't believe I missed the
entire thing. I can't imagine what all my relatives think. What
kind of person am I? I try to be a good person, but I'm driven to
my passion—climbing. My decisions here have nothing to do with
Charlie, but my passion to climb and to be an adventurer. If I could
climb, explore, and travel 365 days of the year, I would. But it would
be nice to do it with someone you love. Hopefully that will be . . .
Charlie?

CHRIS AGONIZED OVER HER DECISION to stay on the expedition, though
overwhelming factors tipped the scales. Having just summited Mount
Everest in May, Chris offered the clients on Cho Oyu confidence they
were in the presence of an extraordinary mountaineer. Her name was
the incentive for paying large sums of money for the trip. Leaving them
in the care of talented Sherpas and other high-altitude workers for the
remainder of the expedition was possible but would have disappointed
clients who had paid for the experience of climbing with her. If she had
decided to leave, Chris would have spent days downclimbing, then more
days hiking from base camp back to civilization, followed by yet more
days in transit to a city large enough to board a plane home. Missing
her father's final days and his funeral were a near certainty, no matter
what she did.

In a contest between where she wanted and needed to be, the mountains had won.

CHAPTER 12

SHISHAPANGMA

AFTER JUST A FEW DAYS of rest following their separate attempts on Cho Oyu, Charlie and Chris began their first joint trip. While many couples would opt for a day hike or maybe an overnight at a nearby bed-and-breakfast, Chris and Charlie went slightly more ambitious. With little more than an email inbox full of correspondence and a few brief days together in Salt Lake City, they set their sights on Shishapangma, the world's fourteenth tallest mountain, located just northwest of Mount Everest and Cho Oyu.

Though neither Chris nor Charlie had been there, they both preferred to climb the peak alpine style. Climbing light meant leaving behind oxygen canisters, fancy coffee, extra gear, and a sense of doubt about success or failure. Confidence was essential. And climbing alpine style meant they relied on each other entirely for the greater part of the journey. Along with sleeping bags and pads, cookstove, essential food, and climbing gear, they carried Charlie's favorite tent, a cheap model from Walmart that was actually two child-sized tents strapped together. He had cannibalized the set of tent poles, added a tarp as a storm fly, and meticulously waterproofed it before the trip. The resulting shelter was infamous with his Telluride friends, who treasured the fact that Charlie refused to spend money on a fancier version. They coined it his "kiddie tent."

As both Chris and Charlie so often did, they recorded their climb in journals and notes. Chris's words touched on humor and emotion, while

Charlie's recorded more factual details that would later be published in climbing journals.

[Charlie] On October 2 we hike from Nyalam for two days to reach base camp on Shishapangma's south side. Chris and I pitch our tent not far from a memorial chorten to Alex Lowe and David Bridges, tragically killed the year before while attempting the face we hope to climb. Since we are quite acclimated from Cho Oyu, Chris and I spend only one day at base camp before heading up to start climbing.

The south face of Shishapangma is over 2,000 meters high. It was first climbed in 1982 by a strong team of British alpinists; since then a few other routes have been done. Chris and I hope to do a new line to the left of the British route, but after a day at the base contemplating conditions we change our plans and decide to repeat the British route instead, as it looks safer.

On October 7 we begin our climb. Crossing the glacier, we head up a rocky rib that defines the lower part of the route. The climbing is easy, but after some time we rope up. With Chris in the lead, we climb simultaneously, clipping the occasional fixed gear or placing ice screws. Just before sunset we arrive at our first bivouac and pitch our small tent on the crest of a wildly narrow ridge.

We lie in [our sleeping bags] till the sun hits our tent the next morning. With me in the lead, we continue up steep snow slopes. After lunch, Chris takes over the lead and climbs through a section of mixed terrain, which proves to be the technical crux of the climb. In the midafternoon, we discover an ice cave, dug out by a Korean team that had successfully done the route earlier in the season. We settle in for our second bivvy.

Next day, it's a relatively short climb to another ice cave at 7,650 meters. We stop here and rest up for our summit push the next morning.

At 5 a.m. we leave this shelter with only light packs. As the climbing appears to be easy, we even dispense with the rope to save weight. So far the weather has been ideal, but this morning high winds whip off the summit—it seems like a storm is moving in. Nevertheless, we carry on and arrive at the top at 10 a.m. in blustery winds and mist. We snap a few photos and without further dallying, cruise back to our high camp. We pick up our stash here and continue down to the lower ice cave and crash for the night.

The storm has not materialized, so the next day we continue our descent in balmy weather. At the foot of the mountain we pause for a long rest, then work our way across the loose moraine towards base camp which we stumble into right at dinnertime.

The following day a friend heads down to town to fetch yaks, which come a few days later. We arrive back in Nyalam twelve days after leaving. Soon we are back into the hustle and bustle and chaos of Kathmandu, and I long to return to the big mountains soon.

• • •

[Chris] Charlie and I had a great time on the climb. We hiked into base camp on the first and second of October. The third was a rest day. Camp 1 was our kiddie tent and Camps Two and Three were snow caves that the Koreans had built. On the 10th we left our snow cave at 5:00 a.m. as it was being spin drifted. Summited at 10:00 a.m. What can I say next. It was great climbing with Charlie. No criticisms from him. He let me lead most of the time. We shared cooking responsibilities. I even cooked at Camp 3 because the Koreans left a stove and fuel and a Therm-a-Rest at Camp 3 . . . score!

Charlie hardly eats anything. Maybe that's why I'm so strong . . . I eat! At Camp 3 Charlie woke me up around 11:00 p.m. and said, "We're gonna suffocate if we don't shovel out." I had put a Therm-a-Rest over the snow cave entrance to prevent the snow from coming in with the wind, but the entrance was being filled in. Charlie got up at 1:00 a.m. to clear the hole. I was so glad he was so willing. I had cooked that night and didn't feel like shoveling. I was in a stupor.

At 5:00 a.m. we left for the summit. We climbed unroped. I topped out of the couloir first and was met with fierce winds.

Charlie caught up and I was thinking about turning around, but he
didn't mention it so we continued on. We topped out by 10:00 a.m.

When Chris and Charlie stood atop Shishapangma, Chris became
the only living woman and only American woman to have summited
six 8,000-meter peaks. There is no evidence that she celebrated or even
realized the accomplishment. Instead her thoughts were squarely in the
one place she felt she should have been were it not for her deep desire
to climb—Appleton, Wisconsin.

TWO WEEKS TO THE DAY after Chris had set foot on top of Shishapangma,
she browsed the shelves at her hometown Barnes & Noble. Autumn had
come to the Midwest, though the temperature was 62 degrees and felt
vastly better than the wind-blown nights on the mountain. She picked
up a book on public speaking. As strong as she was as a climber, the art of
talking in front of crowds hadn't come easily. She frequently butchered
idioms, and her unvarnished delivery included her strong Wisconsin
accent sprinkled with a string of "ya knows." *Smart Speaking: Sixty-
Second Strategies* found its way into her basket.

A month had passed since her father's death. Chris still thought
about how she hadn't been there when it seemed to matter most. Her
mother Joyce had let it go, understanding that it had been too difficult
for her daughter to get off the mountain in time to get back for good-byes
with her father. Now that Chris was with Charlie, his soulful, deeply
philosophical angle of looking at the world was quietly influencing her.

"Charlie always said that the Buddhists he'd met on his travels
'lived their religion' on a daily basis more than any other religion he'd
observed," said Ginny, Charlie's sister. "He loved to visit monasteries
because he felt the monks were often the most educated people in some
of the countries he traveled to."

Chris was spending more time with Geri, talking about similar,
deep issues. The two would linger for hours with a bottle of red wine
in front of Geri's fireplace, talking about life. "She became much more

introspective after Keith and her father died," Geri said. "She was an old soul, with endless curiosity about life."

Back in the bookstore, Chris wandered to the stacks that held books on religion. *Buddhism: A Way of Life and Thought* caught her eye. The cover image was a gilded Buddha draped in robes. Inside the book jacket, the description offered an overview of the "teachings and practices of the Buddhist sects now prevalent in the United States." She bought it. Buddhism wasn't totally unfamiliar to Chris. Each trip to Asia had brought her in contact with intriguing concepts, and Hinduism and Buddhist influences continued to weave their way through her expeditions—from the rituals practiced by the Sherpas to the mountains themselves, many of which were considered holy and thus not as accessible for Western climbers.

Among the practices that Chris became most familiar with through her climbs was *puja*. Traditionally Buddhist or Hindu in origin, puja is a ceremony that includes reflection, chanting, and offerings designed to show reverence to the divine. Prior to each attempt of large peaks in Asia, Chris would join in puja with her teammates. Oftentimes such expeditions would include a monk who presided over the ceremony. A shrine was erected, complete with pictures of holy monks, loved ones, and offerings of food. At the base of the altar, the mountaineers placed their ice axes, boots, and crampons to be blessed. Strings of prayer flags encircled the altar, each leading to a stupa in the center. Each color on the flag carried a different meaning: yellow for earth, green for water, red for fire, white for air, blue for space.

The air in camp filled with smoke as Sherpas busied themselves burning small fires with juniper branches. As cymbals clashed, the monks chanted prayers, most designed to ask the gods for permission to climb the mountain and for safe passage. Sometimes there were more general words of advice to the climbers: requests cloaked in prayers for mountaineers to be respectful of the mountain while on the journey, and to think about world peace and humankind living together in harmony. Handfuls of rice were tossed in offering. Toward the end of each ceremony, barley flour was spread on the climbers' faces as a sign of long life, and the monks provided a wish to "live until your beard turns old and grey"—a blessing that made Chris stifle a giggle.

An expedition member on one of Chris's trips fondly recalled puja: "The Tibetan Buddhist puja is an enjoyable, casual, and yet very meaningful affair. The reverence for life is displayed and celebrated with laughter and humor throughout these ceremonies. I know all of our team were impressed with how organic the whole experience seemed. After the ceremony, the dancing, eating, and drinking gave everyone a chance to hang out more with our expedition staff and that bonding was a highlight for all." The practice of puja is so vital to the ascent itself that many climbers experience a shift in their emotional awareness once it's completed. The scent of burning juniper boughs becomes a visceral sensory reminder much like the aroma of pine needles and sap to a child experiencing Christmas.

RISING TO AN ELEVATION OF 10,300 feet, the Uncompahgre Plateau cuts across one hundred miles of western Colorado. From the ranching community of Norwood, the vistas are striking. It's a wide expanse of dry mesa speckled with the sort of life that can survive the altitude and the temperature shifts. The plateau is home to limitless opportunities to hike and climb, which made it the perfect playground for Chris on her now-frequent visits to Charlie.

Finding she could continue to run Mountain Madness in Seattle while spending time in Colorado, by 2001 Chris had gradually accepted both the Norwood lifestyle and Charlie into her world. Though the purchase of Mountain Madness had secured her place professionally in Seattle, Colorado had long spoken to her on a personal level, and she relished the chance to explore it with Charlie. Their match worked. Though she was more of a high-altitude mountaineer and Charlie more of a rock climber, there was enough overlap in their preferred styles and personalities to solidify their bond. They both focused intensely on their own pursuits and found great joy in simple things. They both loved to laugh and teased each other endlessly. Chris had an impish grin and sparkle in her eye that infected Charlie, and the two would often crack up over things other people found nonsensical. Their admiration for each other grew. While Chris's relationship with Keith had been competitive at times, Charlie's quiet self-confidence made her feel an equal. They had great respect for each other, and it allowed them room to grow.

Charlie's friend Joel recalled, "Charlie was steady and reliable. The way he got excited about things was subtle. He didn't need conversation to be about him and he didn't need to drive it. He was at peace with silence in a way that most people find uncomfortable. He accepted the quiet. With Chris, he was true to his essence." After all the girlfriends of the past, it appeared that Charlie had met his match. He brought her home to Oregon to meet his sister Ginny and she in turn visited them in Seattle at Chris's home. On one such visit, Ginny opened a book Chris had been reading. Instead of a bookmark, out fell a pile of love letters Charlie had written to her.

Together, Chris and Charlie became a powerful duo who cared little about notoriety. Charlie's devotion to getting others hooked on the sport of climbing was in full swing with a new partner. Sensing Chris's hunger to learn more about rock climbing, he dove into the relationship like no other. Chris totally absorbed his teaching, just as she had with Keith and his lessons on mountaineering. Charlie and Chris explored the valleys of southwestern Colorado, put up new routes, and worked on their skills. Charlie and his friend Damon Johnston built Chris a special wall so she could work on holds and angles that would allow her to improve her climbing and tackle more difficult routes. "She soaked it up and really increased her skills tremendously," Damon recalled. "She had great balance, but she'd tire after a while and get frustrated with herself. She had a hard time embracing things as a learning experience and felt like a failure sometimes."

Ambitious and a visionary in his own way, Charlie flourished having a partner as driven as Chris. She was the louder voice in the partnership yet trailed him in pure climbing ability. He fought to understand his relationship with her, learning to let her sulk when she stumbled and providing encouragement but not placating her.

And always, she was able to laugh and enjoy being laughed at. "She was a magnet for cactus," remembered Damon. "I've never known another person who's fallen or stepped or sat on cactus as much as Chris."

As she spent more time in Colorado, Chris's circle of friends increased. Having heard about Chris from Charlie for months before actually meeting her, his friend Julie Hodson was initially wary. Charlie had described Chris as laid back, a fantastic climber, and completely lacking in ego. She sounded too good to be true. "I mean, he talked on and on about her," Julie recalled. "Endlessly. Until finally one day I was going to meet her when we went ice climbing. She and Charlie had beaten my partner and me to the spot. I remember walking up to the ledge and hearing her voice before I saw her. 'Charlie, throw down the rope, will ya?' That's all I heard, but her Wisconsin accent was unmistakable. I'm from Wisconsin, too, though Charlie hadn't mentioned that connection before we met. I knew immediately, even before I saw her, that we'd be friends. When I finally met her, she noticed I had a Green Bay Packers sticker on my helmet, and that was it."

BY 2002, CHRIS HAD BEEN with Charlie two years. She moved to Norwood part time, buying a small house a few blocks away from him. Maintaining her own space was critical, as was the ability to continue her trips back and forth to Seattle to oversee Mountain Madness. On one such trip to Seattle, Chris sat at her desk working, papers covering every inch of the flat surface: invoices from vendors for oxygen cylinders, drafts of the next brochure, phone messages from journalists requesting interviews. The phone rang late in the day as Kili Sherpa, who was waking up in Kathmandu, called in for updates.

Standing nearby, the office bookkeeper noticed Chris glancing at something in her bottom desk drawer. With the phone propped on her shoulder, Chris scribbled notes on a piece of scratch paper, shifting her gaze again to the open drawer. A slight smile, natural yet private, held itself as her eyes lingered. Chris rose to find something in a file cabinet, leaving the room and the drawer accessible. Intrigued, the bookkeeper stapled a receipt to the latest wave of paid bills, then walked to Chris's desk to deliver it.

Staring up from the desk drawer was a handsome man on the cover of a 1993 issue of *Climbing* magazine. The man wore a multicolored headband with pink sunglasses draped around his neck by a blue cord. His hair was dark, still many years away from the salt and pepper it would become. The magazine tagged the climber, who was featured in the cover story. "Travels with Charlie: At Home on the Ranges, Boulders, Ice, and Rock with Charlie Fowler."

CHAPTER 13

THE CALL OF K2

THE WORLD'S FOURTEEN 8,000-METER PEAKS are located in Asia, situated either in the Himalayas bordering Nepal and China or in the Karakoram Range straddling Pakistan and China. For Chris, the appeal of being the first female to summit all fourteen was waning. Now thirty-four, she had claimed six of the big peaks. With Charlie as her partner, the prospect of chasing more seemed less enticing. His fervent pursuit of slightly lower mountains in unknown places in Asia had caught her attention. Though she was the only living woman to have climbed six of the fourteen, Chris began to see a quieter future in Colorado.

From a practical standpoint, her name recognition and reputation were enough to sustain the Mountain Madness reserves. Clients requested trips that she led, requiring that she put in face time once a year on a big expedition. Between these trips, however, there were few 8,000-meter peaks that inspired her. Except one.

Beyond the glitz that is Mount Everest stands the peak that's often called the "Savage Mountain." Though it trails Everest in height by roughly eight hundred feet, the technical challenges are far greater, the risks exponentially higher. Described as a "cone of ice and limestone," K2 is a mountain inviting many superlatives: the most extreme weather conditions, the toughest altitude adjustments, the most complexities in terms of pure climbing. Widely considered one of the most difficult mountains in the world to summit, K2 claims one life of every four who attempt it, putting it second in the "death-to-summit" ratio, just behind Annapurna. "I've called it the Holy Grail," said climbing icon Ed Viesturs, who is the only American to have climbed all of the world's 8,000-meter mountains. "[For] a mountaineer, it's the total test of your ability, not only technically, but endurance, patience, and your willingness to get slapped in the face repeatedly by the mountain, go down, regroup, and go back up."

By 2002, only five women had reached the summit of K2, and of those, only two made it down alive. The memory of seeing British climber Alison Hargreaves perish on K2 in 1995, when Chris was on neighboring Broad Peak with Keith, was a constant reminder of the dangers she faced in her chosen sport. Still, the prospect of challenging themselves with something so mythical drew the attention of both Chris and Charlie. "It's just something I want to climb," she said in an interview with the *Billings Gazette* leading up to the trip. "It has nothing to do with wanting to be the first American woman . . . I'm going to give it my best—I always do—but it's not 'summit or die.'"

The two planned their expedition for summer 2002 and aimed to do it all without the help of porters, fixed camps, or oxygen. Charlie was just coming off a successful bid on Everest in May and was already acclimatized when he met up with Chris. Of all the routes possible to ascend K2, Charlie and Chris intended to take the least attempted and steeper route known as the South Southeast Spur or the "Cesen Route," named for the Slovenian climber who first attempted this route in 1986 but did not summit, leaving that accolade to a Spanish-Basque team eight years later. Were Charlie and Chris successful, it would be the first North American ascent of this line. "I'm really excited about this expedition," Chris said. "We plan to reach the top by going light and fast, and keeping it safe and simple. But the mountain always has its own agenda. We just hope it matches ours."

IF EVER THERE WAS A place on Earth where the laws of the mountain collide with faith, it is K2. Those who perish on the mountain are often left there by necessity. The strength required to simply sustain life is too overpowering to consider exerting the additional energy needed to bring a body down. Instead, deceased mountaineers are often wrapped in sleeping bags or tarps and left to become encased in ice.

For certain religions, this reality is particularly difficult. Believing cremation releases the soul to be reincarnated in another body, Hindus must help their dead complete this cycle. Likewise, the Buddhist philosophy is one of spiritual rebirth, with the body being merely a vessel for the spirit. Returning the body to the earth through cremation is the preferred method of continuing the cycle of life, as is sky burial (exposing dismembered corpses to sacred vultures) among Tibetan Buddhists. On other, more accessible mountains, such as Everest, families of climbers with wealth pay high-altitude porters to retrieve bodies, often hiring the same companies that attended the climb in the first place. For other families, their loved ones' bodies remain on the mountain, somewhat like sailors buried at sea, washed back into the landscape they adored.

Unlike burial at sea, however, bodies left on K2 resurface over time. The mountain is so steep that frequent avalanches and rockfall churn the dead into pieces, scattering body parts, clothing, and personal effects down K2 until they are spread all over the glacial moraine from base camp to a section of the mountain known as the Abruzzi Spur. Though frozen for years, the warm summer months melt even the thickest of ice chunks landing at the base of the mountain. What results is a revelation, year after year, of tragedies from prior decades, making the base of K2 feel more battlefield than nature's playground. The task of burying the remains of deceased climbers is left to the living. Based on clothing or equipment found nearby, some climbers are identified. Others are not. The remnants are often buried under a memorial not far from the base of the mountain, which endures as the ultimate reminder to those attempting K2.

Its namesake is Art Gilkey, a young American geologist who joined a team to climb K2 in 1953. Gilkey was not the first American to die on K2, but he lost his life during the third American attempt, an endeavor Americans hoped would rival Great Britain's triumph on Mount Everest a few months earlier.

Though the team's attempt began strong, at 25,500 feet the notorious storms of K2 rose up, stranding team members in tents for days. When they emerged, Gilkey attempted to stand and collapsed. The team doctor was quick to diagnose the condition as thrombophlebitis—blood clots caused by dehydration, oxygen deprivation, or long periods of immobility.

Gilkey's teammates were resolute. While the summit of K2 meant the world, the team's response was unanimous: they would do whatever it took to try to save Gilkey's life, as every one of these men, individually and collectively, had a strong moral compass. They placed him in a sleeping bag, wrapped him in a tent, and began lowering him on belay, sliding him on ice and snow. As the climbers crossed a sheet of ice, one slipped, causing a series of collisions with roped teammates. In total, six climbers began a perilous slide. In what became known as the "Miracle Belay," climber Pete Schoening saved all six men. Schoening securely wrapped the rope around his ice axe and hips. To further add security, he leaned against the top of his ice axe and wedged it against a rock that prevented the ice axe from being pulled out from the mountain. Schoening's mountaineering prowess saved all six men, including Gilkey in his protective bag. Many of the climbers had been seriously injured, however, so they secured Gilkey to the mountain with two ice axes and went to set up camp and tend to the wounded. When they returned a short time later to try to move him to the tents, his body was gone.

What happened in Gilkey's final moments is known only to the mountain. Perhaps he was swept away by an avalanche. Others speculated that he'd cut himself loose from the rope to save his teammates from continuing his rescue. The only truths were what remained. Bits of his clothing, blood, and sleeping bag were found all the way down the mountain. The porters on the team built a memorial out of stones for Gilkey, leaving his personal possessions not too far from where K2 Base Camp stands today. It was not only a testament to death but to the power of benevolence in a sport so often seen as selfish. The Gilkey Memorial has become holy ground. The stone cairn has grown in size and is now adorned with shreds of *khatas*, white silk scarves presented as a sign of respect. Seen from a distance, the conical formation glimmers if the sun catches it just right. The glimmer originates from dozens of steel plates taken from expedition cook tents, each inscribed with the name of a climber who perished on the mountain.

CHARLIE AND CHRIS MET UP in Pakistan on June 7, 2002, Charlie from Kathmandu and Chris from Seattle. Though Charlie was already acclimatized from his Everest summit, Chris needed time to catch up. Neighboring Broad Peak served as their practice field. Stationing themselves out of K2 Base Camp, Chris and Charlie planned to take several short trips up and down Broad Peak in preparation for the greater challenge on K2.

As usual, the red tape that had preceded their trip was extensive. Each expedition was required to have a permit to climb the mountains in the area. As a two-person team, Chris and Charlie opted to piggyback onto the existing permits of other teams. It was a workaround that allowed them to maintain their ability to climb legally but act independently from the others on the permit.

Press coverage in advance of their K2 trip had been high. The mountain was well known and should Chris land on top, it would be yet another monumental achievement. Regular expedition dispatches published online fed the hunger of those anxious to be part of the couple's highs and lows. For the first time, Charlie and Chris shared the task of writing the dispatches.

June 8, 2002
Christine and I arrived in Pakistan the other day. We have been buying some food and making last-minute arrangements. We are anxious to get to the mountains and will fly to Skardu tomorrow morning. Last night we had dinner with Nazir Sabir, the first Pakistani to climb Everest (on an expedition led by Christine a few years ago).
—*Charlie*

• • •

June 20, 2002

We arrived at K2 Base Camp yesterday, after a nice trek up the Baltoro Glacier. We have found the local Balti people to be very friendly and helpful—no hassles so far. We did a recon to the base of the SSE spur this morning and have decided to attempt a route up the south face, following the Polish line or perhaps another variation nearby. Tomorrow we will climb to approximately 5,800 meters to assess conditions and to acclimate. We are both feeling great and highly motivated!

—Christine and Charlie

• • •

June 22, 2002

Yesterday we climbed a line to the right of the original Polish route on the south face of K2. We left a tent, food, fuel, and gear at 5,700 meters. The snow conditions were fairly good and allowed rapid progress.

Today we are resting at base camp with beautiful sunny skies. Tomorrow we plan to climb to about 5,900 meters and bivvy. The following day we plan to climb to 6,400 meters and bivvy again. From here we hope to do a recon of the route above before returning to base camp.

We are having a great time with everyone at base camp. We are acclimatizing well and feel strong.

—Christine and Charlie

• • •

June 26, 2002

Last Sunday we climbed to 5,900 meters and established our Camp 1 on the south face of K2. Unfortunately the weather deteriorated and we descended late in the evening back to base camp. The weather has been unstable since then. We had our puja on Monday. Lhama Jangbu performed the ceremony. He was a team member on our recent Everest expedition and is now climbing with a Spanish team on K2.

Last night it snowed a foot. We woke to find our mess tent collapsed from the weight of the snow.

We are enjoying base camp life by playing cards, reading, and taking short hikes. Tomorrow we plan to hike to Broad Peak Base Camp and stash gear at the base of the mountain in anticipation of our acclimatization climb.

—*Christine and Charlie*

• • •

July 20, 2002

We just returned from a successful [acclimatization] climb on Broad Peak. On July 15th under cloudy, dark skies, we climbed to the 6,400 camp on Broad Peak. The weather reminded us of a normal Washington Cascades day. The next morning greeted us with clear skies and crisp air. We climbed higher to 6,800 meters, where we dug a platform and set up camp. Later in the day we climbed higher to 6,900 meters and scouted the route above. From there we descended back to camp and enjoyed the rest of the afternoon sun. The next day we moved our camp to 7,300 meters. We cut a platform for our tent in the icy slopes beneath the summit pyramid. We brewed hot drinks, made dinner, and prepared to go higher the following day. We woke up at 11:00 p.m. to cloudy and stormy skies. We felt it would be difficult to navigate higher, so we made it a rest day. The skies cleared in the evening. We received word by radio that the Koreans and other members of the K2 International expedition were going for the summit of Broad Peak from 6,400 meters in the morning.

We left our camp at midnight to climb toward the top. We took turns breaking trail in the deep snow. The Koreans caught up to us at 7,700 meters and took over making the trail. We reached close to 7,800 meters when our friends from the K2 International team caught up. At this point, just below the col, we ran into poor snow conditions and everyone decided it was safer to descend. We were back at our tent by 6:00 a.m. We warmed up a bit before breaking down camp and returning to K2 Base Camp. It took us the rest of the day to get there, since we were carrying heavy loads.

Our plans are to rest for the next five to six days at base camp drinking plenty of Starbucks coffee and eating a lot. After our climb

*on Broad Peak we feel we are sufficiently acclimated for an attempt
to summit K2. Now we just need to be well rested before our K2
attempt. We received news that the Tibetans made a summit push
on K2 today. They reached approximately 8,400 meters, fixing
rope through the bottleneck and reported knee-deep snow. They
turned around because they were exhausted and encountered high
winds, it is reported.*

*Our plans are still to climb the south face via a variation to the
Polish route. We hope to climb to our stash at 6,400 meter around
July 26th. Weather permitting, we hope to make the climb in five
days, but we are prepared to spend more time on the face if necessary. We are not using fixed ropes, oxygen, or porter support.*

*Now it's back to drinking coffee, lots of reading, and preparing
for our climb ahead!*

—Christine & Charlie

• • •

July 26, 2002

*Today is our sixth rest day in a row, since we returned from our
acclimatization climb on Broad Peak. We've just had four days of
snowy, windy, and cold weather. Yesterday was the first day the
sun came out.*

*We received some bad news on the 21st—a liaison officer [govern-
ment official designated to accompany climbers] from the Tibetan
team fell from just below Camp 2 down to the base of mountain. He
died instantly. The liaison officer, who had elected to climb with the
Tibetans, was a captain in the Pakistani military. All the expeditions
came to the assistance to carry the body back to base camp.*

*Many expeditions have become discouraged with the weather
and the latest death, and have decided to abort K2. The Tibetans,
both remaining Spanish teams, and Henry Todd's international
team are all leaving in the next few days. The only teams left now
are the Mexican-Spanish, Japanese, and our small camp, including [alpinist] Simone Moro. The Japanese have left base camp
today for the summit of K2, and we plan to start up K2 tomorrow*

ourselves. The weather doesn't look too stable with high cirrus clouds forming, but we will go up in any case, and see what happens. We do receive weather forecasts here via email, but the forecasts have proven to be very inaccurate, so it is tricky to judge when we should begin climbing. Ideally we need about five days or so of good weather for a summit attempt, but lately we have only seen short periods of good weather—a day or so at the most.
—Christine & Charlie

• • •

July 29, 2002
The Spanish climber Luis Fraga's line of porters passed by our tent this morning under cloudy and snowy skies. The Spanish team was the last of four expeditions to leave K2 base camp in the last few days. The Tibetans, the two Spanish, and Henry Todd's International teams have trekked out to Askole in the last four days, leaving K2 Base Camp similar to a ghost town. It has snowed for five days straight. Doubts of a summit attempt have started to enter our minds. The Japanese, Spanish-Mexican, Charlie, and I are the last to reside at base camp. The Japanese team is finished on K2 and will be leaving on the 4th or 5th to attempt Gasherbrum II. Then there will be only five climbers here at base camp to climb K2: Three members in the Spanish-Mexican team and us.

One of the Pakistan rules of climbing in the K2 area is that all expeditions must have a liaison officer present with the team. A liaison officer is an officer within the Pakistani military that stays with the expedition and sees that the expedition is abiding by the climbing rules. He acts as a correspondent to the Ministry of Tourism if a request needs to be made from the expedition. When Henry Todd left, we were signed off to the Japanese liaison officer. Now the Japanese want to leave as early as the 4th or 5th. According to the rules, we are required to leave with the Japanese liaison officer. We are trying to work out an option to stay longer, but it's hard to justify the fight when the weather is so miserable. We may try to push our stay for a few days longer to allow us one more summit push. However, we would need the weather to change in the next couple days.

Overall there hasn't been much progress on K2 this season, except for the Tibetan team. They arrived at base camp late May. It wasn't until July 20th, when they got as high as 8,400 meters under marginal conditions. The Tibetans reported that on their descent they took seven hours in whiteout conditions to locate their high camp. The Japanese expedition spent this past week at Camp 2 (6,900 meters) on the Abruzzi Ridge route waiting for clear skies for an attempt at the summit. They gave up and are coming down.

The snow continues to fall and load the slopes higher on the mountain with deep snow. Above 6,500 meters the snow has been reported as "unconsolidated, sugary, and knee-to-waist deep." It may take several days of sunny weather for the slopes to become stable enough for safe travel.

—Christine

• • •

August 1, 2002

Charlie and I are leaving for our summit push tomorrow morning and plan to take five days to reach the summit. We will carry food and fuel for eight days. The weather looks promising. Today is partly cloudy and cool. We heard the Japanese are still at Camp 2 and have not given up. Our liaison officer made us call for our porters, so this will be our last try for the top.

—Christine

• • •

August 8, 2002

We are back down safely at base camp after an unsuccessful attempt on the summit of K2. On August 2 under clear skies we climbed to 6,400 meters on the south face of K2. We found the snow conditions good with firm-to-knee-deep snow. We found our stash of gear buried under a thick layer of ice, and it took us a couple hours to recover it. The next day we climbed with heavy packs on a delicate corniced snow and rock ridge. It took several hours. Due to the lateness of the day and the snow conditions, we decided to camp at 6,700 meters.

Early morning on August 4, we traversed under a giant hanging serac. We were exposed to icefall for about thirty minutes before climbing slopes under the SSE ridge to gain the Cesen route (the SSE spur). The weather to the south looked bad with dark clouds forming. We had a difficult time finding our way to the ridge and were moving slowly. With high winds coming off the summit and the uncertain weather, we decided to turn around. We descended to the site of our 6,700-meter camp. Due to poor snow conditions, we decided to spend the night here. On August 6, we descended to base camp. Our cook met us at the bottom with cold drinks and a warm greeting. We heard that the Mexican-Spanish team also came down on the 6th due to weather after making a carry to their 6,900-meter camp.

The weather fooled us, because the last two days it has been beautiful. We can't speculate on how high we would have climbed if we had continued. Unfortunately, we will not have an opportunity for another try.

We had lunch yesterday with the Japanese expedition. Wonderful folks with much climbing experience. Last night the Mexican-Spanish team invited us for dinner. They plan to continue to climb on the SSE spur.

We enjoyed our climbs on K2 and Broad Peak this season. We got a lot of climbing in with only a few additional rest days. We can't understand why everyone left base camp so early this season. Climbing in the Karakoram one must be patient and sometimes one must wait out the weather to be successful. The weather in August is looking good so far. We wish we could stay longer, but our porters are expected on the 9th of August.

We look forward to our next climbing objective. There are so many mountains to climb and many without permits or liaison officers to deal with.

—Christine

DISAPPOINTED MORE BY THE POLITICS than their climbing performance on K2, Chris and Charlie returned to Colorado. Asked about the experience later, Chris said, "I used to feel I had to make the goal; I pushed and pushed. Over time, I've started to back off because so many friends and acquaintances have died climbing. I'm learning to listen when things aren't progressing right."

It would be another fifteen years until dual-citizen Vanessa O'Brien would become the first American (and British) woman to successfully summit K2 in 2017. Like Chris, Vanessa came to the sport later in life, having already achieved success in the business world before turning her attention to mountains. "By the time K2 entered my radar," Vanessa said, "I was amazed that no American woman had ever summited. Christine had six 8,000-meter peaks to her name and if I were lucky, K2 would be my fifth. The way I looked at it was what had happened with Chris and Charlie in 2002 was simply bad luck—they climbed in a year of no summits on the mountain. Since 1986, there were twelve years of no summits, ergo, almost a forty percent chance in any one year of not seeing the summit on K2. It took me three consecutive years to get my summit, and luckily, I discovered my love of Pakistan along the way."

Similar to Chris, who preferred to climb with little support, Vanessa returned after her first attempt to lead her own expeditions. She sought out the services of a local logistics provider, one who knew his way around the Pakistan Alpine Club for permits, who could secure the services of experienced low- and high-altitude porters, and who could safeguard transportation to base camp. She was directed to the man who'd become well-respected since his own Everest summit in the year 2000 as the first Pakistani. He'd grown a successful mountaineering company since then and when it came to K2, there was nobody better. Nazir Sabir was her man.

"I poked around and learned that Chris had led Nazir to the summit of Everest and that pretty much sealed the deal," Vanessa recalled. "It was an amazing fact. This Pakistani man being led to the top of Everest by a woman just blew me away. I told him, 'Nazir, we have to meet.' I knew he understood the strength of women." The gregarious mountaineer understood that women could be just as successful as men on

K2. Perhaps, as Vanessa suspected, he had come to his belief by way of something the founder of Pakistan, Muhammad Ali Jinnah, once said: "There are two powers in the world; one is the sword and the other is the pen. But there is a third power stronger than both, that of woman."

About Nazir, Vanessa said: "Here was a man, so confident and strong in both his career as well as his masculinity. It didn't take long for my immense admiration to form. Nazir knew I needed to call the shots and it didn't intimidate him that I was female. He revered women. He just got it." On July 28, 2017, Vanessa's black and yellow down summit suit offset the colors of the American flag as it blew against her thighs. She stood on top of K2, leaning into the wind. In succession, she held up the British flag and then the Pakistani flag in honor of the opportunity she'd been given in the country she'd come to admire. Together, these flags represented friendship, peace, and solidarity.

Record books, countless articles, and awards ceremonies appropriately honored Vanessa's achievement. Aside from K2, her climbing résumé ballooned with notable climbs all over the world, including a Guinness World Record for climbing the highest peak on every continent in 295 days. Despite that, she was humble about her latest title and recognized the woman who'd just missed it. "I came back after I'd summited K2 and gave a speech to the American Alpine Club," she said. "I put up a picture of Chris. Just a radiant photo of her on a mountain. I said to the audience, '*This* is who should have had it first. Christine Boskoff should have been the first American woman to summit K2.' I spoke the truth. I always felt Christine should have had the summit."

CHAPTER 14

NORWOOD

It is not the critic who counts; not the man who points out how the strong man stumbles, or where the doer of deeds could have done them better. The credit belongs to the man who is actually in the arena, whose face is marred by dust and sweat and blood; who strives valiantly; who errs, who comes short again and again, because there is no effort without error and shortcoming; but who does actually strive to do the deeds; who knows great enthusiasms, the great devotions; who spends himself in a worthy cause; who at the best knows in the end the triumph of high achievement, and who at the worst, if he fails, at least fails while daring greatly, so that his place shall never be with those cold and timid souls who neither know victory nor defeat.

—Teddy Roosevelt (from a handwritten entry in Chris's journal)

WITH A WEALTH OF CLIMBING, warm weather, and the man she loved, Chris eventually made Norwood and Charlie her home, as she noted in her journal: "Charlie has become a part of me. I feel him even when he's on the other side of the world." She'd been at the helm of Mountain Madness in Seattle for more than five years, which was long enough to now spend significant time away from the office, turning over daily operations to Mark Gunlogson, who'd been hired in 1994 by founder Scott Fischer. To stay somewhat on top of the business, she needed only a laptop and the quiet space of the small home she'd bought near Charlie. The "satellite office" was in full swing by early 2003.

[Chris] We officially declared an opening of a small office in Norwood. I love Colorado and will never move back to Seattle. I love the small town. I love my friends, my relationship, my home, my travels, my job. I know that at any moment things can change, so I realize I must find happiness within and not through others, through events or material things. It's difficult at times, though, with the pressures at Mountain Madness and my low self-esteem. I'm trying to achieve peace of mind.

THOUGH SHE'D ATTAINED GREAT SUCCESS in many areas of life, Chris was human. Self-doubt in the areas of business, personal relationships, and perhaps even her climbing kept her constantly striving for more. Her years at Mountain Madness had brought her fame, a decent income, and meaningful relationships. The expeditions continued. Interviews persisted along with the cover stories and flashy photo spreads that made her cringe. But by 2005, Chris seemed to measure her success by how well she helped others to fulfill their dreams.

As she wrote in her journal: "I realize I play a role in people's lives, and I want to continue to give back. To help people achieve their dreams, reach their goals and have the experience of a lifetime."

JOYCE FELD WAS IN HER late seventies in 2005, but her age was no deterrent for a trip with her daughter. She sat next to Chris as they sped through Europe in their rental car. "We just landed in Paris, got into a car, and off we went!" Joyce recalled. She was nestled into an armchair in her apartment at a retirement home in Appleton, flipping slowly through photo albums showing the two of them in Germany and Italy. Now she was a dozen years older, with freshly permed white curls, a perfectly matched outfit, and a full dish of candy on the coffee table. The hall was draped with a Tibetan *thangka* painting that Chris had brought back from her travels. Reflected on an opposite wall was a framed quote from a passage in the Bible.

Joyce and Chris's bond had strengthened since the death of Chris's father in 2000. The generations separating the two women had been significant. The norm for women when Joyce was young was a career path in nursing, teaching, or managing a household, while Chris's options seemed limitless. Over time, Chris saw her mother lose the inhibitions of her era and embrace greater freedoms. Joyce was energized, and she and Chris found a new connection as independent women. An understanding about Chris's mountaineering had found a comfortable space in Joyce's life. She'd met Charlie and approved, both as a boyfriend and as a climbing partner for Chris. "He was quiet and patient," Joyce recalled. "I bossed him around one day about how to take the best pictures until I caught myself and remembered he was a photographer!" She laughed at the memory. "He took that well."

The May 2005 mother-daughter trip to Europe was a highlight for them both. Although she would be climbing Everest a second time in a few weeks' time, Chris downplayed it so that Joyce remembered it as a mere side excursion that Chris "tacked on to the end of our trip." More important than mountains and fulfilling the dreams of others, in that moment, Joyce and Chris were simply fulfilling their own.

SEVERAL WEEKS AFTER THE EUROPEAN trip ended, Chris was on Everest. The weather gods were not cooperating, and the window of time to summit was shrinking. Veteran mountain guide Willie Benegas was concerned. Having spent plenty of time acclimatizing, the Mountain Madness team he and Chris were leading had only a few days left before their permit ran out. To make matters more difficult, Willie and Chris weren't aligned on strategy. The more cautious of the two in terms of technical risk, Willie felt overwhelmed by Chris's certainty that the team could summit based on their overall physical condition. "She was very focused on the physical strength it would take to summit," he recalled. "But I was very focused on risk avoidance and running a smooth machine. I wanted things triple-checked and she was a strong, go-get-it lady. These methods were just in conflict."

With the Khumbu Icefall melting a little more every day and the danger of crossing it increasing, Willie and Chris took a day of rest to refocus. Joining other guides and Sherpas, the two hiked to a site for bouldering a short distance from base camp. The outing served to help them pass the boredom of base camp and hone their skills. Climbing ten- to twelve-foot rocks, without ropes as she often did in Colorado with Charlie, Chris seemed at peace. "She was full of joy there," Willie said. "We spent part of the day rock climbing. We brought a picnic. It was just a simple day, but she was content to live that way. She would have been happy to have a bowl of rice every day for the rest of the expedition."

The winds that had kept teams from summiting finally abated. Willie and Chris reconciled their vastly different strategies, pulling the best parts of each into a plan. A finer pair could barely have been imagined: Chris with her notable status as the American woman with the most 8,000-meter peak ascents, and Willie with his deep climbing accomplishments including speed records and first ascents of some of the world's highest mountains. Together, on May 30, 2005, the two stood once more on top of the world.

"I still use that experience as an example to others of how it can be good to have different points of view when trying to reach a shared goal," Willie said. "She was one of the first female guides on Everest, and she worked in a purely male environment. But the fact that she was a woman wasn't an issue for me. My approach was effective, but I understood the reality. The truth was, she was stronger than me."

THE YEAR 2006 WAS GOING to be monumental. Chris had talked of moving the company entirely to Colorado, but for now Mountain Madness was staying put in Seattle and she was thinking of getting an MBA to boost her business acumen. Three trips in summer and late fall would provide a mix of guiding work and personal travel with Charlie. She'd bought twenty-five acres of land outside Norwood with views over the Uncompahgre Plateau. With Charlie, she had house plans drawn up for a future home, large enough for both of them.

"Charlie was ready to settle down and travel less," recalled Ginny, Charlie's sister. "Chris was special and he wanted to make it work with her."

In the weeks leading up to her Russia and Asia travels, Chris's journal bubbled with a mix of business brainstorming and personal reflections. A Goals List included items such as:

Climb 5.11 consistently
Ice climb WI4 consistently
AMGA certification
Mountain Madness $2M by December 2007
Summer 2008 in the Cascades
Learn Spanish, be fluent by 2009
Contribute 20 percent to 401K

On the page next to her Goals List, Chris scrawled an entry referencing her life thus far:

I decided to compose a journal of my experiences in life. Not to brag about my accomplishments, but to find out how to inspire others and motivate people to do great things and to cherish others.

I remember when Keith and I first bought MM [Mountain Madness]. I remember looking up at a "Make it Happen" poster and thought, "What have *I* done?" My life was about to change significantly. The tragedy of my husband's death was the turning point in my life. After nine years of running the company and eight years on my own, I find myself a stronger, more secure, and focused individual. I realize I am the only person responsible for my destiny. I have obtained a new respect for others, cultures, customs, and life. I now have focus with my life as a business owner, guide and climber.

IN THE SUMMER OF 2006, young mountaineer Meagan McGrath flipped through her contact list until she found Chris. After several trips with Mountain Madness, Meagan had gained the experience she needed to be able to climb Everest without a guide. "The trips with Madness were phenomenal. They had a great ethos. They valued safety and had a high regard for the environment. I'd had both Charlie and Chris as guides, and they both taught me how to be a better climber." Though Meagan had crossed paths a couple of times with Chris, she wasn't sure Chris would remember her. Still, the need to touch base felt urgent. "She and the other guides there had taught me so much," Meagan said, "and I was planning to take all that knowledge to attempt a summit of Everest. I just needed her to know what an influence she'd been on me."

Reaching Chris on the phone, Meagan ran through her words of praise. Chris remembered her, thanking her for the call. "Before I hung up," Meagan said, "I remember asking her what gave her the courage to quit her job and climb full-time? What made her chase the dream? She just said, 'Meagan, you just have to do it. Just go do it.' She was so matter of fact. Life can be complicated, but for her it was very simple. She'd found something she loved to do, and she didn't care what anyone else thought of it, nor if she was constantly praised for her achievements. I don't think she fully realized the impact she had on other people. I'm just very glad I had a chance to tell her."

STEAM ROSE FROM THE MUG of coffee on Mark Gunlogson's desk in the cozy Mountain Madness office. It was early, before the rest of the staff had arrived. The recently acquired office was a 650-square-foot house situated in an eclectic neighborhood of West Seattle. Chris's long stays in Colorado were so frequent that she'd given up first-floor space herself and instead spent time in a room in the unfinished basement when she was in town. She was there, in July 2006, planning for her upcoming trips.

Sifting through the stack of files he'd laid out, Mark scribbled a checklist of items to discuss with Chris.

Mount Elbrus/Russia logistics
Clients for Cho Oyu
2007 Everest update
Holiday party
Financials

Mark's tenure at Madness had been a dozen years. Originally hired by Scott, he'd been a guide first, then moved into operations. He'd been there through the ownership transition from Scott to Keith and Chris, smoothing the edges for staff when Keith's bold personality became difficult to bear. To anyone with basic knowledge of the company's inner workings, it had been years since Chris ran the show. Her alliance to the business was clear, but it was Mark who oversaw every piece of the daily workings and had done so since Keith passed away. In recent years, Chris had made him president of the company. The title mattered, though the income both of them drew from co-leading the business would never be substantial. Neither of them was in this for the money or the glory. The draw of the 8,000-meter peak expeditions remained a focus by necessity, but it was clear that both Chris and Mark would rather be exploring somewhere far away and much more under the radar. They partnered well, spent company dollars wisely, never climbed together, and rarely socialized outside of the office.

Kicking off his sandals, Mark stretched his long legs under the desk. At forty-four, he was late to fatherhood with two young daughters under age six. Though he didn't climb as much as he had in his twenties, his appearance suggested he could be on the nearest rock within an hour. His build was lean, a climber's physique stretching to 6'2". His sandy hair was speckled with white. He wore metal-rimmed glasses, an untucked T-shirt, and a slightly youthful look that was nerdy yet warm and unintimidating. Mark chuckled easily, was steady, mild-mannered, transparent, and fully unmoved by the inflated climber egos he sometimes encountered.

Chris appeared from the basement with a mug in her hand. Stepping over to fill it at the coffee pot, she then plopped down in the chair across from Mark. Over her shoulder on the wall hung a few of Scott's possessions. Old pitons, an ice hammer, one of his backpacks, and a down jacket.

"Okay, so you've got a few big months coming up," Mark started.

"Indeed," she agreed. "It just sorta happened that way, didn't it? I wasn't planning on Elbrus, but I think it will be good prep for Cho Oyu, and I like climbing with Ted." Ted Callahan had led expeditions for years with Mountain Madness. He was now based in Kyrgyzstan. Chris took a sip of coffee and leaned back in her chair. "I bet he has stories to share!"

"No doubt," Mark said. "So you'll be in touch after you leave Russia and then via sat phone from Cho Oyu?"

"For sure. And from Kathmandu. I'll connect with Kili and let you know how we're doing on supplies there before I leave." Chris had three clients for Cho Oyu: Wolf, Eric, and Mark. It was a good group—three solid dudes. "Experienced. No drama. I think this'll be an easy one."

"I suspect base camp will be generally crowded this year," Mark said, "but that's a nice-sized group. Just four of you."

Chris was not planning on the expedition being difficult as long as the weather held. The climbing with Charlie afterward was also pretty straightforward.

"Right, so that's in Western China," confirmed Mark. "You guys have been there before. Taking on a third trip is a stretch, but I know you can handle it."

It did feel long to Chris, but she said, "I'll be fine." She wanted to figure out a basic idea for the office holiday party in Seattle before her trip to Wisconsin. A low buzz of chatter filled the office as staff and guides began to trickle in for the day. Knowing Chris was in town, the days started early so the staff and guides could be in her midst.

"Oh, one more thing," Chris said. "I've been asked to speak at a women's group of some sort and do some mentoring with them. But I don't know..." her voice trailed off.

"Not interested?" Mark asked.

"Well, more like not enough time. Will you cover me?"

Mark paused, looking up over his glasses to see if she'd been struck by the irony in her request. Chris stared back at him, awaiting a response. "Chris. Context. I'm all about girl power, but I don't think I meet the baseline criteria."

Her momentary miscalculation sent the two of them into laughter. Catching her breath, Chris said, "So we're good? Got what you need for the next few months?"

"Yeah, we're good," he replied as Chris walked out. Mark scratched off a couple of items on his checklist. In the margin he wrote: "Back by Christmas."

"COME ON, TED," CHRIS WHISPERED. "I can just get on your shoulders." The night before climbing to Elbrus Base Camp, they'd stayed out too late. Now in the chilly Russian midnight, the guesthouse holding their beds for the night was locked.

"You're joking, Chris. Can't we find some other way to get in?" He knew before she answered where this was headed. The glint in her eye calmed him.

"I'll just pop in the window and open the door for you." Looking at him with conviction, she placed her hand on his shoulder, gently pushing him lower so she could step up.

Marveling at her free spirit, he kneeled and sank a little into the soft ground. "Oh god, all right. Up you go. Don't hurt yourself."

"I'm totally fine. Let's do the damn thing." Dirt from the bottom of her shoe smeared onto the shoulder of his T-shirt as she pushed off and up through the window. Callahan heard a *thump* followed by silence until she appeared at the door to the guesthouse. Triumphantly, she waved him in, still giggling at the absurdity. "Not bad for a thirty-eight-year-old, huh?" she whispered.

"Impressive," Callahan said. "Also, typical. You're going to dust me on this climb, aren't you? Leave me with the slower climbers and just kinda do your own thing, aren't you?"

"We shall see. This is one of three trips, ya' know? Cho Oyu with clients in a couple weeks and then meeting Charlie after that."

"Exactly. Pace yourself."

"No problem," Chris said, opening her bedroom door and flashing her bright smile as she closed it.

Callahan entered his room and crawled into bed, mapping out the next day's climb in his head. As always, Chris was in the lead, slowing down for nobody.

CHAPTER 15

CHO OYU

BY THE END OF AUGUST, Chris had summited Russia's Mount Elbrus with Ted Callahan and was on her way to Nepal. She connected with her three clients in Kathmandu, checked in briefly with Kili Sherpa, and proceeded to Lhasa, Tibet. Before beginning their climb of Cho Oyu, several days of low-key activity busied the group of four: touring Potala Palace, residence of the Dalai Lama until the 1959 Tibetan uprising; bargaining for jewelry in the market; short day hikes; a visit to Tashilhunpo Monastery. Then onward: the drive across the Tibetan Plateau, a mix of barren mountains and raging rivers, with a gradual ascent to Chinese Base Camp, the first stop on the journey by foot to the top of the 26,906-foot mountain.

The ascent to Cho Oyu is gradual, its gentle slopes fusing into other peaks. Located on the border of Tibet and Nepal, it's just twenty miles west of Mount Everest. The place felt familiar to Chris. She remembered clearly being here with Keith. Cho Oyu was his only 8,000-meter summit and one she'd visited now several times.

Among those attempting to summit Cho Oyu in 2006 with a different guiding company was American Samantha Larson. At seventeen, she was new to the sport of climbing but like Chris, a natural. In the years that followed, Samantha would become the youngest person to climb the Seven Summits, the highest mountain on each continent. "I was young in 2006 and not clued in to mountaineering yet," she remembered. "I didn't know much about Chris, but I remember talking to her a little on the way to base camp and it really resonated with me that she was a woman doing big expeditions but not making a big deal about it. As a teenage girl, it meant a lot to me to see her as a leader on the mountain and universally respected at base camp. It was clear she was a trailblazer."

Samantha, her father, and scores of other mountaineers with various guiding companies made the three-day trek to advanced base camp (ABC), a rocky field dotted with brightly colored tents. While Chris's three clients began the process of getting their bodies used to the altitude, Chris launched another series of dispatches. Unlike those from K2 back in 2002, which were written for a general audience following Chris and Charlie's ascent, these missives were lighter and targeted family and friends proudly tracking their loved ones up the mountain from thousands of miles away. Using a satellite phone to transmit them back to the United States, short dispatches were posted each day online. Chris worked hard to give each a flavor of life at base camp.

September 5, 2006

Another fun day here at Chinese Base Camp (CBC)! Once again our ritual wake-up: hot washing water and fresh coffee greeted us at 7:30 a.m. There were a lot of yaks around base camp to carry loads to the intermediate camp, halfway point from CBC to advanced base camp (ABC). Yaks can carry up to 50 kg loads and are very hearty animals.

After breakfast, which consisted of omelets, toast, and cereal, we got our gear together for our skills review training this morning. We reviewed ascending and descending fixed lines, so we are all clear on how our climbing systems will work on the mountain. Everyone did well, so with the extra time, we reviewed crevasse and rope rescue skills as well. After a nice lunch, we rested up for our move to intermediate camp tomorrow. Everyone is feeling good and our hopes are that we can stay healthy for the entire trip.

Until tomorrow!

—Chris

· · ·

PREVIOUS PAGE: *Chris in her element on Careno Crag, Leavenworth, Washington, 2006* (Sean Courage photo)

TOP: *Chris and Keith at the summit of Kala Patthar overlooking Mount Everest, late 1990s* (The Boskoff Collection Archives)

LEFT: *From Appleton East graduate to trail-blazing mountaineer* (The Boskoff Collection Archives)

TOP: *Chris and Kili Sherpa (red shirt) with his family in Kathmandu, 1998* (The Boskoff Collection Archives)

BOTTOM: *Scott Fischer (black tank top) with Keith and Chris Boskoff at Broad Peak Base Camp, 1995* (Mountain Madness Collection)

Chris and friend after climbing Snow Creek Wall with Jane Courage (Jane Courage photo)

TOP: *Jane Courage and Chris perfecting their edgy look* (The Fowler Collection Archives)

BOTTOM: *Joyce and Chris on a mother-daughter adventure in Europe, 2005* (The Boskoff Collection Archives)

TOP: *In the Khumbu Valley, late 1990s* (The Boskoff Collection Archives)

BOTTOM: *Chris in a moment of contemplation at Everest Base Camp* (Mountain Madness Collection)

A youthful Charlie Fowler on the Diamond, Longs Peak, Rocky Mountain National Park (The Fowler Collection Archives)

TOP: *Chris on the summit of Mount Everest, May 2000* (Photo by Andrew-Lock.com)

BOTTOM: *Chris and Charlie on Touchstone Wall in Zion National Park* (Photo by Joel Coniglio)

September 6, 2006

We are at Intermediate Camp tonight. It's a clear night, a full moon, and Cho Oyu is towering above us. We have had great weather so far.

We woke early, so we could dismantle camp. Our gear was weighed to make loads for the yaks to carry. Since the last time I was here, much has changed. There is no longer a river crossing, but two new bridges have been built. The trail has also been widened to accommodate vehicles to get into Intermediate Camp.

We now have a sunglass saga going on here at camp. Wolf made the mistake of giving a couple yak herders good sunglasses and now all the Tibetans want some. They have been stopping by our dining tent pointing to their eyes asking for glasses. Unfortunately Wolf has given out all of his extra pairs of glasses.

Tonight we celebrated my thirty-ninth birthday a day early. I was completely surprised by the cake that our Sherpas Myla and Babo made.

All the best!

—Chris

. . .

September 8, 2006

Today was a rest day at ABC. This morning we set up our communications/recharging station, organized our high-altitude food and equipment, and tidied up ABC. Wolf and Mark went for a socializing walk and met up with our German friends. Eric was the only one to take a shower; let's hope the rest of us do the same tomorrow!

There is still a lot to do here at ABC to get it more like home. Our local staff members are moving rocks around to get the kitchen in good shape.

This afternoon I went to a meeting to discuss how the fixed line will be installed in the next several weeks. After dinner tonight we watched a movie, Fahrenheit 9/11.

We plan to rest one more day at base camp before moving uphill. It's good to acclimatize well before climbing higher. We are happy that there are no headaches or coughs here at camp.

Good night from ABC!

—Chris

· · ·

September 10, 2006

We had a big day today. After breakfast we left for Camp 1 at 8:15 a.m. We hiked on the moraine until the base of the mountain, approximately 18,800 feet. We climbed up to intermediate camp at 19,300 feet and arrived around 10:45 a.m. After a short break we hiked to just below Camp 1, approximately 20,200 feet. We hung out until noon before heading back to ABC. About forty-five minutes before reaching ABC, it started snowing. Undi [one of the group's high-altitude team members] greeted us just before ABC with hot drinks. Everyone did well today. We nicknamed Eric "the rabbit" for his everlasting energy. After a late lunch we crawled into our sleeping bags to relax before dinner tonight.

Tomorrow morning is our puja, a Buddhist ceremony asking the Gods for good luck and health on our climb of Cho Oyu.

Cheers!

—Chris

· · ·

September 11, 2006

Last night we watched the movie Forrest Gump *before retiring for the evening. It snowed lightly most of the night.*

We had some sunshine this morning as we prepared for our puja. A lama performed the ceremony. We brought our ice axes and crampons to be blessed. After a half an hour of chanting Buddhist prayers and throwing rice, we broke into the Coca Cola, PBR, and snacks. We raised the prayer flags over base camp. The wind blows the Buddhist scripts that are written on the flags into the sky. We had many other expedition teams celebrate our puja with us.

After a late lunch, Wolf went on his gossip walk and Mark listened to the BBC, so at dinner tonight we received the current gossip and international news, respectively.

We'll have another rest day before moving up the mountain.

—Chris

• • •

September 16, 2006

Hello from ABC!

We had a successful acclimatization climb. After spending two nights at Camp 1 (6,400 meters / 20,900 feet) and climbing to 6,800 meters above the ice cliff, we are now back at ABC. Wolf was quoted as saying the climb over the ice cliff was the hardest thing he ever did in his life! The ice cliff did present a bit of airy traversing with a strenuous seventy-degree section at 22,000 feet. The oxygen-rich air feels like we are at sea level compared to where we were for the last few days. This morning we left Camp 1 after breakfast. It took us about 90 minutes to get down. Undi met us twenty minutes from base camp with juice and Coca Cola.

After a delicious lunch of fries and hamburgers, everyone took showers and washed clothes. Mark and I played a lengthy game of chess. Let's just say the person who won has a name that starts with "M." Tonight it's pizza, chips, and wine for dinner before the feature movie Austin Powers: The Spy Who Shagged Me.

We plan to have two more rest days before heading up the mountain. Our plan is to have one more acclimatization outing by sleeping at Camp 2 (7,100 meters) and returning again.

All the best,

—Chris

• • •

September 18, 2006

Today is our last day of rest before heading up the mountain again. It's been slightly snowing and cloudy yesterday and today. We spent the last two days playing cards and chess, resting, reading, and eating. Wolf and Mark have been playing some competitive games of chess. Currently Mark is the Cho Oyu MM champion of 2006, but things can change.

This morning we reviewed the use of oxygen for summit day. We checked out our masks and regulators to make sure they will work correctly and ensured everyone had the right size mask to fit their face.

Our Sherpas, Undi and Myla, left today for Camp 1. They will also stock our Camp 2. Tomorrow we will head up the mountain for two nights, a night at Camp 1 and 2. We will be back at ABC on the 21st.

That's it for now!

—Chris

. . .

September 21, 2006

We just returned safely from our last acclimatization climb. We timed it perfectly, since it just started snowing very hard today. We heard bad weather will persist for another three days.

We climbed up to Camp 1 on September 19th. September 20th we climbed to Camp 2 and considered it one of the hardest days on the mountain. Both Wolf and Mark said this was the hardest day of their lives. We arrived at Camp 2 around 3:30 p.m. It took us seven hours. Everyone did well considering it being our first night at 7,100 meters. This was Wolf, Eric, and Mark's personal high-altitude record!! Wolf had a little vomiting spell due to the high altitude but felt better afterward. We all slept on and off throughout the night.

After hot drinks and a small breakfast we departed Camp 2 at 9:15 a.m. We were all a bit fatigued, except for Eric of course. He enjoyed rappelling over the ice cliff as part of the descent. Myla met us about forty-five minutes from ABC with hot and cold drinks. At this point the snow was coming down steadily. We arrived back at ABC by 2 p.m. Babo welcomed us back home with a delicious lunch.

Now we are ready for our summit attempt. We plan to rest for the next three days and watch the weather for a good window.

Cheers!

—Chris

· · ·

September 23, 2006

Another snowy windy day at ABC. Today is probably the worst day since our arrival here. Fortunately we have a nice heated mess tent to hang out in.

Last night we went to dinner over at the German tent. The leader of the German expedition, Reiner, was an exceptional host. The dinner, drinks, and company were a blast!

Other expedition news: Wolf also took a shower yesterday, so it leaves only Mark as the one not to sit next to at dinner. Mark is still the Cho Oyu Chess Champion of 2006. Eric is trying to take over the title today, but it doesn't look too hopeful. Wolf is currently preparing for his summit attempt by snoozing in his tent today.

I met with a few of the other expeditions to figure out when other groups are planning their summit attempts. Our plan is to wait until the weather gets better and snow conditions above Camp 2 improve.

Signing out!

—Chris

· · ·

September 26, 2006

Hello from sunny ABC!!

Well, sunny skies greeted ABC today. It was the first clear day in six days. We had been receiving conflicting weather reports about today's weather, but today's report was right on the spot! The good weather lifted everyone's spirits here at ABC. Snowball wars were uncontrollable! We even played the game of getting the snowball into Wolf's tent, since he left the fly open. Fortunately for him we all missed! Our entire group also took advantage of the warm weather and took showers and washed clothes.

Undi and I met with other groups who still are attempting the summit. We worked out a plan for the next several days if weather and snow conditions high on the mountain look good. Our plan is to move up to Camp 1 on Thursday the 28th, and if everything works out we would be summiting on the 1st of October.

Tonight our group watched the movie Rudy. *It was a great movie and very motivational.*
—*Chris*

. . .

September 28, 2006
We all arrived at Camp 1 today—it seems that more groups have decided to go up and summit the same day as us because the trail has been quite busy. We are having soup and snacks before dinner and hopefully everyone will sleep well. Our Sherpas have gone up to Camp 2 tonight to stash at Camp 3 tomorrow. Over and out.
—*Chris*

. . .

September 29, 2006
Hi everyone, this is Chris calling in for the Cho Oyu dispatch. It is September 29th and we made it up to Camp 2 today. It was cooler than the last time we came up because there was a slight wind. We are settling in at Camp 2 and are having a dinner of burritos. Tomorrow, if everything goes well, we plan on going to Camp 3.
—*Chris*

. . .

September 30, 2006
Hello, this is Chris calling. We are at Camp 3 gasping for air at 7,500 meters. Our plan is to get up at around 11:00 p.m. today, make water, and start out for the summit at around 1:00 a.m. If every-thing goes well, we plan on summiting at around 9:00 to 10:00. We will report again from the summit if our satellite phone is working. We are all doing well considering the altitude and will call again soon.
This is Chris, over and out.

. . .

October 1, 2006
Hey, this is Chris on October 1st. Just wanted to let you know that our entire group—Mark, Eric, Wolf, Myla, and myself—summited at 8:00 a.m. on Cho Oyu. We left camp at 1:00 a.m. with great con-ditions. Everyone did well and we are now safely down at Camp 3.

We will be moving down to Camp 2 today. It was a good summit day and we had a lot of fun. We will call in again later.
—Chris

• • •

October 3, 2006
100 percent success rate on Cho Oyu and all back at ABC!
Our entire group is back in ABC after a safe and successful climb of Cho Oyu. Wolf had stomach issues the entire time, so put in an extra effort by making it to the top. Undi, Eric, and I saved weight by not bringing a sleeping bag to Camp 3 and had a very memorable cold night there.

Our summit day was very rewarding. We woke at 11 p.m. by making hot drinks and breakfast. Wolf's breakfast didn't sit too well with him, and it came up shortly afterward. High altitude affects your digestion, so it's quite common for people to lose their appetite or to throw up.

We left for the summit at 1:00 a.m. with our headlamps on. Our group climbed relatively quickly. As usual, Eric was right on my heels and not even breathing hard. Everyone enjoyed the rock band section of the climb with its mixed rock and ice and near vertical part. By daybreak we were already on the summit ridge leading up to the summit plateau. We had one of the best morning sunrises that I could remember. The morning sun on the surrounding mountains was breathtaking. Wolf with his usual optimism expressed his enjoyment at this point. Mark must have had a shot of Red Bull, since he and Eric were first to the summit. We realized we were at the summit when Everest, Lhotse, and the entire Western Cwm was glaring us in the face. This was 8:00 a.m. After summit photos, we were ready to head down to the oxygen-rich air below us. It took us three hours to reach Camp 3 even though we stopped a few times to take in the Himalayan mountain range around us.

Once we arrived at Camp 3, both Mark and Wolf flopped in their tent. Our goal was to reach Camp 2, and Eric, Undi, and I had no intention to sleep another night at Camp 3 without our sleeping bags, so we took apart Mark and Wolf's tent with them in it. This encouraged them to pack up and head down. We spent the night at Camp 2 at 7,100 meters, which felt like sea level compared to Camp 3.

Yesterday was a long day. We all cleared everything from Camp 2 and brought it down to Camp 1. From Camp 1 it took us 4 1/2 hours to reach ABC when it normally takes 1 1/2 hours. Our cook helper, Pemba, met us about forty-five minutes from camp with juice, Coke, and beer. Of course we invited friends who we knew from the mountain to join us as they hiked by. We toasted our success as the sun was setting behind the mountains. It was a beautiful sight to remember.

We were one of the first groups to summit Cho Oyu this year! I think what was so exceptional is that all of the smaller groups here at ABC worked together to organize the fixing of the lines to make the route to the summit possible. When small groups or individuals work together, it can make a big impact or make things possible.

We had a pre-celebration dinner last night. As normal, our cook Babo made an exceptional dinner! We were all too tired to celebrate past 8:30 p.m., even Eric!! Today is showers and resting. Our depart date from ABC is on the 5th and back to Kathmandu on the 6th.

Until tomorrow!

—Chris

• • •

October 4, 2006

Our final day here at Cho Oyu ABC! We are all excited to get back to Kathmandu and depart back home or to our next adventure. Everyone is busy packing up equipment here at camp. Tomorrow we will depart camp after breakfast.

Today we will have our final card matches and relax with Cho Oyu towering above us. The winds have picked up significantly and it seems the summit window has closed for the season.

Last night we had our celebration dinner with champagne and toasted our success! We stayed up late and played cards. It was a beautiful starlit night with a three-quarter moon and Cho Oyu lit up.

We say hi to our family and friends. We will see everyone soon!
Cheers!
—*Chris*

CHRIS AND HER TEAM NARROWLY avoided witnessing tragedy from Cho Oyu Advanced Base Camp. Nangpa La, a glacial pass of ice at 19,000 feet, is clearly visible from ABC ("Nangpa" in Tibetan means "insider," while "La" means "pass"). For centuries, the smooth contours of Nangpa La allowed pilgrims and traders free yet still perilous travel between Tibet and Nepal. Once a sovereign nation, Tibet fell under the control of the People's Republic of China in 1959. Since then, the route has become an icy escape path for Tibetans seeking refuge in Nepal and India. By 2006, Nangpa La was heavily patrolled by the Chinese Border Patrol. With the Summer Olympics being held in China in 2008, the possibility of refugees fleeing the country threatened the image Beijing wanted to portray. Chinese Border Patrol agents were given orders to shoot any refugee trying to cross Nangpa La.

On September 30, as Chris and her team prepared to summit, a line of roughly seventy Tibetan refugees was fleeing their homeland via Nangpa La. Without warning, Chinese Border Patrol fired on the group, shooting a seventeen-year-old Tibetan nun in the back and killing her almost instantly. The event, in full view of climbers resting at ABC, created chaos. Though it was clear the Chinese had committed a massive breach of international human rights, many mountaineers backed away from reporting the incident to the international media. Fearful of repercussions from China, the climbing teams at ABC felt a layer of silence settle over them. The atrocity thus became invisible.

Veteran guide Luis Benitez reached Chris at Camp 1 on the descent with her team. It was two days after the shooting and he'd been vocal about the need to notify the press, but still the incident had gone largely unreported. Standing in an intense windstorm outside expedition tents, Luis spoke to Chris and several other guides briefly about what had happened. "I told her I wasn't sure she wanted to go down yet," he said. "I was sure ABC would be swarming with media. I suspected Chinese soldiers would be everywhere. She'd be walking into a mess."

Expedition team member Wolf recalled what happened next: "We got to ABC and nobody was talking about it. Then we heard rumors that the people shot were human traffickers. We weren't sure what to believe. It wasn't until I got back to the States that we heard the truth."

Overcome by what had happened, Luis Benitez abandoned his summit attempt. Returning to ABC, he broke the news to online media and promptly landed in the middle of a firestorm. Many of his fellow guides lashed out at his actions. Others remained silent. "Chris would have spoken up about what happened at Cho Oyu once she got back to the United States," Luis said. "She'd done a ton of work with nonprofits on behalf of impoverished women and children in Asia, and she would have been upfront. Chris had a barometer when it came to things that mattered most." In service of these beliefs, Chris had begun volunteer work with an organization devoted to improving children's literacy in developing countries. Sitting on their board of directors, Chris spent late-night hours preparing speeches designed to bring in donor dollars at fundraisers and promote the charity climbs she led.

Politics was perhaps the least appealing part of Chris's work, though her travels forced her to frequently face sensitive issues. The topic came up with her mother from time to time, the two of them saddened that places of such wonder could be tainted by strife. "She hated war," Joyce said. "She saw the beauty in the mountains, not the bullets."

CHAPTER 16

OFF THE GRID

ON ANY GIVEN WEEKEND IN the majestic Cascades of Washington State, hundreds of climbers descend on trails to practice their sport. Equally bustling are the base camps at Everest, Cho Oyu, and many other mountains around the world that have been discovered, named, photographed, climbed, littered upon, cleaned up, and ultimately brought into the spotlight. With endless pockets of unknown peaks and luminous beauty, western China has long called to adventure-seekers less interested in those spotlights. In particular, a 500-kilometer area stretching from Dege County, Sichuan, in the north to Shangri-La City, Yunnan, in the south is home to the Shaluli Shan, *shan* meaning "mountains" in Mandarin. It's a landscape on the eastern Tibetan Plateau filled with peaks that have been called the "Tetons on crack" for their dazzling, craggy beauty.

One of the earliest explorers of the region was Tamotsu Nakamura, a Japanese climber who started coming there in the early 1990s. After several trips, he boldly stated in 2003: "Some convince themselves that veiled mountains in the greater ranges are an experience of the past. But [the eastern] Tibet [Plateau] has an incredibly vast and complex topography that holds countless unclimbed summits, and beckons a lifetime's search. The peaks there are stunning and magnificent, and many of them will remain enigmas for generations."

To get to the area, a typical launching spot for Westerners is the massive Chinese city of Chengdu. From there, the province of Sichuan spills west into the mountains before hitting the city of Kangding. A natural border, the city contains a distinct mix of Han Chinese and Tibetan cultures. Over time, the Chinese government has implemented a policy of developing its western edges known as the Great Western Development Strategy. The policy incentivized Chinese to move farther west, infusing small Tibetan cities such as Kangding with Chinese growth, architecture, and infrastructure. The result is an odd mishmash of loud, Western amenities with traditional Tibetan influence such as small monasteries housing Tibetan prayer wheels of all sizes, spun by children and pilgrims alike.

Once west of Kangding, Tibetan culture is firmly rooted and the landscape opens up into sweeping, vivid green grassland panoramas, many speckled with Tibetan farmers and hundreds of grazing yaks in the summer months. Nomadic tents are planted along fields, each tent carefully constructed with yak wool. Herders spend their days tending to the animals that feed on the lush grasslands. When the weather cools in the autumn, the nomads travel to better feeding grounds for their herds.

The villages along the road west of Kangding gradually reach an altitude of ten thousand to eleven thousand feet. There the architecture is entirely Tibetan, and the region is known as Kham, one of the three traditional regions of Tibet. The buildings have simple stone or clay walls with flat roofs. In the more ornate homes, elaborate wood carvings decorate windows and doors. In nearly all cases, colorful Tibetan Buddhist prayer flags fly from the rooftops. At the center of nearly every Tibetan city is a hub of activity with trucks selling the day's harvest of vegetables, and groups of Tibetan nomads on motorcycles in town on supply runs. The time needed to "run into town" is now cut in half with motorcycles replacing horses. It's still rare in these parts for locals to encounter Westerners, and practically impossible to communicate when they do. All Tibetans in China have been forced to learn Mandarin as part of their formal education, but in the far western reaches of Sichuan, Tibetan is still the dominant language.

For certain avid Western mountaineers, such rare interactions provide incentive to travel farther, endure more discomforts, and risk more unknowns than they would traveling a well-worn path elsewhere in the world. The Tibetan Plateau contains fascinating people, culture, and challenges. Rushing streams are adorned with wooden footbridges, each bursting with tattered prayer flags tied on year after year. It beckons with desolate rocky outcrops on the sides of roads. And in every direction of the Shaluli Shan in this part of western China, a feast of mountains explodes in every direction, all waiting to be treasured. Of all the jewels in the Shaluli Shan, several call to climbers for their particular challenge and splendor, and Genyen Peak, rising to 20,354 feet, leads this list.

WHILE CHRIS FASTIDIOUSLY RECORDED NOTES and thoughts as they traveled, Charlie stayed true to character with only brief email messages to friends. Months later, it was revealed by *Alpinist* magazine that before he'd left to meet Chris, he'd written a nine-thousand-word first draft of an article about his life as a climber. The final passages of Charlie's work were eventually published, setting forth bits of his philosophy and making an offering to those who knew them both.

K2 was a harsh lesson. We were fit, acclimated, and climbing in good style on a fine route but got shut down by bureaucratic, arbitrary rules. I've always felt mountains belong to everyone and government management should be limited to protecting important cultures and resources. Mountains are not a commodity to be bought and sold. "Freedom of the Hills" is not a cliché. It's my credo.

I've always looked to the future and been skeptical of tradition, while trying to learn from the past. I long to return to the wild country of Tibet and Patagonia, those vast lands that feel like home. I want to share my knowledge, following the example of modern-day explorers like Tamotsu Nakamura.

Lately I've been looking homeward for inspiration and challenges. Surrounded by a mythic history and ancient culture, the American Southwest remains wild and remote, free from excessive rules and regulations and prime for exploration and adventure. A small group of friends and I have been establishing dozens of new climbs from the desert to the mountains in remote southwestern Colorado.

Throughout my life, climbing has been a progression. I've slowly built on past experiences, learned from friends and mentors, trained hard, and done my homework. As a guide, I progressed down the same path, but ultimately guiding is about helping others fulfill their dreams. To fulfill my own dreams, I chose to follow in the footsteps of the great French guide Gaston Rebuffat, who made the transition to writing and films and reached more people in the process. Now I spend my days reading and writing and filming and climbing as much as I can.

I have an insatiable appetite for knowledge. Long ago I realized mountaineering is the best education for me. I need to travel around the world, passing through the exciting, dirty, and dangerous cities with a friend or two by my side. Somehow we find our way to the towns and then to the small villages and trek through the pristine meadows to the glaciers and on to the summit. Thanks to my education as an alpinist, there is not much I can't see or experience of this small, lonely, fragile planet.

—Charlie Fowler

BY NOVEMBER 7, 2006, CHRIS and Charlie had already climbed two peaks in remote parts of western Sichuan. The first was a second ascent of Haizi Shan, also known as Yala Peak. At 5,280 meters, it was a mountain that Charlie had eyed for years. Chris captured the experience in her climbing journal:

October 22, 2006
We left HC (high camp) at 5:00 a.m. I started out breaking trail, then Charlie led, and I took over again toward the last couloir. We reached the ridge at 1:15 p.m., the entire time mostly in the clouds. Two pitches with rope. Took us an hour and forty-five minutes to reach the top at 3:00 p.m. On the way down, lightning and thun-

*der. Downclimbed the entire route except one rap and left one pin.
Reached HC at 7:00 p.m. Ten hours up. Four hours down.*

The second objective was Yangmaiyong, a 5,958-meter peak on the southern rim of the Shaluli Shan. The pair stopped short, turned back by thin snow over rock slabs that made them both wary about the stability of their next steps. Chris wrote:

*November 4, 2006
Woke up at 2:55 a.m. Left camp at 4:10 a.m. Two hours we were above col. Waited for sun for forty-five minutes. Climbed another thirty minutes. Hit dead end on unprotectable snow over rock. Turned around 5,400 to 5,500 meters. Downclimbed to High Camp. Waited until 5:30 p.m. to descend to base. 3.5 hours camped at lake around 10:30 p.m.*

WITH THE WEATHER TURNING, CHRIS was anxious to get home. She'd been gone since August and had climbed her way through Russia, Nepal, and now China. As promised, Chris checked in with Mountain Madness from China. In email messages to friends and colleagues, she mentioned being tired, something many of them remember as an uncharacteristic comment. "She was tired and she missed her mom," said Jane Courage, Chris's friend and climbing partner. "She wanted more than anything to come home. She was burned out and wanted to get out of China. But god our last conversation was full of laughs, too. It was her mom's birthday in mid-November, and she had arranged to send her a giant teddy bear. She couldn't wait to hear her reaction."

Before heading to the Genyen Valley with Charlie, Chris had one final call to make.

"SO YOU'LL BE HOME FOR the holidays, right Chrissy?" Joyce Feld asked. The call from her daughter sounded like it had originated right next door and not from the other side of the world.

"Absolutely, Mom," said Chris. "I'm going to try to get home earlier than I planned. Charlie and I just have one more climb."

"And your guiding went well?"

"Really well. I'm good at what I do, Mom."

"I know you are. The best."

Chris knew she wouldn't be able to call her mother on her birthday, November 17. "We'll be in a remote area, Mom. But I'll be thinking of you."

CHAPTER 17

GENYEN

The power of such a mountain is so great and yet so subtle that, without compulsion, people are drawn to it from near and far, as if by the force of some invisible magnet; and they will undergo untold hardships and privations in their inexplicable urge to approach and to worship the center of this sacred power.

—Lama Anagarika Govinda

WITH THEIR FINAL CLIMB REMAINING, Chris and Charlie extended their visas. Their departure date was now December 4, 2006, giving them plenty of time to return to Colorado before Christmas. Chris would have ample time to get to Seattle for the Mountain Madness holiday party she and Mark were planning. Then to Wisconsin for a visit with her mother. The jumping-off point for their last climb was the city of Litang, 250 kilometers north of where they were currently based in the city of Yading. Before heading to Litang, they returned to a guesthouse in Yading where they'd stored their duffels prior to climbing. When they arrived, the guesthouse manager was gone. So were their bags. From Chris's journal:

November 6
The caretakers said they didn't know where the bags were. We called the police and got the local head of the town involved. Still

no luck finding bags. Some Chinese people helped us translate and had us call the American consulate. The consulate was very helpful and called the local foreign office, who called the police here to solve the problem. The local head guy got the caretakers to admit they had the bags, but they wanted 300 yuan (about $38) for returning them to us. We paid, but eventually the head guy got us the money back. We stayed in Yading for the night, in the lodge next door for 30 yuan (about $3.75). Happy Ending.

Two Americans climbing in remote parts of Sichuan was an oddity the American consulate didn't usually encounter. Yet they had come through and provided proper assistance. The interaction with the US government that day was Chris and Charlie's last known correspondence with other Americans in China.

LITANG, CHINA, AND APPLETON, WISCONSIN, are separated by 7,272 miles. Chris felt called to both. Aside from their roughly similar populations, fifty thousand to seventy-five thousand, the cities bore little to no resemblance to each other. Litang's streets were an explosion of both Chinese and Tibetan influences. The residents were nearly 95 percent Tibetan, though Han Chinese had begun to bring their culture and businesses into the rhythm of daily life. Street signs were posted in both Tibetan script and Chinese characters. The villagers still brought horses through town, though piles of parked motorcycles crowded the sidewalks. Concrete, Communist-style buildings bumped into one another but were adorned with Buddhist prayer flags blowing from spires on their roofs. Elaborate Chinese-style red doors plated with gold adorned even the most simple houses, while only a few feet higher, their eaves gave shadow to the distinctive Tibetan knot symbol painted just below on the house siding.

Nestled among radiant green hills, the city of Litang moved slowly. A main street was lined with shops carrying groceries, electronics, and school supplies. Frequenting the establishments were local Tibetan men and women in traditional dress. The women wore dark, ankle-length robes called *chubas* tied with sashes. Some were covered with *pangdens*—beautiful multicolored aprons, which signified their status as married women. The Tibetan men wrapped themselves in thick jackets and hats with wide brims for sun protection. At nearly thirteen thousand feet, Litang is one of the world's highest settlements and beyond the height of Lhasa, Tibet. As the birthplace of the seventh Dalai Lama and the tenth Dalai Lama, the city's most recognized sight is Litang Monastery, founded in 1580. In 2006, the monastery was home to more than four hundred monks, many who strolled the city streets in flowing crimson robes.

On November 8, 2006, Chris and Charlie arrived. Their local bus pulled down the long road weaving through downtown. Having stayed in Litang before as they'd crisscrossed this part of China, they knew where they were headed, and their host, a Tibetan local, was waiting for them. Ji'an and his wife lived on the main street and ran a small restaurant and guesthouse. His thick, black hair matched dark eyes, which sparkled when he laughed. He was trim, full of good humor, and soft spoken, deferring to his wife when it was clear she had something to say. A solid eight inches shorter than him, Ji'an's wife nonetheless had a commanding presence. She wore a long-sleeved shirt covered with a striped *pangden*, and sturdy, modern tennis shoes. Around her neck was a brightly colored choker with turquoise and red beads. In their mid-forties, the Tibetan couple was without children and spoke only Tibetan, creating a rich game of charades for all as they tried to communicate with Chris and Charlie. Though they'd learned the very basics in Chinese from years of travel, neither Chris nor Charlie spoke Tibetan, aside from the generic greeting of *tashi delek,* meaning "good day" or "blessings."

When traveling, Chris and Charlie needed little in the way of accommodations. The 20 yuan (roughly $2.50) per night price for a bed was plenty. Over the course of three nights and three days, as Charlie and Chris planned their climb, Ji'an and his wife got to know them. By the time they left, Ji'an and his wife understood the nuances of the couple's relationship. The notoriously thrifty pair of climbers would each drink just one bottle of beer at night and split the dinner tab "down to the last yuan" depending on who ate how much.

On the night of November 10, Tibetan dumplings with potatoes were served. It had become Chris and Charlie's favorite meal. Ji'an knew little about Westerners, and even less about climbing, but he noted the stash of crampons and ropes. When he and his wife talked with Chris and Charlie about where they wanted to go, he wasn't surprised. Though the language barrier was firmly intact, the destination was clear with the help of maps, pantomiming, and laughter.

Ji'an remembered the couple seeming tense that night but also excited about their upcoming climb. "They were in good spirits and had a delicious home-cooked meal," he said. "They asked about the price for a ride to the trailhead, and I told them I'd take them. They'd been waiting for a bus for a few days, but I offered to take them myself the next morning. And I gave them a discount because they had stayed in our home and become friends."

It was arranged. Charlie and Chris would leave their duffels with Ji'an, calling him when their climb was over and they wanted to be picked up. The ride to the village of Lamaya was four hours west of Litang, and from there, they'd hike two hours before beginning their climb from Lenggu Monastery. Built in 1164, the monastery is surrounded on every side by exquisite peaks, with Mount Genyen rising slightly higher than the rest. At a height of 13,615 feet, the monastery is one of the highest in the world, increasing its isolation and mystique. White concrete walls pair with dark framing. Gold spires top the roof, a traditional Tibetan Buddhist touch. The monastery survived total destruction during the Cultural Revolution of the 1970s, and much of the inside was rebuilt in the 1980s. The monks who live at Lenggu spend most of their time meditating, reading scriptures, and tending to the wild blue sheep that live in the hills nearby. The monks living at the monastery believe it is part of their role to keep watch of majestic Mount Genyen.

AS JAPANESE CLIMBER TAMOTSU NAKAMURA described it: "The highest peak in the region, Mount Genyen (6,204 meters) is a divine (sacred) mountain which was first climbed in 1988. However, more than 10 untouched rock and snow peaks over 5,800 meters await climbers . . . and the scenery surrounding the Lenggu Monastery amid spiky rock pinnacles is truly enchanting." Treading into the stunning Genyen Valley, Charlie and Chris were entering space that had been visited by Buddhist pilgrims for centuries. Rare plants and animals scattered the landscape. Rivers running from the mountaintops are considered holy waters and call locals to bathe for purity.

The region is part of a larger area covering 1,200 square kilometers that, according to Makamura, weaves together "rigid snowy mountains, perennial glaciers, rushing streams, thick forests, rich meadows, ancient monasteries and tranquil villages where people appreciate its scenery, receive its blessings and thus acquire supreme states of mind." In short, the area had everything Chris and Charlie wanted, including tranquility and a spiritual draw. Whether to undertake a climb of a "holy mountain" had long been debated in the mountaineering community. To climb was to seek solitude, perhaps at the expense of treading lightly on ground that others wouldn't touch because of their reverence for the mountain. Balancing these issues is part of a larger challenge that will always be a subtext of the narrative for climbers.

As anthropologist Sherry B. Ortner described in *Life and Death on Mt. Everest: Sherpas and Himalayan Mountaineering,* "The spirituality and transcendence of mountaineering contrasts with the crass materialism and pragmatism of modern life. Climbers see scaling walls as a solitary affair, disconnected from history and culture, sociality and politics. We seek a pristine and isolated wilderness in which we may find awe, wonder, inspiration, thrill and authenticity. The sublime adventure would not be possible, however, without the amenities of modern life—adequate leisure time, social safety nets and the expendable capital necessary to build skill and buy gear. Far from erasing history, climbing depends on it."

Many Buddhists believe that the power and beauty of these divine locations are places where masters achieve spiritual realization. As such, climbers are often denied access to the faces of these mountains and merely allowed to take a clockwise circumambulation of the base in a pilgrimage known as *kora*. Often this involves a full-body prostration over the entire distance of the path, many times on rough terrain covered with rock and scaling high passes. This is the case for nearby Mount Kailash, a 21,778-foot peak universally known to be closed to mountaineering because of its holiness.

The morality of climbing sacred mountains will always be largely defined by personal judgment. Deciding how to approach a mountain's sanctity depends on a number of factors, all considered and then sprinkled onto a sliding scale of individual logic. To square spiritual principles with their desire to climb, some mountaineers opt to stop just short of the main peak or to only summit a subpeak as a sign of respect. In other cases, expensive permits are sought from local authorities to legitimize the climb. In still other instances, such as with Mount Genyen, the mountain may be remote enough that its sacred status is not widely publicized. Regardless of how mountaineers weigh these issues, it is mountains like Genyen that will forever make those decisions difficult.

The mountain itself is part of the Genyen Massif, a group of mountains separated slightly but still connected to a larger range, in this case the Shaluli Shan. Each face of the mountain showcases diverse natural beauty. Along the northern slope of Mount Genyen, wildflowers in season decorate the edges of lush grassland leading to a clear blue-gray riverbed with a sandy bottom. This side of the mountain is covered with boulders leading to scree fields as the mountain rises above tree line. On the southern slope, snow and ice cover the mountain year-round. From every direction standing on the valley floor rise sharp peaks that have rarely been touched by climbers. It's an alpine rock paradise.

By the time Chris and Charlie arrived in the Genyen Valley in November 2006, the main peak of Genyen had been summited just twice, first by a Japanese party in 1988 and a second time in May 2006 by an Italian team. The Italians had visited the monks at Lenggu Monastery at the base of the mountain. Expedition leader Karl Unterkircher reported: "Our association with them became friendlier day-by-day. They told us of the origins of the valleys, in accordance with their religion, and how the mountains that rise opposite the monastery are sacred, because they cannot be reached by people, particularly Genyen with its snow-covered north and northeast faces."

Several days later, the Italians reached the top of Genyen, where they opted to stop just short of the highest point out of recognition of the mountain's sacred status. Though the group felt confident they'd created a bond with the monks and hadn't been disrespectful, several mountaineers who arrived in October 2006 reported the opposite. The monks reportedly told this group that they were upset that Genyen had been summited. Thus the latest group responded by vowing to climb lesser peaks in the area and to encourage future climbers to be respectful of established customs and sacred peaks.

HAVING CLIMBED ALL OVER THE world, Chris and Charlie knew the risks involved in taking on their latest challenge. The usual dangers applied, generally falling into two categories: things that could be controlled, and things that could not. In the first category were such things as not being properly acclimatized, feeling emotionally or physically overtired, having improper training, and not having the right technical skills or equipment. For Chris and Charlie, most of these areas seemed properly addressed.

Beyond the bounds of their control were such challenges as changing weather conditions, the possibility of falling, and perhaps the most unpredictable of all risks—avalanches. Coming in a variety of forms, avalanches can pose threats in a number of conditions. The most deadly type of avalanche, a slab avalanche, is triggered when a weak layer in the snowpack has a compression failure that propagates under a bonded layer of snow (a slab), releasing the slab lying on top of it. Something as simple as a skier stepping in the wrong place in the wrong conditions can trigger a slab avalanche. Those who trigger the avalanche are often within its perimeter and caught within moments, the first sound being a distinct *whump*. Though many slab avalanches are triggered by skiers or snowboarders, mountaineers can also be at peril with cornices or seracs often starting these avalanches when they break off on overhanging ridges or glaciers.

Other types of avalanches can happen as well. Wet avalanches occur when the air temperature rises and the snow melts, and then releases. These avalanches occur at lower speeds and are easier to predict than slab avalanches. Loose snow avalanches, or sluffs, can be released naturally and usually involve small upper layers of dry, powdery snow that break free when a climber or skier is crossing a slope. In these avalanches, death can occur by partial burial or by being swept down steep terrain, falling and suffering catastrophic injury.

Though Genyen was a relatively untested mountain, Chris and Charlie had turned back at obvious dangers just weeks before on a climb of Yangmaiyong. With time expiring on their visas, they were ready to explore the unknowns of this mystical valley.

SNOW WAS FALLING AS CHARLIE and Chris reached Lenggu Monastery on November 12, 2006. To save energy, they'd hired horse packers to carry their backpacks for part of the two-hour trek from Lamaya. As they walked, the group converged with herds of yak, each burdened with supply bags. Their owners were riding ponies, and Charlie exchanged greetings in Tibetan with them as he passed. He had studied Genyen from every angle and spoken to mountaineers who had experience in nearby areas. The dangers and the rewards were clear to him.

As part of their duty, the monks felt obliged to share thoughts with this latest round of climbers. As in so many situations where language, culture, and spirituality collide, the truth of what transpired when Charlie and Chris arrived at the monastery has different interpretations.

IT HAS BEEN A DOZEN years since Charlie and Chris passed through and spoke with the monks, but the head monk at Lenggu wasn't reluctant to discuss their visit. Sitting at the end of the nave in the monastery, he wore a closely cropped buzz cut and a bright smile. A gold watch offset the yellow sash in his traditional maroon robe. His Mandarin was strong, though he used it only with non-Tibetan-speaking visitors who passed through infrequently.

"When they arrived," the head monk recalled, "we told them it was dangerous to climb Genyen. We advised against climbing because Genyen has natural dangers that would prevent them from getting to the top. It's too fierce and too big." With regard to the language barrier, he turned to other monks who'd gathered and then translated for them in Tibetan. The monks grinned, finding bits of dark humor in the prospect of such important messages being lost in translation.

"Yes, that's right," he said. "I don't think they spoke much Chinese. And we do not speak any English. So perhaps they didn't understand."

CAPTURING VISUALS AS PART OF their travels was second nature to both Charlie and Chris. Hundreds of hours of video footage and thousands of pictures filled their homes. Each trip was catalogued to be shared with others when they returned. The trip to Genyen was no exception. Video from their days on the mountain captured perfectly their shared love of adventure: the turns in the weather, the meals they ate and the gear stored snugly in backpacks, glimpses into their humor, the splendor of the alpine landscape.

Speaking to each other as they take turns acting as videographer, Charlie and Chris take us along on their climb up this majestic peak.

BELOW THE MONASTERY, THE RIVER pours over boulders as the two survey their options. To get to the other side where they'd set up camp requires a crossing. Finding a fallen tree to serve as a bridge, Chris scrambles across first, coaxing Charlie.

"Here's Charlie, crossing the river. Hopefully he won't fall in!"

Lowering himself to hands and knees, Charlie strings bags around his neck. Gripping the tree, he makes it to the other side. The look on his face is one of satisfaction as he gives Chris his quintessential smile, raising his eyebrow and dipping his head, whispering, "I did it." He plops the pack into the brush, eyes cast upon Genyen, which is now in full view. The target is clear. The ski hat he wears collects snowflakes, its tassels bobbing side to side.

Chris looks up at the peak through a monocular. "The only thing that's still a question is that very top serac. I'm sure we can get over that, though." At 20,354 feet, Mount Genyen is exquisite. Entirely covered in fresh snowpack, the contrast with the blue skies behind it is stunning. Charlie and Chris are at home, hundreds of miles from other Westerners, with only the possessions on their backs and each other.

Camping that night in the woods, Chris discusses what they'll bring. Enough food for seven days, and a few extra days' worth in case of weather problems. Five ice screws. Rock protection.

"Just trying to go as light as possible," she says. "Can't wait to go."

DAWN BREAKS THE NEXT MORNING, November 13, 2006. Charlie works the video camera, with Chris in the lead. She's carrying a walking stick as she maneuvers around boulders and up the northeast face of Genyen. As they reach a ridge at 4,600 meters, the terrain is desolate. There are no signs of vegetation. Only gray rock, scree, and snow. After a day of climbing, they make camp in an outcropping. Their dome tent hugs the mountainside, surrounded by snow.

On November 14, 2006, sunrise gives way to brilliant blue skies. Charlie is melting snow for their water bottles. Breakfast was oatmeal; its remnants coat the side of a tin bowl lying on a green sleeping bag at the bottom of the tent. "Maybe to a higher camp today," Charlie says. "Hopefully the last camp before the summit." He starts up the slope, an ice axe in each hand. Before long, the snow is ankle deep.

Chris's breathing becomes more noticeable as they gain altitude. They're over 4,900 meters now, and the monastery is a mere speck at the end of the riverbed as they look down the valley. As the video camera pans upward, the clouds move quickly past the peaks on the opposite side of the gorge. The goal is the col just below the northeast ridge. It's a suitable place for high camp before the blast to the summit the next morning. The snow is now knee deep.

Sitting on his backpack in the snow, Charlie rests and studies the weather. Both ice axes are planted in the snow behind him. A fleece jacket is tied around his waist. Crampons are strapped to his boots. "Taking a break on our way to our high camp," he says. "Pretty nice weather so far. A few clouds rolling in, but so far, a good day. Good snow conditions today. Great views up here, too. Spectacular peaks everywhere we look."

Charlie glances at the camera only momentarily so he can take in the views. He seems transfixed, and Chris shifts the camera to follow his gaze across the vista of Genyen Valley. Snow is no longer falling, but simply spinning downward in small bits as Charlie's boots press into fresh layers. He's traversing a funnel steadily, the goal of high camp just above. With Charlie in the lead breaking trail, the two continue. A moraine is off to their right, a pile of dirt and debris that would be easier to climb but would take much longer. Instead, they climb up the chute, being sure to walk carefully, checking the stability of the snowpack.

Unroped, they take careful steps, sinking into hip-deep powder. The sound of the river rushing has long disappeared. Now the only sound is Chris's gentle breathing as she steadies the camera strapped on her chest and grips her trekking pole. Out of nowhere, blackness fills the screen along with a light crackling sound. A brief, inexplicable flash of light appears before the video turns off.

Silence.

STEAM RISES FROM THE CUPS of yak butter tea on the table in the monastery. Reading a traditional sutra, a Buddhist scripture, one of the monks pauses, realizing the date is November 17, the day the two Western climbers said they'd walk back past the monastery and down the valley. The monk adds firewood to the stove. He fills a large silver kettle with water and places it on the stovetop, planning ahead. The climbers might need boiled water for their bottles. The journey back to Litang is long and the sun is already drifting lower.

Goats wander in and out of the communal reading room. Their presence is unnoticed as the monk closes his eyes and falls asleep. Waking an hour later, he considers where the climbers might be this evening, now late in their intended stop. Perhaps they took a different route out of the valley. The monk finishes his readings and hears the evening call to meditation. The sun is nearly below the horizon as he steps out of the warmth and heads across the courtyard to the assembly hall. Tucking arms into his robes, he looks up at the peak of Genyen, bathed in gold light with layers of white snow covering every inch, untouched. *There is no more beautiful place in all the world*, he thinks. *The two Westerners are lucky to have been here.*

The monk finds a spot in the assembly hall. He sits on a thin mat, legs crossed. With hands in prayer, he is at peace, imagining Chris and Charlie watching the sunset.

MORE THAN SEVEN THOUSAND MILES away, the same day is just starting in Appleton, Wisconsin. Joyce Feld dresses and fields calls from her three sons wishing her a happy eightieth birthday. Putting on her favorite sweater, she looks out the window in time to see a flower delivery truck pull up. Stepping out of the truck, the driver looks terribly overburdened and she laughs at his haul, wondering if he has the wrong address. Joyce opens the door.

"A delivery for you, ma'am," he says.

"Are you sure? This is—"

"If you're Joyce Feld, I'm sure. Someone sure hit a home run with this one!" He hands her a dozen red roses and a positively enormous teddy bear. His blond fur melts against a red, stuffed fabric heart sewn onto his hand and pressed against his chest.

Juggling flowers and the bear, Joyce looks him over, knowing that her grandchildren will squeal when they see him. The card reads: "Happy Birthday, Mom! I'll be home on December 22! I love you! From Chrissy, your favorite daughter." Plunking the bear onto the couch, Joyce shakes her head and wonders how in the world her daughter pulled this off. Halfway around the world on top of some mountain. At thirty-nine, Chris is now the same age that Joyce had been when she gave birth to her daughter. They lived such different lives but are now tangled as tightly as a thin chain necklace.

By the end of the day, Joyce's cheeks ache from smiling as she sizes up her new furry housemate. Her daughter, her baby, her Chrissy, was thinking of her. Just as she promised she would be.

CHAPTER 18

QUESTIONS

TELLURIDE, COLORADO. DROPPING FROM THE clouds, a commuter plane approached Montrose Regional Airport in southwestern Colorado. The moon was nearly full and passengers gazed out windows, admiring the light on the mountaintops below. It was December 4, 2006. An hour due south in Telluride, Damon Johnston checked his email, wondering when he'd hear from Charlie and Chris about a pickup at the airport. Their flight was due any day, but Damon hadn't heard a word from his friends in several weeks.

Also curious was Chris's friend Angela Hawse. The duo was planning to go climbing together, but Chris had been uncharacteristically silent in response to her inquiries. Angela got Damon's number from Mark Gunlogson at Mountain Madness and gave him a call to see if Charlie had been in contact. Nothing, he told her, though Charlie had promised to let him know when they'd need a ride. Damon's email inbox was filled with the usual messages, but nothing from Charlie. He wondered if he should check in with Ginny, Charlie's sister, or perhaps directly with Mountain Madness. He'd give it another day. He'd hear something soon. After all, Charlie Fowler was too frugal to miss a flight.

Back at the airport, the plane landed and passengers streamed off, heading for reunions with friends and family. Suitcases spilled onto the baggage carousel. Missing from the pile were two oversize duffels scheduled for this flight, each carrying a yellow Mountain Madness luggage tag with the owner's name attached. Also absent were the owners of those bags, whose names had been called several times at the gate in Denver before the jetway door had been closed.

"Passengers Christine Boskoff and Charlie Fowler, please report to the gate immediately for final boarding."

SEATTLE, WASHINGTON. JOYCE FELD KNEW her daughter. She called without fail when her far-flung travels were finished and she was heading home. This time, the phone had been ominously quiet. Reaching Mark at the Mountain Madness office in Seattle, Joyce received a glimmer of reassurance and a couple of theories. Perhaps they'd done an extra climb or gotten off the last mountain later than planned. Mark vowed to let her know immediately when he received word from her daughter. The bear from Chris still sat on her couch, his expression inscrutable.

Mountain Madness had been here before, though the circumstances were different. Ten years earlier, in 1996, the media glare had been intense. Company founder Scott Fischer had done everything he could to promote the expedition to Mount Everest. The regular electronic dispatches had allowed minute-by-minute coverage, including the tragic outcome that had taken Scott's life. Mark thought back to those fateful hours with the media horde stationed outside the office waiting for news. Today's technology was light-years beyond that, and the players were different, of course. Charlie and Chris were more interested in taking adventures as quietly as they possibly could.

It was December 6. Having heard nothing from Chris, Mark asked his office manager to call the airlines to see if Charlie and Chris had been on their scheduled flights. Perhaps they'd missed their connections and been unable to make calls. He got on the phone himself, checking with a few friends to see if they'd heard from the couple. By December 8, the Mountain Madness emergency procedures manual sat open on Mark's desk, and the US Consulate in Chengdu, China, had received a missing person's report.

DAVE JONES HAD COME ON as the chair of the board of Mountain Madness after Scott passed away. Chris had always been clear about having him help build a business that could "support her habit." As a serial entrepreneur, Dave understood the hunger that drove people to achieve their dreams. He'd worked to help grow the company and set up systems that weren't intuitive for a staff that preferred the outdoors to spreadsheets. His demeanor was as calm as his 6'4" presence was commanding. Getting ahead of the media, Mark reached out to Dave for guidance. Chris's persona wasn't as large as Scott's, but a decade later, his death remained a pivotal event in the mountaineering community. Mark wanted to be prepared for whatever was ahead.

Dave's office was located in a high-rise in downtown Seattle, with views overlooking the ferry docks and Elliott Bay. He listened intently as Mark ran through the past few days, the steps they'd taken, and the assumption that news would break shortly that the owner of Mountain Madness was missing in China. Taking in each detail, Dave grew increasingly worried. Though steady by nature, he felt his stomach turn as he listened to the information Mark laid out.

"What the hell?" Dave said. "Didn't she give you her travel details, Mark?" He stepped toward the window and stared out at the bay.

Mark's eyes were heavy with concern after several sleepless nights. "Listen . . . I'm not her travel agent. Nor her husband. She gave me a general idea that she'd be home by Christmas and that's all I needed."

"And no itinerary?"

Mark bristled at the accusation that he should have known where they were, and now felt irritation mixed with panic. "No, Dave, come on. You know how the two of them travel. This isn't exactly checking into a Holiday Inn." He was certain Chris and Charlie didn't know where they'd be going each day. "They were probably staying in guesthouses. Or in the homes of people they met on the street."

"I know," said Dave. "I know you're right. They're unconventional. Chris has always been this way. The two of them together, even more so."

"Also this is a fucking personal trip," Mark mumbled. "I don't ask other employees to tell me where they're staying and what they're seeing when they go on vacation."

"Fair enough. This is how she does it. She just prefers to go—"

"Remote," Mark interrupted.

"Beyond just remote, Mark. Way beyond that," said Dave. "She prefers to go to the edge of the map." He sat down in his desk chair. To his right lay a pile of client files he suddenly knew would remain untouched. As chair of the board, it was his responsibility to drop everything and focus on bringing Chris home. "We've gotta find them," he said. "It has to be possible."

Dave offered his office as a command center of sorts, with its conference room, huge whiteboard, and extra phone lines. "It's more space to breathe," he said. "Your staff doesn't need to be around what might hit the fan."

"Can do," said Mark. "I can get things together and be back down here in a few hours."

"And Mark," offered Dave, "bring a string of prayer flags. The room is going to need a little . . . life."

BY THE EVENING OF DECEMBER 8, the staff at Mountain Madness was consumed. Desperate to find clues to Chris's whereabouts, they turned to email messages she'd sent from China. A few discussed the upcoming spring trip to Everest. One mentioned the staff holiday party. Another . . . Genyen.

At 3:09 a.m. Seattle time on December 9, Mountain Madness requested help in China. The subject line of the email message read simply, "I need your help." It asked a well-known Chinese mountaineer for assistance in finding information about Chris and Charlie, who were presumed to have gone to the Genyen area. The Chinese climber worked diligently, and ten hours later he responded. He'd checked personally with the chief of the last village before Genyen, who reported that no Western climbers had passed through in recent weeks.

On December 11, an official from the US Consulate in Chengdu wrote Mark. He'd elevated the issue and asked the Foreign Affairs Office to coordinate a search with the local Public Security Bureau (PSB) in Litang. This would include stopping at guesthouses, Lenggu Monastery, and bus stations. If anyone had seen Chris and Charlie, they'd report back.

In the early morning hours of December 13, the lead went dead. The consular official wrote back, indicating that "the Foreign Affairs Office and the PSB say that so far the search teams have not found evidence that Chris and Charlie stayed in Litang. They checked guesthouses and other places foreigners would commonly visit in Litang and also visited Zhangna, Lamaya, and Lenggu Monastery." In fact, though, the monks at Lenggu never received such a visit—a reality that would remain unknown for several weeks. A lie manufactured by the PSB had just derailed the search for Chris and Charlie.

MARK AND DAVE STARED AT the whiteboard in the conference room. One row was labeled "Communications/Command" and another labeled "Action." Email messages had been printed and taped to the wall in an attempt to trace a coherent path. A week had passed since Chris and Charlie were due back. Mark had spoken with Charlie's friend Damon in Telluride who'd turned up similar but inconclusive email messages from Charlie, all sent in early November.

"We're not getting anywhere," said Mark. He'd tried to look slightly more professional in Dave's fancy downtown office, but after a day of frustration, his shirt was untucked and his weariness apparent.

"Agreed," replied Dave. He pushed back from the table, arms crossed. "I don't think it's right to rely on the Chinese to figure this out for us. We need someone on the ground there. One of ours."

Mark considered this strategy. "Well, if we go down that road, there's a cost, literally and figuratively, and we both know it. If we start our own search effort, well . . . I'm not saying I'm opposed, in fact, I'm in favor of it. Just saying we should be ready for the long haul." A search like this would involve the kind of emotional and financial expenditure that Mark knew Chris would be horrified by. "For doing this right. Because you and I both know the reality, Dave. The reality of a recovery operation versus a rescue operation."

Dave tapped his pen against a yellow legal pad on the table. "I realize that," he said, "but we're knee deep in this now. Her mother is desperate and it's amazing the news hasn't hit the mainstream media yet. We can figure out the financial piece. So let's just kick this around a bit. Who've we got over there?"

Mark leaned into his elbows on the table. One of Dave's colleagues walked by, peeking in the glass doors of the conference room and giving a weak smile.

In addition to a few local guides, Jon Otto, a business partner of Mountain Madness, lived in Chengdu. The American ran a climbing school and knew the mountains in Sichuan better than anyone. Problem was, he was currently stateside with his wife and their brand new baby girl.

"I imagine he can help us with logistical support, though. Involve his climbing staff. That sort of thing. I've got a call in to him," said Mark.

"It's something. Let's bring him on board. Anyone else? You got anyone else in spitting distance over there who climbs, speaks Chinese, and would be willing to search for a needle in a haystack?" Dave leaned back, certain Mark would never come up with an individual fitting these requirements.

Mark raised his eyebrows and crossed his arms over his chest. He knew Dave wasn't ready for what was coming next. "I do. I've got someone."

"You're kidding?"

"I'm not." Mark hit the speakerphone button on the conferencing system and dialed the main number for Mountain Madness. The office manager picked up, her voice anxious when she realized it was him. He answered her questions, then got right to his.

"No, no, nothing more new from here. But I need a favor. Will you go into my Rolodex and get me a number. For Ted. That's right. Ted Callahan. In Kyrgyzstan."

COLORADO AVENUE IN TELLURIDE BUSTLED with the winter ski crowd. It was December 15, and tourists strolled up and down the main drag, getting a jump on the holiday. Inside a real-estate office in the middle of town, Damon Johnston looked up from his laptop. Another three people had entered, each wondering if they could help. The conference room he was working from had been turned into a war room, a virtual mirror image of the setting in Seattle a thousand miles away. A mess of papers, maps, a constantly ringing cell phone, and old coffee cups cluttered the farmhouse-style conference table. Huge windows looked out over the box canyon at the end of town.

"Nothing more to do at the moment, I'm sorry to report," Damon said. "Just in a holding pattern." The group asked a few more questions he couldn't answer. Was there someone else they might have left word with? Was there any news on whether they'd obtained a climbing permit? Wasn't it possible that they were just delayed or had lost track of the date?

Damon's responses were not satisfying. Deflated, the group left as his phone rang again. It was Chris's friend Julie Hodson, checking in for an update. Damon told her what they knew, then asked her questions that had already been asked and answered.

"It's making us crazy that we can't find anything more," he said. "You said you heard from her, but nothing definitive, right?"

"Right. Just a quick email saying they were going on one last easy climb," Julie responded.

"Easy, huh? That could mean *genuinely* easy or it could mean . . . "

"It could mean *Chris and Charlie* easy," Julie finished. "Which I realize could mean something totally different to the rest of us. I just can't imagine why they would've missed their flight. Could they have gotten in trouble with the Chinese over the permit issue and been thrown in jail or something?"

"Not sure, but none of it is adding up, Jules. It's too close to Christmas, and she wouldn't do this to her mom. You know Joyce gets nervous about Chris being out there too long." Damon looked out the window at the people heading to happy hour. All of them seemed irritatingly carefree. They had not a thought in the world other than dinner plans and their next day on the slopes.

"I hear you. Let me call Joyce," Julie said. "We've got the Wisconsin connection, which has always been nice for us and maybe it'll be good for her to hear from someone she knows."

"Sounds good. Let's talk tomorrow unless something comes in from Mark tonight," Damon said. At thirty-four, he felt he had aged ten years in just the past week. This was the time of year he thought he'd be ice climbing with Charlie, not searching for him and certainly not stuck inside poring over topographic maps and incorporation documents. The Telluride operation had begun the process of establishing a nonprofit with a temporary umbrella entity to accept donations for the search. Operating under the name "Fowler Boskoff Search Committee," they'd received an initial infusion of cash from friends with which they planned to pay expenses alongside the funds raised by Mountain Madness.

Separated by distance and professional experiences, Mountain Madness's Seattle team and the Telluride team nonetheless sought the same outcome. Constant email messages and phone calls kept them in contact and sharing information as best they could. Joining the Telluride operation was Charlie's friend Keith Brown, a broker's agent at the real-estate agency. With experience both in business relations with China and in military operations, Brown's skill set was well matched to the effort. Organized and disciplined, he was released from his tasks at the real-estate agency and was soon working 24/7 on the search.

In the conference room/command center, Brown walked to the over-size maps of western Sichuan that had been posted on the wall. Charlie's friend Joel had just accompanied law enforcement to Charlie's house in Norwood, breaking in and retrieving Charlie's laptop, hoping to find further clues to their whereabouts.

"Let's talk about where we're at, Damon. The information from Charlie's computer yielded that bit about the Deqin area, yes?"

"Right, yes . . . the intent was somewhat clear," said Damon. "It's an unnamed peak, west side of the Yunnan–Tibet Highway." He had given this intel to Jon Otto, along with directions to send some of his guys to Litang. The consulate told them that they hadn't found anything, but it couldn't hurt to follow up, and Mountain Madness agreed. After all, Chris's email to Mark pointed to Genyen.

Brown looked over his notes and back at the map. "As far as activity on the ground," he said, "we've got that Aussie named Kara in Chengdu who I found. Totally random, but the info she gave us was solid." He had sent out a message to what looked like an expat listserv in Chengdu, saying they were looking for a couple of missing Western climbers. "I guess she was up for a bit of a thrill," Brown said, "because she saw it and nibbled."

It was a big break, especially at the holidays. Kara Jenkinson had seen the message and gone to a backpacker hotel called the Traffic Hotel to check. She'd suspected Chris and Charlie might have stayed there a month ago, which apparently they did. "Emailed me the details," said Brown. "I got back to her right away. Asked her what she wanted for Christmas if she helped us. She said I sounded desperate."

"I'm sure you did," said Damon.

"She seems nice, organized. Zero climbing experience, but I figure Callahan is on his way now and when they meet up, it'll be a decent ground team." Kara spoke Chinese, which was critical. "No way we're getting anywhere without a few people there who speak Chinese," Brown said. "This thing is a fucking train wreck and we need people who understand China and the bureaucracy." He walked back to the table, slumping into one of the chairs and expressed more frustration about Chris and Charlie not getting a climbing permit.

"That's just how Charlie rolls," Damon said. "Permits in China are so damn expensive."

"The whole 'mountains are for everyone' deal," said Brown. "I understand that mentality. Hell, he's a friend of mine, too. It's just . . . if you're not gonna get a permit, be a little more clear about where you're going, ya know? Tell someone. I just wish he would've told one of us . . . " His voice trailed off.

"It's not useful to talk about this now, right?" Damon said. They'd give Charlie hell for it when he got home.

They went over remaining details before their regularly scheduled afternoon update calls with Charlie's sister Ginny, Mountain Madness, and Joyce. Hoping to elevate the awareness level within the Chinese government, the groups were working with inside contacts, including senators, former and current governors, and the US ambassador to China. Both the Seattle and Telluride operations had assigned media reps to handle the expected press blitz. Brown was working on the possibility of MI-17 helicopter flyovers of whatever mountains they narrowed the search to.

Brown had also contacted a local physician with expertise in high-altitude medicine, Dr. Peter Hackett, to develop survival timelines. "He'll get those to us right away in case we're looking at a high mountain rescue scenario. It'll address specific periods of time Chris and Charlie could survive with or without water or snow melt." Brown looked up from his notes and saw Damon staring blankly out the window. A moment passed, both men silent and uninterested in filling the space with words.

Finally Damon spoke. "They're alive. I know they're alive."

"Listen, there's no evidence that they're *not* alive," Brown said. "Until there is, we proceed. Expeditiously. Carefully. I'm not focused on anything except bringing them home, Damon."

Damon's eyes welled up, concentrating on Brown's resolve to keep himself together. He couldn't think about the worst-case scenario. Not yet. There was so much climbing left with Charlie and just as much with Chris. The three of them were a team and just getting started.

Brown dialed the number in Wisconsin and Joyce picked up the phone on the first ring, her thick, eighty-year-old Midwestern accent illuminating the conference room through the speakerphone. Damon, who'd been prepared to answer her questions, felt his emotions bubbling back to the surface at the sound of her voice. He shook his head at Brown.

Taking the cue, Brown jumped in, ready to soften another brutal call. "Joyce! How are things in good ole Appleton this afternoon?"

CHAPTER 19

SEARCHING

CHENGDU, CHINA. ONE WEEK FROM Christmas, this wasn't what Kara Jenkinson had envisioned. Her plan after nearly two years working at an NGO in Sichuan was to spend the holidays somewhere warm and tropical with her sister. Instead, she'd offered to help in the search for two Western climbers after reading a plea from their friends in Telluride—people she didn't know, much less care about. Still, she'd been in need of help herself in situations like this. Lost in China trying to navigate the complexities of Chinese protocol.

Plus, she loved a good mystery. At twenty-nine, she knew the value of being flexible. Her time in China had taught her that her experience there would be only as positive as the opportunities she was open to.

After talking to Keith Brown, Kara had established that Chris and Charlie had stayed in Chengdu, then traveled west eight hours to the city of Kangding. She'd bought three oversize maps of the provinces in China where searchers were focusing. Yunnan, Sichuan, Tibet. Finally, she searched for a proper communications center. Like the operations in Telluride and Seattle, she didn't need much more than a large table, decent Wi-Fi, and a few people who'd be understanding enough to loan her space.

Grandma's Kitchen fit the bill. The expat hangout served burgers, fries, salad, and pizza. There were comfortable chairs and the walls were covered with silly drawings of deer and flowers. It felt homey. Kara had exactly one day to prepare for the arrival of a guy named Ted Callahan who was going to help with the search. She wasn't sure what sort of venue he'd be expecting, but this would have to do.

As it turned out, Callahan had plenty of years in China under his belt. Arriving at Grandma's after his travels from Kyrgyzstan, he shook Kara's hand, then glanced at the menu. "Ah, bottomless cups of coffee. Awesome. This place is gonna work just fine, I think."

It was December 17.

ONE DAY TURNED INTO TWO and then three. Pencil marks were scattered all over the maps on tables at Grandma's. Kara and Callahan worked nonstop, in constant communication with Seattle, Telluride, and the Chinese/Tibetan search teams that Jon Otto had sent into the western reaches of China. The hunt to determine where Chris and Charlie had climbed was maddening, with no genuine information coming from the field. The teams had been thwarted by dead ends and misinformation. Making matters worse, the Chinese police officers assigned to support them seemed apathetic. The potential embarrassment for the Chinese meant they'd tried hard to shift blame and wish the situation away.

Kara closed her eyes briefly as Callahan talked over the list of items they wanted to cover with the consular officer who they were due to meet with that afternoon. Sleep had become secondary to making sure the information chain was fully functioning. The time difference between Chengdu and the United States wasn't allowing any of them a decent night of rest.

"Wait, what did you say? I missed that. Say that last one again," Kara said, opening her eyes. Her ponytail had come undone in the course of the day, leaving strands of auburn hair hanging along the side of her face.

"I said that I think we need to level with him about the frustrations we're having here," Callahan said.

"With the PSB, you mean?"

"The PSB. The Foreign Affairs Office, all of it," Callahan answered. "They're taking down the Missing Persons posters as fast as we can put them up. They're unresponsive and seem completely uninterested in the fact that a couple of climbers have evaporated in their country.

We've got our own guys on the ground working independently and going door-to-door, but we need more help from the Chinese to get this going."

"It's delicate, Ted, you know that," Kara said. "You know exactly how this works. If this blows up, they're at risk of losing face. Obviously they'd rather the whole thing would just—"

"Go away?" Callahan blurted.

"Yes. Go away. We've got climbers invested in this now, too. Chinese. Tibetan. Let's tread lightly. I want Daliu in on some of these conversations. Asu, too." Daliu and Asu were Chinese climbers who'd been deployed by Jon Otto to help the cause. Though Kara and Callahan spoke decent Mandarin, it was Daliu and Asu who were instrumental in smoothing over relations with the local Chinese officials in the villages the search party visited.

"Smoothing over" was harder than they'd hoped.

TWO HOURS LATER, THE MEETING with the American consular officer was over. Far from buttoned-up, the meeting had been casual. The officer seemed inexperienced but enthusiastic. Showing up in sweaty soccer gear after a club practice, he'd come with his Chinese girlfriend in a BMW. Ordering a beer at a pub near Grandma's Kitchen, he complained endlessly about life in China and apologized that the consulate had been short-staffed at the holidays. It was December 20 and much of the consular division had flown to the States or taken time off.

"This whole thing sounds like a total shit show," he said. "Why people go to such extreme lengths to find excitement is way beyond me, but what the hell do I know? I'm just a bureaucrat with a lame post in China."

Callahan and Kara patiently provided a thirty-minute update on the search, ending with their challenges and a list of requests for help.

"I'll tell you straight up, the fact that they didn't get a permit is a bitch," the consular officer reported. His girlfriend sidled up next to him, trying to follow the conversation. "I can understand why they flew under the radar, though. These mountains are easy to access, and getting a permit is pricey. Plus the permit requires you to invest in a liaison officer and a translator and then the costs skyrocket, isn't that right?" he asked.

Kara looked at Callahan, unaware of these ramifications.

"Yeah, something like that," Callahan said. "Plus, it just wasn't the way they liked to climb."

"Maybe not, dude, but I'm telling you the Chinese are probably not too pleased about it and this is part of the fallout. The stonewalling you're getting. They're probably just really fucking pissed that this hasn't disappeared yet."

It was exhausting, trying to get someone to care as much as they did.

"Right. I understand," Callahan said, "but I guess what we're saying is that we've tried to play nice. Now if you wouldn't mind leaning into them a bit. Perhaps let them know that CNN International is on the way."

The consular officer swallowed his last sip of beer. "No shit?!"

"Yeah," Callahan nodded. That ought to get things rolling.

"Airplay always does the trick," said the consular officer. "That and the fact that members of Congress are starting to hear about it. That should do it."

"We appreciate it," said Kara.

"No problem," he replied. "Let's be in touch. I hope you find them. Look like a really sweet couple." He glanced at the grainy photos on the Missing Persons poster. "Actually, one thing I might suggest is better pictures. Color. Close up. That'll help." Throwing a jacket over his shoulder, the consular officer took his girlfriend's hand and they headed out the door.

Kara looked at Callahan and laughed. It was the first real laugh in four days. "What was *that*?" she said.

"Amazing," Callahan guffawed. "That guy was straight out of a John le Carré novel!"

"Exactly. Okay, but here's what I'm getting after listening to him. I want us to stop for a minute. Can we do that? I keep coming back to Genyen, Ted. The PSB officers are dodgy and useless." Kara's eyes were tired but filled with conviction as she explained her point. "Why are we believing the Litang PSB officers who said they already searched the Genyen area? We're believing them over Christine. Her words. Her email said, 'We're going to Genyen.' How much more evidence do we need?"

The PSB claimed they had checked out Lamaya and Zhangna and even went to Lenggu Monastery looking for Charlie and Chris. Kara couldn't get the question out of her mind: "What if they're full of crap?" It was a thought that had been lost in the chaos of the past few days. With information flying as fast as they could keep up with it, the fact that the searchers may have been led to the wrong places based on faulty information had been overlooked.

"Valid point," Callahan agreed.

Freshly animated, Kara stood from the table and began pacing as she talked. "Also . . . we've been operating under the assumption that nobody saw them in any of these locations. Our search teams are out there asking around and nobody's talking. It's like they were invisible, but that's just ridiculous. Of course people saw them. They probably stuck out like sore thumbs. It's just that . . . "

She stopped and turned to Callahan. He looked at her intently, waiting for the conclusion to her thought. "There's no incentive," she said.

"Oh for fuck's sake, that's what we've been missing! There's no incentive," repeated Callahan.

"Damn right there's not. This is China. People aren't going to willingly talk to the police. They need something more. They need—"

"Money," Callahan interrupted. "We need a reward."

"Why the fuck haven't we offered a reward?" Kara yelled, throwing her hands in the air, causing customers to turn and stare.

"It didn't really hit me until now. Money talks and bullshit walks!" Callahan said.

Kara laughed and sat back down. Grabbing a notebook, she started scribbling calculations. "How much? What do you think would get this thing moving? Ten thousand yuan? Twenty thousand?"

"We're assuming that there's funding for this, yes?" Callahan asked.

"Fully. Look, we know the search committees have raised a ton of money already, and what are they spending it on? We're costing practically nothing here," Kara said. "The expenses for the search team members are tiny, and otherwise it's just the cost of our meals and tipping the waitresses every few hours."

Callahan was sure they'd greenlight it. "No doubt," he said. "What about thirty thousand? That is, what, roughly four thousand US dollars?" Kara did the math in her head. "A little less, but yeah. That's a solid number and totally feasible for us to request. For a lead that gets us directly to Chris and Charlie."

They would need a new Missing Persons poster. And clearer pictures of Charlie and Chris. Pictures that show the life in them. Callahan turned to his laptop. "I've got a few that Telluride and Seattle sent after we'd already printed that first round." A few clicks later, his screen filled with both images.

Chris in a red-and-black down jacket and a white Mountain Madness hat. She smiled broadly, and behind her were yellow tents, an indication that she was at base camp on one of her expeditions. Her complexion was rosy, from being so close to the sun. In a separate picture, Charlie looked directly at the camera from a few feet away. He wore a gray Mountain Madness polo and his hair was tousled. Never grinning in photos, he looked dashing and rugged, as if lifted out of the pages of a Patagonia ad.

Kara stepped over to look at the photos. They were the first she'd seen since the initial batch. Leaning toward the screen, she was captivated. These two people she'd known nothing about a few weeks ago had now become her entire life. "Spectacular. They both look like such ... forces. And you're friends with both of them, right?"

Callahan nodded, thinking back to his last moments with Chris in Russia. "Yeah. Charlie was probably my first real climbing hero. I totally look up to the guy. Don't know him as well as Chris, but respect the hell out of him. And Chris, well ... " he stumbled. After running on adrenaline for a week, the magnitude of what he was involved in was staring at him.

"Oh, Ted, I'm so sorry."

"It's okay. It's just a lot to take in, you know? Chris is fantastic. She's genuine and unvarnished and tough as they come. To a fault, sometimes. She just wants to climb. Gets her in trouble sometimes when she's leading clients who are slower than she is."

Callahan explained he had known Chris for six years or so and that she and Mark had hired him to work at Mountain Madness. "I lived in her basement one summer," he told Kara. "She offered me the space and the rent was a case of beer for the entire summer." That was right after Chris had started dating Charlie. "He barely said two words all summer," Ted added with a laugh.

"Not really known to be super chatty," he said. "One morning he got up and I offered him some coffee. He said yes and then started mumbling a long soliloquy about coffee as he went out to his car. Came back inside still mumbling about coffee and holding a mug. The thing looked about a hundred years old. I poured him a mug and he got in his car to go climb. Off he went. That's just . . . Charlie."

Kara laughed, the personalities of the couple sinking into her a bit further. "He's older, right? They aren't married? She was married before, wasn't she?"

"He's quite a bit older, yes. I think he's fifty-two or so and she's thirty-nine. Not married. Not sure if that's in the future for them or not. And yeah, she's a widow. Her husband Keith died in 1999. Suicide."

"Oh god."

"Awful, really. Nobody saw it coming. They'd bought Mountain Madness just a year before."

Kara had done enough homework over the past few days to connect the dots. She'd been a teenager when Scott Fischer had died on Everest but remembered the event and couldn't believe she was here, ten years later, helping piece together a related drama. "Where are they, Ted? Where the hell are they?"

The buzzing of Callahan's mobile phone interrupted their conversation. Picking it up, he looked at the caller ID. Kili Sherpa, Kathmandu.

"Go. Take it," Kara said. "I'll work on this new poster."

Stepping away from the table, Callahan walked to an alcove in Grandma's that provided a bit of privacy. Kili was a friend of his from years of mountaineering and trips to Nepal guiding for Mountain Madness. Knowing how much Kili adored Chris, he steeled himself for the call.

UNABLE TO HIDE HIS EMOTIONS, Kili was distraught. He'd been trying to get a visa to leave Nepal and come to China to join the search for Charlie and Chris, but had been unsuccessful. Now, he offered what he could, which was money. An infusion of several thousand US dollars for whatever was needed.

"What do you need, Ted? Gear? Travel expenses?"

"None of that, Kili. We're doing okay in the money department. We just need to find them, is all."

"It's too long. It's too long now. Her mother is waiting too long, Ted," Kili said in halting English.

Looking over his shoulder, Callahan made sure that Kara was out of earshot. She still had hope, but his was nearly depleted and Kili understood. "It's best you don't come anyway, Kili. You don't want to be here. We'll find them, but I don't want you here when that happens."

Silence occupied the space between Kathmandu and Chengdu. Callahan heard Kili softly crying. His friend, a Sherpa from Nepal, had become a superstar in the mountaineering business thanks to his grit, but also because of Chris.

"I want you to use it for puja," Kili said. "The money I'll send you. Use it for puja when you find them." He could barely talk, but Callahan felt his friend's resolve.

"I'll do that, Kili. I promise." Ending the call, Callahan felt the need for fresh air. He stepped out into the biting, moonless night in Chengdu.

SEVERAL HOURS LATER, CUSTOMERS AT Grandma's slowly departed. For another night, Kara and Callahan had the place practically to themselves. Tonight they'd been joined by Daliu and Asu. The two climbers had been out in western China over the past week and were back in Chengdu to regroup, leaving a few teams still scattered and searching.

The four of them stood over the maps Kara had bought. Each was marked with different colors to indicate places searched and places yet to travel. The Genyen Valley seemed a logical focus once again. And though they needed a thumbs-up from Telluride and Seattle to offer the reward money, the new posters were ready for distribution.

Daliu stepped away, taking a call from one of his team members. A moment later he was back, breaking into the conversation at the table. "I've got something! Listen. One of my guys got something!" He handed the phone to Kara.

Callahan, Asu, and Daliu froze as Kara spoke rapidly in Mandarin. Hearing only one side of the conversation, the news felt promising. "Right. Yes. I understand. So you took it, yes? Okay good. Make a copy and email it to us. Can you do that right away? Tell me again what the wording was?" Kara hugged the phone to her ear, indicating with hand signals that she needed a pen and paper.

Callahan frantically ripped a page out of his notebook and handed her a pen.

"Thank you. Nice work. Yes, I'll get back to you." She hung up the phone, staring at what she'd written. "One of the guys found a note in a guestbook at a place in Litang. Charlie and Chris were there. They signed it. On November 9."

"You knew it!" Callahan shouted. He thumped his fists on the table. "About goddamn time. What did it say?" he asked.

Kara looked over her Chinese characters, translating into English. "It said, 'Great food and people! Enjoyed the food. The mountains around Yading are awesome. Countryside reminds us of home. We'll be back." It was signed "Chris Boskoff and Charlie Fowler. Norwood, Colorado, USA."

"My god," Kara said. "They were there. Litang." She beamed at the assurance that her hunch had been correct.

"Hell, we don't need any more than this," Callahan said. "All of our guys need to be redeployed to Litang. Immediately. As in . . . tonight. Can we make that happen?"

Daliu and Asu nodded. Pulling out their phone lists, they moved away to adjoining tables and began making calls.

"What time is it in the United States?" Kara asked.

Barely 6:00 a.m. in Seattle and 7:00 in Telluride, it was too early to call. "But we can email and then as soon as they're awake, they'll call us," Callahan said.

"All right, you take Seattle and I'll take Telluride?" Kara said.

Divvying up the communication, Callahan was anxious to do more. "I can't sit around Chengdu any longer. Not with this kind of solid lead."

"I agree," Kara said. "First thing in the morning. Take Asu with you. Daliu is wiped out from the past week. I'll keep him here with me."

They had a plan. Callahan would get as far as Kangding the next day. On his own, he'd be prepared to go straight to Litang, fourteen hours of driving, with serious elevation gain. But he hesitated, suspecting he'd be traveling with the CNN crew. "They're gonna need to ascend a little more gradually," he told Kara.

"Oh god, you're right. They've got their claws into this now. They'll want to go with you, but they have no clue what they're in for." She knew that an ascent that quick could be wicked.

Callahan and Kara typed out email messages to Mark Gunlogson and Keith Brown in Seattle and Telluride, respectively, hitting send at the same moment.

LITANG, CHINA. IN HIS COLD-WEATHER gear, Callahan stood with several of the local climbers who'd been a part of the search for Chris and Charlie. The group had agreed to help the CNN crew get images more dramatic than just scenes of door knocking or phone calls. The caravan had arrived in Litang that day, December 22. Now they were on the outskirts of town, with heavy packs and making staged stops to speak with Tibetan yak herders.

The images of a search in this remote part of the world were at odds with those that Americans had seen for the past week. A trio of climbers had been lost on Mount Hood in Oregon. The coverage was nonstop with a search and rescue that involved scores of volunteers, a mass of aircraft, and professional rescue staff. A far cry from the effort in Litang, which consisted of three laptops, four mobile phones, and two dozen Chinese and Tibetan climbers.

"This is outrageous," Callahan muttered. He'd just gotten directions from the CNN crew to look into the tents of local herders. The act felt intrusive.

The group took the short drive back to Litang. There was an evening conference call with Kara to attend to. Several issues needed to be addressed. Callahan made mental notes as the minivan pulled up to the guesthouse. First was to report that reward signs had been posted around town. This meant diplomatic pressure from the US Consulate had been felt and the consular officer was due a thank-you, perhaps another beer when Callahan got back to Chengdu.

Then there was the matter of Chinese sensitivity to the use of the word "Tibetan" in the CNN reporting. They definitely needed to avoid pissing off the Chinese right now. And the CNN crew was a mess. The rise to nearly thirteen thousand feet had taken a toll. While Callahan and the locals felt fine, the CNN reporter, John Vause, his producer, and the cameraman were suffering from altitude sickness and diarrhea.

He'd also want to talk to Kara about other incoming film crews. The clusterfuck this could become made him cringe. They'd need a way to hold other media outlets at bay.

An hour later, Callahan listened with disbelief as she filled him in on the day's events. The reward posters had done the trick, and a driver had come forward in Litang. Ji'an had approached police with the news that he'd hosted Chris and Charlie in his home for several nights, then dropped them off in the village of Lamaya. They'd also left luggage.

"We've gotta get our hands on their bags," Callahan said.

"I've been trying all day," Kara reported. "The police aren't being, shall we say, agreeable."

Callahan was not surprised. "These are the same police that probably never looked for Chris and Charlie in the first place. This entire mess could have been handled a week ago if they'd done their damn job."

"I'll call our guy one more time at the consulate," Kara offered.

"Today, if you can. Call his mobile phone. I know it's late, but it's December 22 and tomorrow is a Saturday." They needed them to put pressure on before Christmas hit. "How are the families doing?"

"Keith and Mark say they're fair," Kara said. "Trying to focus on the news we're giving them. Keeping hope alive, I think."

"They've been through drama like this with Charlie before and he always comes back. Thinking anything different now would feel foreign, I'm sure," Callahan said.

"Yeah, I imagine it would. How's it going with CNN?" Kara asked. They'd had a few nights of coverage on Anderson Cooper's show.

Callahan laughed. "Best way to describe it is that they look like they're on an epic bender." The CNN team had taken a lot of strikes: GI problems, unheated hotel rooms, and terrible food. The search and rescue wasn't providing enough glitz for them, and the conditions in Litang were absolute misery. The altitude was not agreeing with them.

"They're wearing these big, puffy down coats with fur hoods and Vause just keeps sinking into his a little further every day," he said. "Completely puffy and retaining water. Cold and crabby. Look like hell."

"Did you dose them with Diamox?" Kara asked.

"Yup. Did that, but they just need to descend. I'm going to advise them to head back to Chengdu in the morning. I think they'll jump at that recommendation."

IT WAS DECEMBER 23, 2006. The Litang Public Security Bureau had put up a twenty-four-hour fuss but ultimately relented, allowing Callahan to come to the station to open Chris and Charlie's duffels. Approaching the station, he bristled. The PSB hadn't provided any help whatsoever in the search, but it was clear from talking to Kara that they were now trying to claim they had.

The officer assigned to him smelled like smoke. A ring of keys on his belt loop jingled, echoing off the cold, marble floors. Deep red doors lined the hallway, each leading to rooms for inspections, interrogations, or meetings. Hanging above each door were signs with dark blue words in both Mandarin and Tibetan. Han Chinese were in charge here, but Callahan knew that to get this job done, he'd need local Tibetan climbers.

The officer led Callahan around a corner and into a large conference room with bad lighting. There, in the middle of the room, were the duffels.

GENYEN WAS A CERTAINTY. CHRIS'S words had been true from the beginning. Opening her duffel and reading her journal had been confirmation. After phoning Kara, Callahan turned his attention to the Tibetan driver. Ji'an appeared shaken as he was brought into a separate room at the police station. He was dressed in layers to guard against the cold. A head of thick, black hair fell over his ears. Smiling weakly when he saw Callahan, the lines around his eyes deepened.

An interpreter entered, sitting between them to translate the Tibetan to a mix of Mandarin and English for Callahan to understand. The interpreter briefly explained to Ji'an that Callahan was a friend of the missing climbers and had a couple of things to ask. Few questions remained, though even the smallest of details mattered—if not for the search, then for the families.

Over a few minutes, Callahan's picture of Charlie and Chris's last few days in Litang came into focus. Ji'an talked about the time he and his wife had spent with the couple, what the pair ate, and how he drove them to see sights around town. He described their laughter and their excitement about climbing. When Callahan began with questions about the plan for their return, Ji'an slowed his answers. He appeared nervous around the interpreter and answered with brevity.

From the few words, it became clear why he appeared so tired. After not receiving the call from Charlie and Chris that he'd expected, Ji'an and his wife began to worry. He tried to go about his normal life, but one day he saw the signs with their photos. He was illiterate, unable to understand that a reward was attached to information about their disappearance, but he approached police anyway. An interrogation at the police station led to a search at his house. A crime scene, with police collecting hair samples and demanding the bags.

And then, Ji'an said, he refused.

"He refused to give the police the bags?" Callahan clarified with the interpreter. He looked at Ji'an, a proud and poor Tibetan man with everything to lose and nothing to gain from standing up to the Chinese PSB. Ji'an averted his eyes.

"Yes, that's right," the interpreter said. "He said the police came several times to demand them, but he didn't want to give them up. He said his wife was crying because your friends had been gone too long."

"But why?" Callahan asked. "Why didn't he just turn the bags over right away?"

The interpreter spoke a moment, then waited as Ji'an provided the response. Outside the doors, Callahan heard sirens from the parking lot. He leaned forward to catch the translation.

"He says he and his wife still believed they would get the call to come pick them up. He says your friends had become like children to them and they just wanted them to come back."

Callahan and Ji'an stared at each other, no questions left and both anxious to leave. Walking past the conference room on the way out, the contents of Chris and Charlie's duffels were being put back together for shipment to the US Consulate, then on to the families. Pieces of their lives still scattered on the marble floor.

CHAPTER 20

ANSWERS

IT WAS CHRISTMAS MORNING.

In Telluride, Keith Brown was exhausted. His business as a real-estate agent had suffered, along with his home life, since he'd been virtually absent for two weeks straight. The only people he'd had significant contact with were members of the search team.

In Seattle, Mark Gunlogson opened presents between cups of eggnog but felt constantly pulled to email for updates. His two daughters, both under five years old, tried to get their father's attention without luck.

In Chengdu, Kara Jenkinson took a break from Grandma's Kitchen. A friend invited her for Christmas dinner, and while the party carried on all around her, she fell fast asleep on the couch, her mobile phone resting in her hand. Meanwhile, the CNN International team had returned to Chengdu and filed their report, which aired its grim assessment.

No one knows how long they've been in trouble; at least a month, maybe more. A local mountain guide says it would be almost impossible to survive. Still, this against-all-odds search will continue for the next few days in one of the most remote and isolated places on earth.

After spending Christmas Eve in the village of Lamaya, packing supplies to be carried on horseback, Ted Callahan and a team of twelve mostly Tibetan searchers, began the ten-mile hike to Lenggu Monastery at the base of Mount Genyen. Walking in relative silence, the group followed a well-worn trail. The route had been used by Tibetan pilgrims for centuries as their path to the sacred mountain, and along the way Callahan and his group passed three such pilgrims. With each step, they would stop, drop fully prostrate, then stand and repeat the process.

The path gradually rose 900 meters. The terrain was rocky, the color of the hills drained to a pale brown. In the distance, a jumble of gorgeous mountains loomed. It was a massive collection of peaks above nineteen thousand feet, and Callahan imagined being there in better circumstances, just as Charlie and Chris had been, for pure pleasure. He tugged on his backpack straps, impressed with Chris's fortitude in coming on this trip after back-to-back expeditions to Elbrus and then to Cho Oyu.

Approaching a small settlement in the valley, the team met a yak herder who looked at a photo and remembered Chris and Charlie from weeks before. He described seeing them videotape each other along the way. Narrowing in on their goal, the team camped for the night an hour below the monastery.

The next morning, the day after Christmas now, Callahan's hiking poles grazed the dirt as he took steps closer to the monastery. Walking the last hour to Lenggu, the team had run into three Tibetans who'd been sent to Genyen by Jon Otto a few days earlier. They reported that the monks at Lenggu had seen Chris and Charlie on November 12, and that the Chinese police hadn't visited the monastery until December 23. Another puzzle piece snapped into place, sending a moment of nausea through Callahan's entire being. As the tips of his poles marked the path, he felt dread mixed with resolve. Looking around at the vastness of Genyen Valley, he finally accepted that the goal of finding Chris and Charlie alive and bringing them home had changed to simply bringing them home.

To the left, a riverbed wove out of the thin forest. Head down, Callahan began planning the directives he'd give his climbers later that day. *If you find a body, leave it undisturbed. In peace. Take pictures. Record your coordinates. Return to camp immediately.* As his plan became clear, Callahan looked up, momentarily stunned. Lenggu

Monastery rose from the valley floor just ahead of him. Set against glorious, rugged peaks, it looked as if it had been picked out of a dream. The outside walls of the monastery were humble. White, weathered stone set off with crimson pillars. The roof was speckled with gold columns and ornate wood carvings. Surrounding the monastery were dozens of smaller structures, presumably homes for monks.

Knowing Chris and Charlie as he did, not one piece of this picture was out of place. The valley, the mountains, and this remote monastery—every part was the essence of both.

Approaching the monastery, the team met the two monks who'd spoken to their colleagues the day before. Callahan went inside with them, accompanied by Kelsang, one of his climbers, who interpreted from Tibetan into Chinese. The monks wore thick, quilted red jackets over their robes. Sitting in the reading room, they poured yak butter tea as Callahan clarified what he already suspected. Yes, they confirmed, Charlie and Chris had been vague about their plans, simply pointing north of the monastery when asked where they intended to climb.

"Kelsang," Callahan asked, "can you ask the monks if they planned to return to the monastery? And also, snow. Can you ask about the snowfall before and during their visit?"

Conferring with each other, the monks nodded, sizing up Callahan with his Western gear and entourage of a dozen Tibetans waiting outside. Turning to the interpreter, they talked back and forth, recounting the details. Callahan strained to understand the Tibetan, but it was uselessly dissimilar from Mandarin.

"They said your friends indicated they'd be back in four days and would visit the monastery on their way out of the valley," Kelsang reported. "I'm not sure how they communicated that, but that's what they say."

"Four days, okay. Well clearly that never happened," Callahan said. "What about the snowfall?"

"Yes. There was snow when they arrived," Kelsang confirmed. "They say it kept snowing for three days. A total of twenty-three centimeters."

Callahan shifted on the cushion beneath him. Twenty-three centimeters—just about nine inches—wasn't a dumping by Himalayan standards, but the patterns and terrain of the mountains here were unknown to almost all Western climbers. Outside the door to the reading room, he could make out the nearby peak of Genyen, completely blanketed in white. From the proximity of the monastery, the monks were regular spectators to the power of the mountains. At over twenty-thousand feet, Mount Genyen provided a constant source of inspiration and danger. Depending on the winds and time of day, the monks would recognize the familiar sound of an avalanche's beginnings, a muted *whump* or perhaps a striking crack.

"I imagine the monks can hear avalanches from the monastery," Callahan said to Kelsang. "Can you ask them if twenty-three centimeters was enough snow to trigger an avalanche in these parts?"

It was a question Callahan hadn't needed to ask. He already knew the answer and braced for it.

"Yes," Kelsang said softly. "They say it was enough snow. Enough for frequent avalanches."

ACCORDING TO BRUCE TREMPER, AUTHOR of *Staying Alive in Avalanche Terrain*, it is nearly impossible to survive such an event. He described of his own experience:

It was like being stuck in a giant washing machine filled with snow. Hat and mittens, instantly gone. Snow went everywhere: down my neck, up my sleeves, down my underwear—even under my eyelids, something I would have never imagined. With every breath, I sucked in a mixture of snow and air that instantly formed a plug in my mouth and down into my throat. I coughed it out, but the next breath rammed my throat full of snow again. Just when I needed to breathe the most, I couldn't—I was drowning, high in the mountains, in the middle of winter, and miles from the nearest body of water.

As snow roars downward, an initial slab breaks into larger blocks, gathering speed and catching victims at roughly ten miles an hour. Within five seconds, this speed increases to twenty-five miles an hour, making it impossible to hold onto anything. Most likely, victims are hurled against trees and over rocks, causing severe injury and eventually death. Though statistics vary, it's estimated that one-in-four avalanche victims in the United States dies from this type of trauma.

At the ten-second mark, an avalanche is traveling up to eighty miles an hour. As the avalanche slows, the victim has the opportunity to create a pocket of air around her mouth and nose through which to breathe. This can happen if she has enough consciousness to bury her mouth in the crook of her elbow. The timing of this is critical, as avalanche debris will begin to collect and solidify around her even before it has stopped moving completely. While creating an air pocket is essential, the victim is still in grave danger as the avalanche stops. Depending on the depth of her burial, the snowpack around her begins to harden, preventing fresh air from reaching her. The resulting lack of oxygen, however, is not the greatest concern. The more serious concern is the inhalation of carbon dioxide.

As the victim is frozen in place, continuing to exhale, the condensation from her breath saturates the area around her mouth and nose, creating an ice mask. Because ice is less permeable than snow, this mask results in an increase in her intake of carbon dioxide. With less oxygen combined with more carbon dioxide in the blood, it's a race against time. Hypercapnia—excessive carbon dioxide in the blood—causes faster and deeper breathing, anxiety, and impairment of mental function. She will eventually fall unconscious. Trapped in what feels like concrete, 90 percent of those completely buried and not killed by the trauma of the fall will be dead within thirty-five minutes, victims not of suffocation but of asphyxiation from their own deadly carbon dioxide.

Surviving an avalanche can depend on training, equipment, and sometimes plain-old luck. Beyond the physical sensation of being trapped, those who survive often describe the emotional aspect as unforgettable. When ski mountaineering guide Ken Wylie was hit by an avalanche in 2003, instinct and experience kicked in immediately. A shock wave ripped through his gut—he knew instantly what had gone wrong and where things were headed in the seconds to come. What followed was textbook avalanche science, but it was the emotional experience that became the lasting legacy for Ken. What he recalls most from that day is what few textbooks discuss.

As Ken lay trapped, completely buried, he experienced a sensation of weightlessness, as if in a "strangely protected cocoon." Though he had enough air space to survive until rescue, the sensation of being buried left him with a mixture of grief and looming panic:

> It was a feeling of total dread in which I knew the end result for others would be tragic. I knew my life had changed and I wasn't certain I was strong enough to deal with it. Though I was only conscious for a few minutes before I passed out, I went through a full body emotional experience. The avalanche forced me to stop and in the stillness, everything came to the surface. Every emotion I'd ever felt flooded through me. It was like taking a jigsaw puzzle and throwing the pieces into the air. Each piece in laser focus.
>
> It was all right there . . . a profound feeling of humility, deep spirituality, loneliness, regret, fear. Each emotion fleeting, but also completely accessible in a way that I'd never experienced before. I'd been unable in my life to live in the full expression of each emotion, and in the moments of being buried it was almost a feeling of comfort. I was finally able to recognize what was important and see my own truths.

Forty-five minutes passed until Ken Wylie was unburied. Slapped across the face by his clients, he took a breath and woke up.

"STAY SAFE OUT THERE," Callahan said. Five teams of two searchers each assembled around him in the early morning of December 27. "We all know our objectives. Everyone has a specific search area. It's important to stay in pairs and be back before sunset." Kelsang translated and the Tibetans nodded as each team walked in a different direction down the valley. Every assigned path up the face of Genyen was challenging. Climbing over fourteen thousand feet, the searchers scoured the mountain for signs of Chris and Charlie. By 4:00 p.m., Callahan and Asu's teams had returned without news. Then two more, also dejected.

Callahan looked over the barren landscape as 5:00 grew near. From a distance, the last team of Tibetan searchers approached camp. Trying to read their expressions, he came up short until they were just feet from him and he made eye contact with the youngest in the group. The eighteen-year-old spoke only a few words, his voice somber.

"He says he found a body," Kelsang translated.

Though he'd been prepared for the news, Callahan felt time slow down. He heard himself replying but felt disconnected from each word, as if he were listening to somebody else. After a few minutes of debriefing, he stepped away, retrieving his satellite phone from the duffel in his tent. Finding a quiet spot away from the group, Callahan lowered himself onto a boulder. Sunset had passed, leaving the crown of Genyen awash in alpenglow. He leaned over, an elbow on his knee and his hand resting on the five days of red-hued growth on his chin.

Kara answered immediately. He heard no background noise, and knew that Daliu had taken her to a peaceful sitting room in a nearby pub for distraction. As Callahan relayed the details, he imagined her taking in the news.

A crackle on the sat phone interrupted their conversation. "Ted . . . Ted can you hear me? Tell me again. I need you to tell me again. I want to understand." Overtired, she listened as he repeated the update. They'd found a body. They believed it was Charlie. No sign of Chris.

"But why . . . why didn't you find Chris?" Her voice was barely audible. Daliu noticed her eyes welling as she tried to keep herself composed.

"They weren't roped together, Kara," he said, his words barely registering. "The guys looked above and below Charlie, but they couldn't find her. There's snow here. Heaps. And it's going to continue tomorrow. But we'll go back. We'll bring Charlie down and look for her tomorrow. I brought equipment to probe for her body. She can't be far from Charlie."

"And you're sure it's Charlie they found?"

"I think so, but I won't know for sure until I get up there and we dig him out." Callahan looked at the photos on the digital camera the young team member had given him. Charlie's boots and gaiters were visible, backlit against the snow.

"Okay let me confirm what you've told me. The body was found at an altitude of 5,300 meters. Head and torso buried. Modern climbing equipment. Blue gaiters. Gray boots. Crampons," Kara said.

"That's right," Callahan said. "It's all I can give you now until we get him out tomorrow."

There was silence on Kara's end as she took notes. Callahan felt the weight of the phone in his hand, desperate to put it down and be alone.

"Do you have what you need for tomorrow, the supplies . . . ?" she trailed off. They'd need a body bag, but they never got one.

"We asked and they never provided it. We're gonna have to use a fucking tent fly."

Kara's head hurt from trying to keep it together. Daliu sat next to her, his hands clasped as he watched her.

"I need to call the consulate so they can contact the families," Callahan said, his voice quivering. Kara would call the States.

"Kara, this place is breathtaking. I've never seen anything like it. I know they were doing something they loved."

Ending the call, Kara turned to Daliu. He'd only heard half the conversation but needed nothing more. His eyes were full of sympathy. Kara put her head in her hands and took deep breaths, unashamed. After a minute, she looked up at Daliu. Tears dripping down her cheeks, she had calls to make.

"First, this," Daliu said. He passed her a shot of whiskey.

BACK AT GENYEN, CALLAHAN SPOKE briefly to the consulate. Though he knew this was part of their job, he apologized for burdening them with the task of notifying the families. Dinner was being prepared at the campfire as he walked back to his tent to put away the phone. A short distance over a ridge, he could see light coming from the monastery as evening worship started.

Sinking into his sleeping bag in the tent, Callahan was finally alone, unburdened by the tasks of managing, directing, searching, climbing, and wondering. Here, in this moment, he was just a man, emotions raw, weeping, grieving his friends.

SNOW FELL IN THICK FLAKES the next morning, December 28. Between six to eight inches had piled up overnight. Crossing the river, the entire team ascended a steep moraine to a series of flat benches under Genyen's northeast face. Two hours later, Callahan looked ahead and saw the basin containing the body. It lay directly under the summit around the 5,300-meter mark and showed significant avalanche activity. Tracks from the previous day had all but been washed away by more avalanches.

Carefully, Callahan and his team navigated the unstable snowpack. Hearing a *whump*, the team froze, making sure their traverse was still safe as small spindrift slides fell around them. When they reached the body, it was prone and Callahan could see that all limbs were at least partially exposed. The team of a dozen moved to a ridgeline a hundred meters from the body to assess.

"Look, it's not safe for all of us to walk into the avalanche zone," Callahan told Asu. "I think half the team should stay here on the ridgeline just in case another one comes down. There's no fucking need for all of us to be put in danger like that." Callahan and a handful of team members made their way down the ridge and over to Charlie's body. Snow fell steadily, coating their faces as they pulled rope and supplies from their packs.

Turning toward the mountain, Callahan looked up the narrow gully, its pitch roughly forty to fifty degrees. He imagined Chris and Charlie on a drive to establish high camp on the col before a straight shot to the summit the next day. The gully in which the frozen body lay was bounded by rock buttresses on either side, forcing anything that fell from above, whether snow, ice, or rocks, directly into the gully, acting as a funnel. He looked at Asu, who'd gotten to his knees, laying out the tent fly.

"Whatever it was hit fast," Callahan said. "They probably didn't see the cracks above them. This was the fastest line to where they were headed. Might not have had any warning at all, especially if the snowpack looked stable. The thing just hit and even if it wasn't huge, they didn't have a chance."

Asu gestured at one of the backpacks. Callahan reached into the backpack and got out an ice axe. Gently, the team chipped the ice and frozen snow around the contorted corpse until Charlie was revealed.

The fall he'd sustained appeared traumatic, with blood in the snow around his head and several bones that looked broken. His fleece jacket was still tied around his waist and in his hand, Charlie gripped his ice axe, its pick broken. With only seconds to prepare, Callahan imagined him jamming it into a rock crack as the avalanche hit, but the force of the slide being too much to withstand.

Lifting the body onto the green-and-yellow tent fly, the team wrapped him tightly, then tied the fly with rope. Snow continued falling, blurring Callahan's visibility as he looked across the couloir for signs of Chris. They hadn't been roped together, and the video camera, which he suspected one of them held onto as they climbed, was nowhere to be found. Lost forever, perhaps.

By the time a litter had been rigged to transport Charlie down the mountain, Callahan knew the descent would be problematic. Carrying the body would be unwieldy on the slopes, and they'd have to slide it in steep sections. He felt the side of his pack. Lodged between layers of webbing was the probe he'd brought to search for Chris.

Asu saw him struggling with the decision. "Callahan, we can't stay. It's too dangerous. The snow isn't letting up, and it's going to take everything we've got to get Charlie back to camp. We're gonna have to cut trees to get him through the forest and then across that bridge."

Callahan stared out over the gully. "She's here," he said. "She's gotta be here. I don't want to leave her." Lifting the makeshift litter onto their shoulders, several of the searchers were taking timid steps downhill. Loose rocks shifted beneath their feet. Callahan pushed his sleeve back, recording their exact location with the altimeter watch on his wrist.

Tomorrow, he thought. *We'll come back tomorrow, Chris.*

IT WAS NEARLY DARK WHEN the team reached camp just above the monastery. The snow continued, showing no mercy. Callahan's men, exhausted, crawled into their tents. In the distance, he could hear rockfall, indicating the mountain was sending more snow and debris down from Genyen's upper reaches. The avalanches would continue all night and throughout the next few days.

Winter had settled into the Genyen Valley. They'd barely made it in time for Charlie. Conditions were too precarious, and waiting a few days wouldn't do any good. Without a massive burst of warm weather and snowmelt, he'd be risking more lives if he took his team back up the mountain. He knew, falling asleep that night, that Chris would need to wait.

By the next morning, the Chinese police had arrived in droves at the monastery, along with curious locals. Callahan inquired about help getting the body out of the valley and back to Litang and on to Kangding for cremation. Dragged into an outbuilding near the monastery by a Chinese cop, he listened as the cop unloaded. With veins bulging from his temples, the cop ranted at Callahan, covering him in halitosis and flecks of spit. The problems caused by the search and recovery were too great, too embarrassing, too inconvenient. With a menacing tone, the cop was insistent they'd provide no help in getting Charlie's body back to civilization. It would be up to Callahan and his team to find their own way to Kangding.

Retracing their hike back to the village of Lamaya required more than human labor. The team needed a horse. Charlie's body was still frozen solid and the team too wiped out to carry it another ten miles. As Callahan negotiated with locals to rent a horse, it was apparent there were going to be problems.

He got out the sat phone and called Kara. He'd already spoken to her once today, explaining the danger and the impossibility of continuing the search for Chris, given the snow conditions. This conversation would be different.

"Hey, it's me again. You're not gonna believe this," he began. "I need you to verify that we've got the funds to spend eight hundred dollars."

"Eight hundred dollars?! For what?" Kara knew the funds were there but couldn't imagine what he needed them for in the middle of western Sichuan.

"A horse. I need to buy a horse. To get Charlie to the road. From there we can get a van to get us back to Kangding, I'm sure, but right now we just cannot get his body back to the road in Lamaya without a horse."

"But why *buy* a horse? Can't you just rent one?"

Callahan and his team had tried that. "The locals are too freaked out about death," he told her. "They say the horse will be cursed if it carries a dead body. But apparently somehow . . . "

"Eight hundred dollars to buy the horse overcomes those superstitions?" Kara asked, incredulous.

"Something like that. I figure I'll just sell it back at the end of the trail. Probably to the guy I buy it from. He'll make a nice profit and we'll be on our way. God, Charlie is just absolutely hating me for this right about now."

Kara laughed, and Callahan joined her. The moment of humor felt soothing. "Do it," she said. "Buy the horse. And take pictures."

"I shall. I'm gonna have Asu deal with this. I'm terrible with all things equine."

After the horse had been acquired, the team strapped the tent fly carrying Charlie's body onto one side of the creature, counterbalanced by two heavy duffels on the opposite side. The horse seemed irritated at the awkward, heavy load but slowly made its way down the trail to Lamaya.

Three days later, on January 1, 2007, a white van carrying Charlie's body arrived at the mortuary in Kangding. The van had been decorated with red ribbons to guard against evil spirits, and its driver earned a hefty sum. True to his promise to Kili Sherpa, Callahan had monks from a nearby monastery perform puja, a daylong ceremony to bless the spirits of both Chris and Charlie. An autopsy was performed, declaring that Charles Duncan Fowler had died as a result of severe cold, oxygen deprivation, and injury.

Before he left with Charlie's ashes, the monks approached Callahan, sharing their belief in reincarnation, along with the most comforting words he'd heard in weeks. "Do not worry about your friends' bodies, for they are just empty shells now. Their souls are what matter. They are on the way to heaven now and we are working hard to help get them there."

CALLAHAN CLEARED IMMIGRATION AT DENVER International Airport clutching the ashes of his hero. A week had passed since reuniting in Chengdu with Kara and tying up the loose ends related to the search and recovery. Instead of returning to Kyrgyzstan, where he'd been working, he was asked to come to Telluride by friends of Charlie and Chris. A memorial was being held for the couple, and those involved in the search wanted nobody but Callahan to bring Charlie's remains back.

Transiting to his domestic flight from Denver to Montrose, Callahan asked for the film he was carrying to be hand-checked. The TSA agent pushed back, assuring him it wasn't necessary.

"Look, I'm carrying the ashes of my friend and this is his film," Callahan said sternly. "His family really wants to see these pictures, and I don't want to screw it up for them." The TSA officer continued his lecture, raising his voice and drawing the attention of a colleague. Stepping over, the second officer inquired about the disagreement.

Callahan couldn't believe he'd come this far to argue with the TSA. He'd chipped Charlie out of ice, had him cremated, and carried him across the ocean. This was a load of bullshit. He stood his ground. "Listen, I've been on a body recovery in China. This is one of the climbers we found, and this is his film. I want it hand-screened, goddamnit."

Callahan held up the package containing the urn. His face was flushed as he tried to decipher the reaction of this latest TSA officer.

"Who is that? Who's in there?" the officer asked.

"It's Charlie Fowler."

"No shit? *That* is Charlie Fowler? Oh man. Gimme this," he said, taking the bag with Charlie's film and handing it to the other officer. "Hand-check this and cover me, will you? I'm escorting this guy to his next gate." Turning to Callahan, he said, "Follow me, brother."

Callahan nodded with appreciation. Starstruck, the officer reached out and fingered the top of the package in Callahan's arm.

"Charlie Fowler, holy shit. The guy's a legend," he mumbled.

THE SHORT FLIGHT FROM DENVER to Montrose was turbulent. Snow was pounding the Rockies, causing the plane to buck. Yet Callahan was half-asleep. He hadn't slept a full night since leaving Kyrgyzstan in mid-December.

It was now just over a month since Charlie and Chris had been scheduled to land at Montrose. They would have come straight to baggage claim as he was now, walking through a similar crowd of ski tourists heading to Telluride. With a backpack over his right shoulder, Callahan zipped up his jacket all the way to guard against another night of frigid mountain temperatures. The backdrop of the Rocky Mountains was lit in ambers and yellows.

Callahan stepped out of the terminal to await his ride, cradling the package with Charlie's remains in his left arm. Resting in a beautiful rosewood carved box inlaid with mother of pearl, Charlie Fowler was finally home.

CHAPTER 21

BIG LOVE

AS 2007 BEGAN, TRIBUTES TO Chris and Charlie filled newspapers, memorial services, and even the streets of Telluride.

"There were literally women walking along the streets of Telluride crying in those first few days," a friend recalled. "Their husbands would come up to me knowing I'd been friends with Charlie and tell me that their wives were shattered because they'd once dated him. It was surreal." Online climber chat rooms were flooded with stories of both Chris and Charlie, including memories from Conrad Anker and Jenni Lowe-Anker, who'd spent time with the famously private couple. They wrote: "Over the years, we'd see Charlie and Chris in Telluride. They were big love together. Here's to both of them for touching all of our lives. We'll see you out there, dear friends."

At a celebration of their lives attended by both families that winter, Charlie's sister, Ginny, spelled out beautifully what drove her brother to climb, characteristics that were matched in the woman he loved. "I came to the understanding that he was doing what he loved," she said. "Charlie always said it was easier for him to climb than not to climb. It was that much of a passion. He wouldn't have changed anything, and I wouldn't have wanted him to change anything. The only thing he would have changed was that he would have come home with Christine."

As winter melted into spring, the families of Charlie and Chris continued the process of living without them. Both families were ever grateful to Callahan, expressing this to him in handwritten cards:

Hi Ted,

Well, this note is far overdue. But I think of you so very often. Words can never express how much I really appreciate all that you have done for my family and me.

Do you ever get to look up at the mountain where Christine might be? I miss her so much. I wish the time would pass more quickly so I could have her more near. But everyone is so kind, and that helps me a lot. I often try to think, Oh she is just climbing some mountain somewhere, and that helps too.

I was glad I had a chance to meet you in Telluride. Now are you doing some studying or research in China? And how long do you plan on staying there? Will you be the one to help with the search in spring?

Hope everything goes well for you. And I do hope I will hear from you again.

God bless you always,
Joyce Feld

THE BUSINESS OF WAITING FOR Chris's body to be recovered proved agonizing. Ramifications stacked on top of one another, from death certificates that couldn't be produced to a funeral that couldn't be conducted. Grieving felt both necessary and somehow premature. Regular calls continued between Mark and Joyce, both wishing away the snow and ice that still covered the mountain.

Jon Otto, his wife, and baby daughter were soon returning to China, and he continued to direct recovery operations. Without a sliver of opportunity to return to Genyen until spring because of the weather, it wasn't until April that he was able to provide the first bits of hope in an email to Seattle and Telluride. "The plan at this point is to watch the snow and weather," he wrote. "Once the melt-off in Sichuan starts, it progresses rapidly, so this will be our sign that we will have to move in sometime soon. It is important for the search team to go in when conditions permit, and not fit the search around anyone's schedule."

Holding to a schedule all her own, Mother Nature continued to call the shots.

JOYCE'S FRIEND PULLED UP OUTSIDE her house right on time. They had a coffee date, one of several they'd arranged in the spring of 2007 since Charlie had been found and Chris presumed dead. Sticking on the front door was a missed delivery notification slip from a shipping company. Pulling it off, the friend knocked and then let herself in.

"I'm here! Looks like you missed a delivery," her friend said, handing Joyce the note.

Joyce stared at it a moment. Reading and rereading, she looked up. "They say they'll come back in two days," she said. "This is a box I've been waiting for. It's from the consulate.... These are Chrissy's things."

The women looked at each other, both imagining the cardboard box filled with the remnants of Chris's life. Inside were the contents of the duffel that Callahan had unpacked in Litang. Extra socks, rolls of film, a journal, mementos from Elbrus and Cho Oyu. The monetary value of these items was insignificant, but to Joyce the box was priceless.

"Oh, Joyce," her friend said, "you should call them now and see if they can come back with it today."

Joyce made the call, then they settled in for coffee, distracted. She offered news about her grandchildren, then asked about her friend's grandson. Sharing, they marveled at the fact that their daughters had attended the local high school a few years apart, grown up, and gone on to have lives of their own exploring all parts of the world the way they never had.

Looking out the window at her yard and flowers, Joyce said, "I wish Chrissy would've had a baby. I could've taken care of her child now."

Thirty minutes after she'd called, the truck appeared. The delivery woman threw wide the truck doors, lifting out a large box that looked ready to burst. Joyce opened her front door, and the delivery woman muscled it inside. Markings covered the box in both English and Chinese. There were ripped bits of packing tape, several small holes.

Neither woman could take their eyes off the box. Finally, Joyce spoke. "The boys told me I should wait to open it until one of them is here. I guess they don't want their mother to open it alone."

"I think that's wise," her friend whispered.

"When they told me they were sending things," Joyce said, "they said they'd have to wash anything that had blood on it. These are just things from her duffel bag, but I didn't like hearing that other part. About the things that might come later." She turned away from the box, heading back for the living room and her coffee. She mumbled to herself as she walked, a stream of questions that would linger, unanswered. "I really hope she had enough warm clothes on the mountain."

The two women sank into the couch as Joyce finished her thought. "Chrissy hated to be cold."

ASU PEERED THROUGH BINOCULARS, LOOKING out at the northeastern slope of Genyen. It was mid-April but the mountain remained fully covered in snow. Callahan had been required to return to his work in Kyrgyzstan, leaving the job of watching the mountain to Asu and a group of local climbers. He made out the vicinity where Charlie had been recovered. A vast layer of thick white snow lay over the area, covering the rocks and scree from last December.

Knowing the patterns of weather as he did, Asu calculated the likelihood of snowmelt in a month was almost none. Turning to head back down the ridge, he realized he shouldered the burden of making the call to Jon Otto. It then fell to Jon to pass on the difficult news that Joyce would need to continue her vigil.

While she waited, Joyce began the task of planning Chris's memorial service. The cover of the program would have mountains on it. Beginning in a nontraditional way, Joyce planned for guests to watch a short video of Chris shot in the summer of 2006 outside the Mountain Madness office. Chris had been interviewed by three young reporters, and Joyce imagined how guests would laugh as they heard her talk about how crazy it appeared when she'd quit her engineering job and started a career as a climber.

How they'd be amazed when she talked about leading a team of eleven men on an expedition up an 8,000-meter peak. How they'd choke back tears as they watched Chris walk around the Mountain Madness offices and heard her say, "Until I die, hopefully at age one hundred, I'll keep on learning and trying to improve how I run a business and how I treat people.

I have nothing to prove. I just want to be the best I can be. We all search around and wonder where we're going and I just kinda found my place."

The back of the program would include a request that donations be directed to the nonprofit Chris volunteered for, which was already planning to build a school in Nepal in her honor. And a mention of those who preceded her in death. Her father Robin. Her husband Keith. Her best friend, Charlie Fowler.

Afterward they would all have dinner at Vince Lombardi's Steak House, a nod to Chris's favorite football team. It would be a lovely service, if she could only make it a little longer until her Chrissy came home. Supporting her in the long wait was Chris's friend and climbing partner Julie Hodson, who called often.

"Mountain Madness says they're still watching the mountain, Julie," Joyce told her on one such call. "The snow isn't melting fast enough for me."

In Telluride, Julie curled up in an armchair. Fourteen hundred miles from Appleton, she zipped up Chris's down jacket, then wrapped it tight around her knees. The jacket showed signs of overuse. Others hung on the coat rack in her foyer, but this was the only one Julie wore now.

"I'll go get her if I have to, Joyce," she said. "You know, I've booked a trip there in a few months, and if she's not back by then, I'll bring her home myself."

BY EARLY JUNE, THE SNOWS of Genyen had begun to melt. Asu and a climbing colleague carried out another unsuccessful search for Chris's body, but they knew they were closer. A matter of weeks, perhaps, until the snow and ice would reveal her. In the meantime, they found remnants of Chris and Charlie's trek up the mountain: a thin yellow tent pole and a water bottle still filled with water.

All expectations were that Chris would be found in the avalanche zone, a dangerous area with a runout of snow, rock, and ice continuously coming down. The only way to search for her now was to look with binoculars from a high vantage point so as not to get caught in falling snow and rock. Monitoring the mountain had become a full-time job. Jon Otto was back in Chengdu, but busy with his newborn daughter, so he'd ordered two climbers to camp at the base of Genyen with enough provisions to last until Chris was found.

ON JULY 3, 2007, CHRISTINE BOSKOFF'S body was finally discovered. She lay exposed several hundred meters below where Charlie had been found. Resting in a steep part of the glacier in a direct fall line of boulders, she'd sustained multiple injuries from the avalanche. Her body was damaged further from being caught in falling debris over the following months.

A team of climbers— some who'd been a part of the December search, others new—gathered to assess the possibility of recovery. Looking over the mountain from afar, the conclusion was obvious. It was still too perilous. The wet season was in full force, and rain came down steadily. Streams of water flowed along the surface of the glacier, loosening rocks. Loose boulders tumbled randomly down the slope where she lay. Higher on Genyen, the team was unable to see past thick clouds and fog. The likelihood of an avalanche starting from above that the team wouldn't see coming was too great for retrieval. All that was available were interim measures to keep her body safe until a larger recovery could be initiated.

When they decided they'd be able to reach her body, several team members scrambled across the rocks. Moving swiftly, they took GPS coordinates and put her in a body bag. Then, carrying her off to the side and away from danger, they gently placed her on a small, solid ledge below a cliff where she'd be protected. Making a circle of rocks around her body, the team secured her on the ledge, protected from rockfall. Before leaving, they gathered a few personal belongings they would send to Joyce, including a piece of paper on which Chris had recorded her last journal entry, November 14, 2006.

As summer continued, the last of the winter snow melted and the rain causing rock slides began to abate. By the end of August, the time for Chris's recovery was near. With neither Jon Otto nor Ted Callahan available to help, Mark Gunlogson bought plane tickets. He needed and wanted to be there and planned to join Asu and a team of local climbers.

ASU PASSED MARK A PLATE of scrambled egg and tomato, then a bowl of steamed rice. A brief stop for lunch in a small village outside Chengdu was all they had time for. The two were in a caravan of vehicles on the way to Lamaya, still three days away.

"Your guys have been outstanding, Asu. I hope you tell them how grateful we are," he said.

Asu nodded, smiling at Mark. "It's no trouble. Some of these guys were part of Charlie's recovery and they want to see it all the way through."

"I appreciate it," Mark said. "I hope we get together someday under different circumstances."

Pushing back from the table, the two stood up and stepped outside, meeting the others who'd finished lunch and were preparing to get back to the drive. Across the road, three of the climbers who were part of the recovery team emerged from a grove of bamboo trees. One carried a machete and spoke in Mandarin to Asu, who responded with a few sentences. He turned back into the thick of trees and Mark watched, mystified as the climber whacked away at stalks of bamboo while his two teammates stood by to catch them as they fell. In only a few minutes, they had three stalks, each ten feet long and four inches in diameter. With an air of solemn satisfaction, they tied them to the top of the SUV they'd borrowed from Jon Otto.

The caravan continued with Mark and the recovery team bumping along. The three-day drive from Chengdu to Lamaya was more treacherous than Mark had imagined. On the final day, their vehicle rattled over bridges fashioned from logs, nearly dumping them in the river several times. Eventually making it to Lamaya and then completing the long hike to Lenggu Monastery, the team was greeted by the monks and given a place to rest before they began their climb to Chris's body.

Chris's recovery the next day was less snow-covered than Charlie's, but followed a similar path up and back, with Asu in the lead. On September 21, 2007, Christine Feld Boskoff descended her final peak, carried down the mountain, her body cradled securely on the freshly cut bamboo stalks.

SIX MONKS SAT ON THE ground chanting in the shadows of Mount Genyen. Chris's wrapped body lay in front of them as they performed puja. Mark was engulfed by the scent of burning juniper as he stood nearby, somberly watching the ceremony.

Back at camp, logistics were discussed for getting her body back to Kangding the next day. Again they needed a horse, though this time they had been able to rent instead of buy one. Retracing the route Charlie's body had taken nine months earlier, Chris's body was strapped to the horse the next morning. They followed the road to Litang and then to Kangding, where she was cremated in the same mortuary as Charlie had been.

While the decision had been simple for Charlie's family, cremation wasn't a part of Feld family rituals. Joyce considered the options carefully, finally leaning on Charlie's sister, Ginny, for advice by phone.

"She's been on the mountain for so long now, Joyce," Ginny said. "Her body isn't as it was before. You can remember her just as she was in life, beautiful and radiant. It's how I remember Charlie."

"Yes, but it feels so foreign," Joyce said. "I don't know many people who've done that."

Ginny spoke gently, anxious to find the right words, both soothing and convincing. "Maybe it will help to remember that they both loved the cultures and the customs of the places they climbed. In China, this is what they practice. Maybe she would have wanted it this way."

CHRIS'S ASHES TRAVELED FROM CHINA to Seattle with Mark and his memories: "I remember being a fifteen-year-old and my very first climbing instructor telling me something along the lines of, 'Hey, kid . . . if you're gonna be a climber, it's only a matter of time before someone you know dies. Before you lose someone you love.' It turned out to be true, though you're never really ready for it. First Scott and then Chris."

Chris's friend and climbing partner Jane Courage recalled that day with Mark: "Geri and I met him at the airport when he landed. All three of us were shell shocked. I don't think we could talk about what we were feeling because the dam would've just burst."

Geri remembered: "He was totally wiped out. He gave us Chris's ashes and never lifted his eyes."

The urn was a stainless silver container wrapped with a crimson scarf. Geri offered to travel to Wisconsin to deliver it to Joyce. Before she left, she and Jane took Chris's urn to Ray's Boathouse, where Geri had first met Chris years ago during the weekend of Scott's memorial. Then it was one last ferry trip to nearby Orcas Island, where Jane had recently bought a house looking north to Vancouver Island.

"Something inside me knew that she'd never see it in her lifetime," Jane said, "so I needed those few days out there. It was peaceful. A place to unburden our souls. Share our memories. Digest the reality of her absence. You could see Mount Baker. She would've loved it."

And one last dinner date. Sushi, with the urn in tow, sitting on a chair as if Chris were there, dipping salmon into soy sauce. "Chris adored sushi," Geri recalled. "She'd go positively orgasmic over the stuff. There was no question she needed one more sushi dinner."

A few days later, Geri flew to Wisconsin with Chris's ashes. Joyce welcomed her warmly. The two women looked at old photos and shared laughter, in advance of the memorial service. Chris was remembered at Good Shepherd Lutheran Church, then her ashes were buried in the family plot.

Geri spent the night in Appleton in Chris's old bedroom before leaving early the next morning. The large box with the contents of Chris's duffel sat nearby, along with more recent arrivals that had been found near her body. Among the items that had been recovered was the video camera Chris had carried on that final journey up Mount Genyen, its tape filled with the stirring images of Chris and Charlie's final ascent.

CHAPTER 22

LEGACIES

INSIDE THE LIBRARY AT APPLETON East High School there is a collection of commemorative plates. Each plate bears the name and photo of the annual winner of the Patriot Award, the school's highest alumni honor. The award was launched in 2003. As nominations rolled in for the first award, the chair of the committee was dumbfounded. One nomination stood out. "How did we not know this elite mountain climber and Appleton East grad? It was embarrassing and spoke to her humility. We had our inaugural winner. A slam dunk," he remembered. "We couldn't have started the award with anyone better."

Her plate in the library has an amusing pair of photos. The first is her senior picture, class of 1985, her hair in a stylish '80s perm. She's wearing a starched white blouse and a row of pearls. The other photo, in full summit gear on a mountaintop, beaming. Underneath the photos is one of Chris's favorite phrases: *Live your dreams.*

The Appleton East gym is now home to the Christine Boskoff Memorial Climbing Wall. A teenage girl yelps as her foot slips reaching for a hold. Twenty feet below, her classmate belays her, and the instructor calls out encouragement to both of them. Sitting off to the side, watching, is Joyce, who comes every now and then to witness kids climb since the wall was dedicated to her daughter in 2012. It's a wonderful rock wall, painted by a local muralist. On the far left in a long vertical strip is Chris's full name flanked at the bottom by a plaque describing her life and legacy. The rest of the wall is covered with a detailed mural depicting the six 8,000-meter peaks that Chris summited, along with a seventh peak, Mount Genyen. At the top of the wall are two items donated by Joyce: an American flag and one of Chris's ice axes.

The physical education curriculum at Appleton East now has a semester-long component designed to build confidence and outdoor leadership skills in teenagers. Lessons from Chris's life have been woven into the program, keeping her memory alive in the high school hallways. In addition to kayak trips and a ropes course, the students watch the film of Chris's 1999 expedition to Gasherbrum II in the Karakoram. As a culminating event, each student is asked to write a reflective essay touching on what they've learned from studying her life. The best of the bunch are copied and brought to Joyce, who laughs knowing Chris would love the observations. Each one is packed with youthful authenticity, hope, and humor.

Christine taught me that you have to find what you love to do and try to achieve it. Know your limits, but be brave and have courage to try new things.

• • •

To be honest, she looked a lot like Tom Cruise.

• • •

Christine taught me perseverance. She reminded me that people should set their minds to things they're truly passionate about and push until the very end no matter what obstacles you run into.

In the Mountain Madness office, a copy of the letter from Sir Edmund Hillary to Kili Sherpa is framed and hangs on the wall. Kili still assists the company with trips through his own guiding company. His office in Kathmandu has a huge portrait of Chris hanging on the wall. Many of the profits from his work in mountaineering are funneled back into the schools in his hometown of Chaurikharka. "Because of Chris," he says, "I can train and employ kids from the Khumbu Valley as climbing Sherpas. If I'm in the middle of a project that's helping people, I always think of her and it's like she's still giving to these communities she climbed in."

Meanwhile, in a village west of Kathmandu, a small primary school is home to several hundred students. Built in Chris's honor with a donation from Mountain Madness, it's a tribute to the woman who came to Nepal at twenty-six, wide eyed and ready to embrace her new passion.

FROM THE TOWN OF NORWOOD, Colorado, looking east-southeast, a peak of 13,123 feet is visible. It's part of the Uncompahgre National Forest that Chris and Charlie loved dearly. A short distance away is another, slightly higher peak at 13,498 feet. They tower over Elk Creek Basin to the north and the Navajo Basin to the south in the Wilson Massif of the San Juan Mountains. From their summits, one can see three 14,000-foot peaks: Wilson Peak, Mount Wilson, and El Diente.

Though getting an act through Congress to name the peaks was arduous, Chris and Charlie's close friends were dedicated. It seemed fitting to give the mountains permanent names to commemorate Charlie and Chris. They put together a proposal that focused not only on their mountaineering achievements but also on the service the two had undertaken throughout their lives, Charlie through building climbing walls in schools in southwest Colorado and Chris through work with impoverished schools in developing countries.

A spokesperson explained the idea behind naming the peaks: "The peak designations highlight the importance of public lands and give prominence to those who loved wilderness and recreation in the form of rock and ice climbing and mountaineering. Perhaps the designations will excite some young people to learn about and emulate Charlie and Chris, and seek their own paths of adventure, environmental stewardship, and service throughout their lives."

After the federal legislation passed the US Congress in 2019 as part of a bipartisan public lands bill package, the two mountains now look out over generations: Boskoff Peak and Fowler Peak.

TODAY, WHEN YOU STEP INTO the storied Mountain Madness office in Seattle, Chris's spirit is present. The company ethos that Scott Fischer launched and Chris carried on remains: meaningful cultural experiences, intense physical challenges, top-notch guides, good coffee, and striking views are standard on every trek and expedition. And, of course, a good dose of laughter.

Hanging on the wall are Scott's ice hammer and one of his down jackets. Chris's expedition boots share space with some of the artwork she'd brought from Nepal: a *thangka* depicting a Buddhist female protector deity, and a large painting of five Hindu women standing on the bank of a river filled with lotus flowers, the flower of eternity, purity, and peace.

Though Scott and Chris preceded him in the leadership position, the reins at Mountain Madness were firmly passed to Mark, who's now helped the company flourish longer than either of them. As new generations of climbers begin to explore the wilderness, Mark and the staff continue to find ways to inspire them.

WESTERN SICHUAN IS BOTH VASTLY different and much the same as it was in 2006 when Chris took her last steps there. Ji'an, Chris and Charlie's Tibetan host, now has a larger family. He and his wife adopted their two nieces, a nephew, and a yak in 2008. Sitting next to him, Ji'an's wife lets tears run down weathered cheeks while he speaks of the American climbers. "I hope their families have peace now," he says. "What happened in the past is over, and their lives should be without sadness."

Villages near Genyen have become more familiar with Westerners, though it has come at a price. More Chinese police officers pass through, and locals still remember several villagers being temporarily thrown in jail on suspicion of being complicit in the disappearance of Charlie and Chris.

At Lenggu Monastery, the monks continue as they have for centuries: saying daily prayers while the sun rises and falls; tending to the wild blue sheep that roam the steep hills; patiently answering pantomimed questions from Western visitors about their traditions, their beliefs, and the power of the mountain. One of the younger monks glances up, seeing a giant mosquito jockeying for position against a pane of window glass. Reaching up, he catches it in cupped hands. The destiny of this insect is more peaceful than that of one hatched elsewhere. The monk stretches his hands outside the window and releases the mosquito on its peaceful journey back down the Genyen Valley.

Smiling, he goes back to his cup of yak butter tea in silence.

SHORTLY AFTER CHRIS'S ASHES WERE brought home in 2007, her friend Julie traveled to Lenggu Monastery. Her intentions were to be in the spaces where Chris had been, to see and feel the mountain. She traveled with a few friends and one of Chris's trekking poles, a beaten-up metal stick that looked particularly unassuming and that had been inscribed with the word *Everest* on the side. Chris had used it on her summit of the world's highest mountain.

After the laborious journey to the monastery, Julie and her friends sat resting outside while the monks curiously sized them up. One of the monks slid next to her, pointing to his presumably bad knee, and then at Chris's pole.

"I realized he wanted it," Julie recalled. "But there was no way I was giving it to him. None. It was Chris's pole and I just . . . I couldn't let go." Instead, she pointed to a fancy aluminum pole that another member of the group was using. Was he interested in that one, by chance, she offered? The monk laughed heartily and pointed at Chris's pole again, unrelenting in his desire. The back and forth continued a bit longer, neither wanting to give in.

"Suddenly, I had a moment," Julie said. "I don't know where the feeling came from, but I just knew." She squeezed the trekking pole in her hand one last time, then reached out to the monk, passing it on. His face exploded with a mix of triumph and bliss as he accepted it. Julie watched as he turned it over and over, gently running his fingers over the printed letters. Then standing, the monk turned and walked toward the mountain.

Looking up, through the clouds over Genyen, there was light.

AUTHOR'S NOTE

CHRIS BOSKOFF AND I NEVER knew each other, though the trajectories of our lives were remarkably similar.

Our parents both started raising families in the town of Sheboygan, Wisconsin, then moved an hour away to Appleton. We both attended Appleton East High School, though she was three years older than me and our age difference and the size of our school meant that we hadn't crossed paths. In high school, we both played on the tennis team, hung out at the same mall, and learned to downhill at the same small ski resort. From time to time, I'd tag along with a friend when he went to Sunday services at Good Shepherd Lutheran Church, where Chris worshipped and would one day be memorialized.

Chris and I graduated and moved away from Appleton. Both of us were eventually drawn to Asia. In 1994 as she was visiting Nepal for the first time with Keith, I was also there trekking the Annapurna Circuit. The highest pass took me to nearly eighteen thousand feet and my body recoiled from the altitude. Cold, nauseous, and miserable, I swore I'd never climb that high again. Clearly young women from Appleton weren't made for that elevation, I thought.

After settling in Denver, I got married and adopted two children from China at the same time Chris met Charlie, fell in love, moved to Norwood part time, and attempted K2. Her stints in Colorado between expeditions were marked by local climbs she'd often undertake with her friend Julie, who had landed in Colorado because she'd been lured there by one of my cousins.

Mysterious as life is, Chris's existence and our parallel paths were unknown to me for decades. Though I lived in Colorado and spent a year with my family in the part of China where Chris and Charlie frequently explored, I wasn't a climber. I followed the Everest disaster in 1996 and knew the name Ed Viesturs, but Christine Boskoff wasn't on my radar screen. In December 2006, I received a call from my mother about a girl in my high school who'd become a world-renowned climber and then disappeared with her boyfriend in China. My mother and Chris's mom, Joyce, both still living in Appleton, became friendly. Over the next six months my mother's interest in Chris's story grew. She agonized with Joyce the many months that Chris's body could not be recovered. She was with her the day the box of Chris's belongings arrived from the US consulate. By the time she'd attended Chris's memorial service, my mother, a writer herself, was so captivated by Chris's life that she decided to begin work on a book about Chris, a woman so humble that her achievements hadn't been known even in the city where she grew up.

Cheering from the sidelines, I felt my mother's fervor for telling Chris's story. Her wheelhouse was meticulous research, and each time I'd visit Appleton, another pile of file folders would be loaded with articles she'd collected, along with interview notes from people in Chris's life who she'd tracked down and spoken with. The book project consumed weekends and evenings as my mother worked her regular job. By 2010 she'd fully retired, had an outline, and was ready to begin writing the book.

Then my sister noticed it. A tremor in my mother's left hand.

PARKINSON'S DISEASE WRITES ITS OWN script with every person it touches. For my mother, the initial years proved irritating but tolerable. Her slowed movements and increased difficulty in walking were not enough for outsiders to notice, but plenty to gradually limit her ability to work on the book. She and Joyce continued to meet, their friendship having transcended Chris's death and my mother's work on Chris's story.

By 2015, I'd published my own first book and didn't have to look far for a second project. My mother welcomed the offer to help write

Chris's story, though I'm certain it felt bittersweet. Wrapping her arms around a decade of work and passing it on was a mix of courage, grace, a tinge of sadness, and unconditional love. There was an understanding that I would tell the story in a way that differed from how she'd intended. What neither of us could have known at the time was just how deeply I'd immerse myself in Chris's story.

I packed my SUV with Mom's boxes of research and drove from Wisconsin back home to Colorado in 2017. For many months, I carefully reviewed each note, every newspaper clipping and business card. Chris's story didn't take long to pull at my heartstrings and keep me awake at night. The process of poring over my mother's work was emotional, exhausting, and inspiring all at the same time. My family grew used to the box of tissues that sat next to the stack of files on my desk. By now, Parkinson's had stolen my mother's handwriting, but her notes from ten years prior were clear and touching, and included such directives as:

- Research the environmental impact on Everest
- Talk to the man who provided Chris's expedition weather reports
- A world of beauty and danger . . . good possible book title
- Must travel to Kathmandu, Tibet, and Seattle

Beyond the emotional impact, there was a toll on my body. In an early indication that I was physically in Denver, but emotionally on top of a mountain, I noticed I was shivering all day long as I researched Chris's expeditions, even when the temperature outside was 80 degrees. My head constantly ached until I realized that I was breathing in shallow sips just as described in the literature detailing high-altitude cerebral edema.

It all just compelled me to fall deeper into Chris's life and all its facets.

After years of hearing about Joyce, I finally met her in person. She'd moved out of the house that Chris had grown up in and was now living in a retirement home in Appleton. Sitting on her couch at our first meeting, I soaked in the friendship she had with my mother and noticed how similar they were. Both full of warmth, humor, and grace even in the face of loss. Joyce in the loss of her daughter, and my mother in the slow deterioration of her body. Over the months, my visits to Joyce continued without my mother and we developed our own friendship. At the end of each visit, Joyce would encourage me to take care of Mom and see that she came by for coffee soon. Loyalties had grown thick roots over time. Mothers to daughters, Joyce to my mother, and now my own devotion to Chris in telling her story.

Eventually I traveled to China on a pilgrimage to the Genyen Valley, retracing the steps Chris and Charlie had taken. With the assistance of Jon Otto, I trekked to Lenggu Monastery, perhaps hoping the monks would help me place Chris and Charlie's deaths into the right compartment in my brain. I'd spent months listening to stories of trauma, avalanches, and deaths in the mountains. From Scott to Keith to Chris and Charlie. Each loss tragic and equally inexplicable. Somehow I'd become what one person described as "a giant vessel for everyone's grief and struggle." I had more questions than answers, and the journalist in me felt compelled to establish a logical conclusion.

Arriving at the monastery was like stepping into the pages of a fairytale. The cluster of peaks behind the classic Tibetan building were more breathtaking than I'd imagined. After spending so much time looking at dark, grainy photos from the December 2006 search-and-recovery efforts, I was stunned by the colors in the valley. It was June, and the grounds lining the monastery were scattered with exquisite wildflowers.

Chris had spoken many times of her love of the journey. Not only the journey up the mountain, but in occupying herself with the surroundings, the people, and customs of whatever place she traveled. It became clear that this place was the essence of her desire to explore. It exuded peace and healing, with a dose of adventure. I looked up at the summit of Genyen and saw thick layers of virgin snow covering every inch.

The monks remembered Chris and Charlie's brief visit and its dramatic aftermath. To me, their words felt like the closest I might get to a resolution. Sitting with them at the monastery, I knew the monks sensed my urgent need for clarity. Patiently letting me describe Chris and Charlie's fortitude, skill, and character, the lead monk waited, then finally explained Chris and Charlie's deaths matter-of-factly, profess-ing: "Young lady, Genyen is powerful and fierce. Therefore the reason they left this earth is simple. They climbed the mountain and the moun-tain sent them down."

I stared at him, waiting for more, but he just smiled, a gold tooth flashing as he leaned forward and offered another cup of tea. His shaved head dipped as I held out my paper cup to receive hot water. For all the debate and philosophical musings about climbing sacred peaks, the monks at Genyen seemed to have a handle on how simple it was.

That night, sleep never came. I'd been submerged for months in the tales of mountaineering, a mess of exhilaration and grief. Stories of tragedy and blissful moments of summiting. Endless conversations that often ended with my subjects in tears, both happy and sad. Carrying all of it, I felt honored yet overwhelmed at the thought of weaving Chris's story into something meaningful that could be shared with others.

An undeniable hum ran through me as I lay in my sleeping bag. A conversation with the mountain, perhaps, or maybe a negotiation. Equal parts fear and gratitude. At twenty thousand feet, I had no doubt that Genyen was more powerful than any physical creation I'd encountered. My heart raced and my breathing was shallow as I tried and failed to sleep.

Climbing the next day, Jon and I spent two hours on a nontechnical ascent. Up the mountainside, I spotted the avalanche zone where Chris and Charlie's bodies had been found and barked at Jon when I felt us getting dangerously close. The area where Chris had been recovered was coated in scree and recognizable from the photos I'd pored over with Mark and Ted Callahan. Jon and I hugged the ridgeline and found a place to sit. Reaching into the pocket of my jacket, I grasped a small collection of wildflowers I'd picked along the way. I lay them along the top of the ridge, then made a small cairn.

We sat for a long time in silence, Jon concentrating on the path to the summit, me focusing on the debris field where Chris had been at rest alone for so many months. I knew there would be no concrete way to describe the all-encompassing beauty of the scene to my mother or

Joyce once I returned, but I would try to explain what I discovered in those moments.

This perfect mix of majesty and adventure was her elixir.

As we turned to hike down, I stared out at the landscape. Below us, the river had disappeared into a tiny thread. Further east, the monastery was barely perceptible. For an instant, the scene felt familiar. Freezing, I tried to understand why. It took a beat, but then it came to me.

Chris and Charlie's video, the final shot across the same panorama.

ACKNOWLEDGMENTS

I AM DEEPLY GRATEFUL TO a mighty tribe of individuals for their unwavering support as I crafted the manuscript.

The generosity of Joyce, Tom, Sue, and Paul Feld, along with Ginny Fowler Hicks in opening their hearts was humbling and a testament to their love of Chris and Charlie. Mark Gunlogson of Mountain Madness was the first person I spoke with about the project and became my most trusted adviser. He patiently answered every question, providing an escape from the weight of the story with lightness, compassion, and wisdom. Jane Courage and Geri Lesko grounded me with their authenticity and allowed the story to be mine to tell. Our friendships will endure.

Ted Callahan kept me laughing from start to finish, even on the tough days. I feel privileged to have crossed his orbit. Jon and Anora Otto balanced an emotional week in China with radiant moments; while Jon's leadership on our trip to Genyen afforded the space I needed to understand the end of Chris and Charlie's story. Kili and Maya Sherpa graciously opened their home in Kathmandu to me. Over many cups of chai, I learned how alliances, friendship, and love can transcend miles, gender, and culture.

Nicki Jepsen of Mountain Madness kindly offered her thoughts on the first draft; her joyful energy is woven into these pages in ways that will always make me smile. I'm overflowing with gratitude for the guidance I received from Anjuli, Carolyn, Carrie, MC, and Missy, who nurtured my every word. Thank you also to BookBar in Denver for providing a home for writers and readers alike. Amy Smith Bell and Ellen

Wheat deftly molded my words and made them shine. I'm honored that the staff at Mountaineers Books, most notably Kate Rogers, Emily White, and Mary Metz, wrapped their arms around Chris's story.

Many thanks to the People's Republic of China for graciously letting me explore their beautiful country.

Supporting me on my path to tell Chris's story were Mark Kroese, Tom Hornbein, Lance Rosen, the enthusiastic and thoughtful staff at Mountain Madness, Bill Dwyre, Henry Coppolillo, the monks of Lenggu Monastery, Kate Baer, Nicole Tembrock, Megan Eliassen, Dr. Peter Hackett, Katrina Reinsdorff, Michael Croy, Liz Garton Scanlon, Steve Sutcliffe and Julia Loo-Sutcliffe, Alison Levine, Vanessa O'Brien, Helen Sadiq, Da Liu, Dave Ratner, Gao Min, Doug Chabot, Alan Arnette, Chris McNamara, Christopher Stratton, David Anderson, David Diaz, Scott MacLennan, Rongqin Su (Asu), Jeff Smoot, Kara Jenkinson, Ken Wylie, Nima Nuru Sherpa, Stefan Nestler, Tad Welch, and Jim Clash.

The friends and colleagues who shared their everlasting love and admiration for Chris, Charlie, and Scott in these pages include Steve Johnson, Matt Schonwald, Phil Powers, John McCall, Brent Bishop, Willie Benegas, Wolf Riehle, Meagan McGrath, CJ Favour, Shannon Callies, Lisa Coll, Mae Torres, Ji'an and family, Russell Brice, David Jones, Teresa Olding, Peter Habeler, Alex Turner, Angela Hawse, Andrew Lock, Axel Koch, Julie Hodson, Conrad Anker, Jenni Lowe-Anker, Steve Walker, Damon Johnston, Hector Ponce de Leon, Kay LeClaire, Nazir Sabir, Rob Hess, Julie Ruef, Julio Bird, Joel Coniglio, Keith Brown, Luis Benitez, Steve Swenson, Paul Kuenn, Peter Goldman, Nadine Plante, Samantha Larson, and Skip Franklin.

And finally, profound thanks to my family, who fills my world with unconditional love: My parents, Jane and Tony Garton, and my sister, Britt, are a constant source of optimism and strength. My daughter, Eden, is finding her own unique edges every day in magnificent ways. My son, Will, astonishes me daily with his brilliance and humor. And to my husband Ernie, who forever embraces the maps I draw and the journeys we share.

SELECTED BIBLIOGRAPHY

Chapter 2

"C-130J Super Hercules." Lockheed Martin website. www.lockheedmartin .com/us/products/c130.html.

Hempken, Doug, et al. "Climbing in High Cliff State Park, High Cliff State Park." Mountain Project (website), November 20, 2006. www.mountainproject.com/area/105889013/high-cliff-state-park.

EEA Aviation Center (website). www.eaa.org.

Chapter 3

Bhandari, Rajneesh, and Kai Schultz. "Elizabeth Hawley, Who Chronicled Everest Treks, Dies at 94." *New York Times* online, January 26, 2018, www.nytimes.com/2018/01/26/obituaries/elizabeth -hawley-who-chronicled-everest-treks-dies-at-94.html.

Hawley, Elizabeth. "Ama Dablam, Khumbu Valley, Nepal." *Archives of Internal Medicine*, vol. 165, no. 1, 2005, p. 7, doi:10.1001/archinte.165.1.7.

Potterfield, Peter. *In the Zone: Epic Survival Stories from the Mountaineering World*. Seattle: Mountaineers Books, 1996.

Siler, Wes. "Why Mount Washington Kills." *OutsideOnline*, July 19, 2019. www.outsideonline.com/2081256/why-mount-washington-kills.

Zeller, Chris. "Climb Rigid Designator, CO Ice & Mixed." Mountain Project (website), April 13, 2005. www.mountainproject.com/route/105747449 /rigid-designator.

Chapter 4

Birkby, Robert. *Mountain Madness: Scott Fischer, Mount Everest & a Life Lived on High*. New York: Citadel Press, 2009.

Blum, Arlene. *Annapurna: A Woman's Place*. Berkeley, CA: Counterpoint, 1980.

Frohlick, Susan. "'Wanting the Children and Wanting K2': The Incommensura-bility of Motherhood and Mountaineering in Britain and North America in the Late Twentieth Century." *Gender, Place & Culture*, vol. 13, no. 5, 2006, pp. 477–490., doi:10.1080/09663690600858820.

Minhas, Salman. "South-Asian." *The South Asian* (blog), January 2004. www.the-south-asian.com/july-aug2006/Women-climbers.htm.

Mitchell, Melanthia. "Climber's Peak Performance an Inspiration to Young Women." *Spokesman-Review* online, June 30, 2009. www.spokesman.com/stories/2005/aug/07/climbers-peak -performance-an-inspiration-to-young/.

Musa, Ghazali, James Higham, and Anna Thompson-Carr. *Mountaineering Tourism*. London, England: Routledge Press, 2015.

Noble, Chris. *Women Who Dare: North America's Most Inspiring Women Climbers*. Guilford, CT: FalconGuides, 2013.

O'Brien, Vanessa. "Mountains Have No Ceilings." National Women's History Museum (website), October 10, 2018. www.womenshistory.org /articles/mountains-have-no-ceilings.

Sawe, Benjamin Elisha. "The Tallest Peaks In The Karakoram Range." WorldAtlas website, April 25, 2017. worldatlas.com/articles/the-tallest -peaks-in-the-karakoram-range.html.

Zuckerman, Peter, and Amanda Padoan. *Buried in the Sky: The Extraordinary Story of the Sherpa Climbers on K2's Deadliest Day*. New York: W.W. Norton, 2013.

Chapter 5

"Broad Peak FAQ." alanarnette.com (website). www.alanarnette.com /climbs/k2bpfaq.php.

"Broad Peak." Peakware (website). peakware.com/peaks.php?pk=389.

Hartemann, Frederic V., and Robert Hauptman. *Grasping for Heaven: Interviews with North American Mountaineers*. Jefferson, NC: McFarland, 2011.

Jordan, Jennifer. *Savage Summit: The Life and Death of the First Women of K2*. New York: HarperCollins, 2005.

Rose, David and Ed Douglas. *Regions of the Heart: The Triumph and Tragedy of Alison Hargreaves*. New York: Simon & Schuster, 2001.

Salam, Maya. "Overlooked No More: Alison Hargreaves, Who Conquered Everest Solo and Without Bottled Oxygen." The *New York Times* online, March 15, 2018. www.nytimes.com/2018/03/14/obituaries /overlooked-alison-hargreaves.html.

Yurtoğlu, Nadir. "Asia, Pakistan, Broad Peak Ascents, Attempts and Tragedies." *History Studies International Journal of History*, vol. 10, no. 7, 2018, pp. 241–264, doi:10.9737/hist.2018.658.

Chapter 6

"Cho Oyu." *Encyclopædia Britannica Online*, www.britannica.com/place /Cho-Oyu.

Chapter 7

Drescher, Cynthia. "This Is the World's Most Dangerous Airport." *Condé Nast Traveler* online, October 5, 2016. www.cntraveler.com /stories/2016-04-12/this-is-the-worlds-most-dangerous-airport.

"Gokyo and Associated Lakes." Ramsar Sites Information Service (website). rsis.ramsar.org/ris/1692.

"The Ice Fall Doctors That Make Everest Climbing Possible." *Climbing* online, October 24, 2016. www.climbing.com/videos/the-ice-fall -doctors-that-make-everest-climbing-possible/.

Chapter 8

Ascent on G2: One Woman's Journey to the Top. Directed by Robert Yuhas, Robert Yuhas Productions, 1999.

Chapter 9

"Biological Adaptability: Adapting to High Altitude." Palomar College website. www2.palomar.edu/anthro/adapt/adapt_3.htm.

Bernardi, L., et al. "Hypoxic Ventilatory Response in Successful Extreme Altitude Climbers." European Respiratory Society website, January 1, 2006. erj.ersjournals.com/content/27/1/165.long.

"Christine Feld Boskoff: Mount Everest Makes 15 Peaks." *Kitsap Sun* online, May 26, 2000. products.kitsapsun.com/archive/2000/05-26/0064 _christene_feld_boskoff_mount_eve.html.

Dappen, Andy. "Christine Boskoff: A Life in a Day." *Wenatchee Outdoors* online, January 6, 2019. wenatcheeoutdoors.org/2017/01/06/christine-boskoff-a -life-in-a-day/.

"EPAS1 Gene—Genetics Home Reference—NIH." *U.S. National Library of Medicine*, National Institutes of Health, ghr.nlm.nih.gov/gene/EPAS1.

House, Steve, and Scott Johnston. *Training for the New Alpinism: A Manual for the Climber as Athlete.* Ventura, CA: Patagonia Books, 2014.

"Oxygen Levels at High Altitudes—Altitude Safety 101." Center for Wilderness Safety website. www.wildsafe.org/resources/outdoor-safety-101 /altitude-safety-101/high-altitude-oxygen-levels/.

Chapter 10

Ament, Pat, et al. "Charlie Fowler: A Climber's Life." *Climbing* online, January 24, 2007. www.climbing.com/news/charlie-fowler-a-climbers-life/.

Benge, Michael. "Travels With Charlie." *Climbing*. September 1993.

"Charlie Fowler Community Hero." *Telluride Daily Planet* online, January 25 2007. www.telluridenews.com/the_watch/news/article_a9f89c21 -b90c-5109-8e56-e0c13a4f6e79.html.

Fowler, Charlie. "Rumors of the Fall." *Alpinist* online, March 1, 2007. www.alpinist.com/doc/ALP19/sidebar-rumors-of-the-fall.

Martin, Claire. "Taking the Fall." *Denver Post* online. extras.denver post.com/empire/feature.htm.

Meadow, James B. "Fowler Always Blazed Own Trail." *Rocky Mountain News,* January 15, 2007.

Takeda, Pete. "The Real Thing: Charlie Fowler." *Rock and Ice*, April 2007.

Chapter 12

"Croagh Patrick and Other Sacred Summits." *Croagh Patrick and the Islands of Clew Bay* (blog), December 24, 2017. thereek.com/2017/06/14/croagh-patrick-sacred-summits/.

Dharmalata. "What Is a Puja?" The Buddhist Centre website, May 24, 2017. thebuddhistcentre.com/coogee/what-puja.

"Everest 2013: Base Camp Puja." *The Blog on Alanarnette.com*, May 27, 2016. www.alanarnette.com/blog/2013/04/09/everest-2013-base-camp-puj/.

Kopeckova, Liba. "Uncompahgre Plateau." SummitPost (website). www.summitpost.org/uncompahgre-plateau/871513.

"Puja: What Is Puja?" Freer/Sackler Museum for Asian Art website. archive.asia.si.edu/pujaonline/puja/background.html.

Ross, Nancy Wilson. *Buddhism: A Way of Life and Thought*. New York: Vintage Books, 1981.

Chapter 13

Branch, John. "Deliverance From 27,000 Feet." *New York Times* online, December 19, 2017. https://www.nytimes.com/interactive/2017/12/18/sports/everest-deaths.html.

"The Miracle Belay." *Gripped* online, December 30, 2013. gripped.com/profiles/miracle-belay/.

"Most Dangerous Mountains In The World: Top 5." Mpora (website). mpora.com/mountaineering-expeditions/most-dangerous-mountain#E12uVrsexVTVe37w.97.

"The Mountain Madness K2 2002 Expedition." Everest News (website). www.k2news.com/k22002/k202cbdis2.htm.

O'Brien, Vanessa. "Mountains Have No Ceilings." National Women's History Museum (website), October 10, 2018. www.womenshistory.org/articles/mountains-have-no-ceilings.

Pohkrel, Rajan. "Vanessa O'Brien, John Snorri Set Record as 12 Scale Mt K2." *THimalayan Times* online, July 29, 2017. thehimalayantimes.com/nepal/vanessa-obrien-john-snorri-set-record-as-12-scale-mt-k2/.

Rowell, Galen A. *In the Throne Room of the Mountain Gods*. San Francisco: Sierra Club Books, 1986.

Stone, Larry. "Summiting 'Savage Mountain': The Harrowing Story of These Washington Climbers' K2 Ascent." *Seattle Times* online, September 12, 2018. www.seattletimes.com/sports/god-were-going-to-get-the-mountain-40-years-later-k2-ascent-that-included-seattles-jim-wickwire-remains-magical/.

"Surviving." K2Climb (website). www.k2climb.net/expguide/surviving.shtml.

Thompson, Elaine. "Seattle Mountaineer Sets Sights on K2." *Billings Gazette* online, May 9, 2002. billingsgazette.com/news/features/outdoors/seattle-mountaineer-sets-sights-on-k/article_bb91e232-0c1e-557d-97af-8469ce02074f.html.

Wilkinson, Freddie. *One Mountain Thousand Summits: The Untold Story of Tragedy and True Heroism on K2.* New York: Berkley, 2011.

Yuasa, Mark. "K2 now atop her list of mountain aspires." *Seattle Times* online, January 20, 2002. community.seattletimes.nwsource.com/archive /?date=20020120&slug=outn20.

Chapter 15

"Cho Oyu Expedition" description on the American Alpine Institute website. www.alpineinstitute.com/catalog/cho-oyu-expedition/.

Green, Jonathan. *Murder in the High Himalaya: Loyalty, Tragedy, and Escape from Tibet.* New York: PublicAffairs, 2011.

Chapter 16

Bartley, Nancy. "Search Called off for Seattle Climber in China." *Seattle Times* online, December 29, 2006. www.seattletimes.com/seattle-news /search-called-off-for-seattle-climber-in-china/.

Cameron, Gwen. "Nakamura: Sichuan's Most Outstanding Unclimbed Peaks." *Alpinist* online, June 9, 2010. www.alpinist.com/doc/web10s /wfeature-nakamura-sichuan-unclimbed-peaks.

Costa, Marcos, and Bruce Normand. "Haizi Shan, West Face." *American Alpine Journal* online, 2015. publications.americanalpineclub.org /articles/13201213338/Haizi-Shan-West-Face.

Humphrys, Tess. "Sleeping under Yak Hair: Life with Gansu's Tibetan Nomads." Lonely Planet website, July 7, 2017. www.lonelyplanet.com /articles/sleeping-under-yak-hair-life-with-gansus-tibetan-nomads.

"A Journey to Western Sichuan, A Return Visit to the Shaluli Shan Reveals Troublesome Changes in the Mostly Unclimbed Peaks of the Litang Plateau, China." *American Alpine Journal* online, 2011. publications.americanalpineclub.org/articles/12201107700/A-Journey -to-Western-Sichuan-A-Return-Visit-to-the-Shaluli-Shan-Reveals -Troublesome-Changes-in-the-Mostly-Unclimbed-Peaks-of-the-Litang -Plateau-China.

Chapter 17

"Asia, China, Sichuan, Shaluli Shan, Genyen, North Spur; Sachun, East Face, Attempt." *American Alpine Journal* online, 2007. publications.americanalpineclub.org/articles/12200740800/Asia-China -Sichuan-Shaluli-Shan-Genyen-North-Spur-Sachun-East-Face-Attempt.

"Avalanche Types." SLF (website). www.slf.ch/en/avalanches /avalanche-science-and-prevention/avalanche-types.html.

"Avalanche." Avalanche (website). avalanche.org/avalanche-encyclopedia /avalanche/.

Bernbaum, Edwin. *Sacred Mountains of the World: With a New Preface.* Berkeley, CA: University of California Press, 1998.

Mott, Nick. "In the Bear's Lodge." *Alpinist* online, June 26, 2017. www .alpinist.com/doc/web17c/wfeature-in-the-bears-lodge-tcl-alpinist-57.

Ortner, Sherry. *Life and Death on Mount Everest*. Princeton, NJ: Princeton University Press, 1999.

"Types of Avalanche." Ultimate Ski (website). www.ultimate-ski.com /features/off-piste-skiing-freeriding/types-of-avalanche/.

Youbin, Sun. "Mount GENYEN the 13th Goddess." *Shanghai Daily* online, August 9, 2010. https://archive.shine.cn/feature/Mount-GENYEN-the -13th-goddess/shdaily.shtml.

Chapters 18–20

Anderson, Dave. "Tibet {Unclimbed}." *Rock and Ice*, January 16, 2014.

Beckwith, Christian. "Body Found; Fowler's or Boskoff's?" *Alpinist* online, December 28, 2006. www.alpinist.com/doc/ALP18/newswire-body -found-fowler-boskoff.

Callahan, Ted. "The Snows of Genyen." *Climbing* online, originally published May 7, 2007; updated December 19, 2015. https://www.climbing .com/news/the-snows-of-genyen/.

Stark, Peter. *Last Breath: The Limit of Adventure*. New York: Ballentine Books, 2002.

Tremper, Bruce. *Avalanche Essentials: A Step-by-Step System for Safety and Survival*. Seattle: Mountaineers Books, 2013.

Tremper, Bruce. *Staying Alive in Avalanche Terrain*. Seattle: Mountaineers Books, 2018.

Chapter 22

"The Fowler-Boskoff Peak Naming Proposal." Telluride Mountain Club (website), July 16, 2019. www.telluridemountainclub.org/fowler -bookoff-peak-naming-proposal/#prettyPhoto.

ABOUT THE AUTHOR

JOHANNA GARTON is a mother, author, and cross country coach who has played many roles throughout her life. A graduate of the S.I. Newhouse School of Public Communications at Syracuse University, she also has a law degree from DePaul University College of Law. As an AmeriCorps VISTA member in Chicago, Johanna worked on behalf of refugee survivors of torture at the Heartland Alliance. She has served on the Colorado Governor's Commission on Community Service and taught advocacy and legal issues for nonprofits at Regis University. Several years of living and working in Asia, including time in China with her husband, son, and daughter, inspired her to write her first book, *Awakening East*. She and her family live in Denver. Find her online at johannagarton.com.

recreation • lifestyle • conservation

MOUNTAINEERS BOOKS is a leading publisher of mountaineering literature and guides—including our flagship title, *Mountaineering: The Freedom of the Hills*—as well as adventure narratives, natural history, and general outdoor recreation. Through our two imprints, Skipstone and Braided River, we also publish titles on sustainability and conservation. We are committed to supporting the environmental and educational goals of our organization by providing expert information on human-powered adventure, sustainable practices at home and on the trail, and preservation of wilderness.

The Mountaineers, founded in 1906, is a 501(c)(3) nonprofit outdoor recreation and conservation organization whose mission is to enrich lives and communities by helping people "explore, conserve, learn about, and enjoy the lands and waters of the Pacific Northwest and beyond." One of the largest such organizations in the United States, it sponsors classes and year-round outdoor activities throughout the Pacific Northwest, including climbing, hiking, backcountry skiing, snowshoeing, camping, kayaking, sailing, and more. The Mountaineers also supports its mission through its publishing division, Mountaineers Books, and promotes environmental education and citizen engagement. For more information, visit The Mountaineers Program Center, 7700 Sand Point Way NE, Seattle, WA 98115-3996; phone 206-521-6001; www.mountaineers.org; or email info@mountaineers.org.

Our publications are made possible through the generosity of donors and through sales of 700 titles on outdoor recreation, sustainable lifestyle, and conservation. To donate, purchase books, or learn more, visit us online:

MOUNTAINEERS BOOKS

1001 SW Klickitat Way, Suite 201 • Seattle, WA 98134
800-553-4453 • mbooks@mountaineersbooks.org • www.mountaineersbooks.org

An independent nonprofit publisher since 1960